CONTENTS

HEARING DATES

OPENING STATEMENT

JUNE 19, 2003

JUNE 26, 2003

WITNESSES

JUNE 19, 2003

CONSULAR IDENTIFICATION CARDS

HEARING

BEFORE THE

SUBCOMMITTEE ON IMMIGRATION, BORDER SECURITY, AND CLAIMS

OF THE

COMMITTEE ON THE JUDICIARY
HOUSE OF REPRESENTATIVES

ONE HUNDRED EIGHTH CONGRESS

FIRST SESSION

JUNE 19 AND JUNE 26, 2003

Serial No. 31

Printed for the use of the Committee on the Judiciary

Available via the World Wide Web: http://www.house.gov/judiciary

U.S. GOVERNMENT PRINTING OFFICE

87–813 PDF WASHINGTON : 2003

For sale by the Superintendent of Documents, U.S. Government Printing Office
Internet: bookstore.gpo.gov Phone: toll free (866) 512–1800; DC area (202) 512–1800
Fax: (202) 512–2250 Mail: Stop SSOP, Washington, DC 20402–0001

COMMITTEE ON THE JUDICIARY

F. JAMES SENSENBRENNER, JR., Wisconsin, *Chairman*

HENRY J. HYDE, Illinois
HOWARD COBLE, North Carolina
LAMAR SMITH, Texas
ELTON GALLEGLY, California
BOB GOODLATTE, Virginia
STEVE CHABOT, Ohio
WILLIAM L. JENKINS, Tennessee
CHRIS CANNON, Utah
SPENCER BACHUS, Alabama
JOHN N. HOSTETTLER, Indiana
MARK GREEN, Wisconsin
RIC KELLER, Florida
MELISSA A. HART, Pennsylvania
JEFF FLAKE, Arizona
MIKE PENCE, Indiana
J. RANDY FORBES, Virginia
STEVE KING, Iowa
JOHN R. CARTER, Texas
TOM FEENEY, Florida
MARSHA BLACKBURN, Tennessee

JOHN CONYERS, JR., Michigan
HOWARD L. BERMAN, California
RICK BOUCHER, Virginia
JERROLD NADLER, New York
ROBERT C. SCOTT, Virginia
MELVIN L. WATT, North Carolina
ZOE LOFGREN, California
SHEILA JACKSON LEE, Texas
MAXINE WATERS, California
MARTIN T. MEEHAN, Massachusetts
WILLIAM D. DELAHUNT, Massachusetts
ROBERT WEXLER, Florida
TAMMY BALDWIN, Wisconsin
ANTHONY D. WEINER, New York
ADAM B. SCHIFF, California
LINDA T. SÁNCHEZ, California

PHILIP G. KIKO, *Chief of Staff-General Counsel*
PERRY H. APELBAUM, *Minority Chief Counsel*

SUBCOMMITTEE ON IMMIGRATION, BORDER SECURITY, AND CLAIMS

JOHN N. HOSTETTLER, Indiana, *Chairman*

JEFF FLAKE, Arizona
MARSHA BLACKBURN, Tennessee
LAMAR SMITH, Texas
ELTON GALLEGLY, California
CHRIS CANNON, Utah
STEVE KING, Iowa
MELISSA A. HART, Pennsylvania

SHEILA JACKSON LEE, Texas
LINDA T. SÁNCHEZ, California
ZOE LOFGREN, California
HOWARD L. BERMAN, California
JOHN CONYERS, JR., Michigan

GEORGE FISHMAN, *Chief Counsel*
LORA RIES, *Counsel*
ART ARTHUR, *Full Committee Counsel*
CINDY BLACKSTON, *Professional Staff*
NOLAN RAPPAPORT, *Minority Counsel*

ISSUANCE, ACCEPTANCE AND RELIABILITY

THURSDAY, JUNE 19, 2003

HOUSE OF REPRESENTATIVES,
SUBCOMMITTEE ON IMMIGRATION,
BORDER SECURITY, AND CLAIMS,
COMMITTEE ON THE JUDICIARY,
Washington, DC.

The Subcommittee met, pursuant to call, at 2 p.m., in Room 2237, Rayburn House Office Building, Hon. John Hostettler (Chair of the Subcommittee) presiding.

Mr. HOSTETTLER. The Subcommittee will come to order.

In the wake of the attacks of September 11, the Federal Government has reassessed almost every aspect of American life to ensure that our country and its people are protected against terrorist threats. This Subcommittee has played an active role in that effort. We have learned from those attacks and from other attacks carried out by aliens in the United States over the past decade that those who have come to our country to do us harm have identified and exploited weaknesses in our law enforcement efforts generally and in immigration enforcement specifically.

In the past few months, increased attention has been directed to the law enforcement and national security implications of local acceptance of consular identification cards. By way of background, consular identification cards have been issued by foreign governments to their nationals living abroad for over a hundred years.

Historically, foreign governments have issued these cards to enable their citizens abroad to seek consular assistance when they needed help. Since early, 2002, however, those cards have served a new purpose. This is when the Mexican Government redesigned their consular identification card known as the Matricula Consular and began promoting it for local acceptance in the United States.

Those efforts have largely been successful. To date, more than 402 localities, 32 counties, 122 financial institutions and 908 law enforcement agencies accept the Matricula for identification purposes.

Those documents are accepted for several different transactions. They can be offered as identification at the police stops, to open bank accounts, to register for local services, to qualify for subsidized housing and even, reportedly, to board airplanes.

Over the past 2 years, more than a million and a half Matriculas have been issued by Mexican Government agencies in the United States. Mexico's success in promoting its consular identification document has prompted other countries to follow its lead. Guatemala has begun to issue consular identification cards to its citizens in our country, and several other countries are planning to do the same.

As the issuance and acceptance of those documents has become more widespread, however, criticism of the documents and of domestic acceptance of the documents has increased.

One of the main objections that has been raised against local acceptance of the cards is that such acceptance encourages illegal immigration to the United States. With limited exceptions, all aliens who are legally present in the United States possess either U.S. Government issued cards or passports, documents that are commonly accepted for many transactions. Critics have argued, therefore, that the only aliens in the U.S. Who need identification, additional identification documents, other than passports and U.S.-Government issued documents, are those who are illegally here. Many have therefore questioned why a country that expends so much energy and money to protect its borders would go to such effort to make it easier for aliens illegally in the United States to remain here.

It has also been argued that domestic acceptance of consular identification cards in the U.S. Possess a law enforcement and national security risk because the documents themselves are not reliable or secure. These critics assert that the processes that foreign governments have instituted for issuing consular identification cards are susceptible to fraud and that the stated procedures for issuance of the documents are not uniformly followed.

Critics have also argued that there are no safeguards in place to ensure that multiple cards are not issued to the same individual and that there is no centralized database of the cards that foreign government agents have issued in our country.

The lack of such safeguards is an issue because reports indicate that counterfeit Mexican birth certificates are readily obtainable. For example, in September, 2002, the largest stash of counterfeit documents in Washington State history was seized. Police and Justice Department agents found specialty papers to print Mexican birth certificates along with other documents and $10,000 worth of computer equipment.

Because the issuance process for consular identification cards are not always followed and because the absence of safeguards on those processes, critics have argued that cards have been issued to applicants who have few, if any, identifying documents. There appears to be some merit to these claim. This Subcommittee has received credible reports about aliens who have been arrested carrying multiple consular identification cards bearing their own pictures but different names.

Of particular note is a memo sent by the Border Patrol agent in charge in Riverside, CA, to the sheriff of San Bernardino County, who was considering allowing his deputies to accept the Matricula. The patrol agent in charge explained that his office had arrested many Mexican aliens who had in their possession multiple valid Matriculas in different names. These arrestees included one known alien smuggler with an extensive criminal history found in a house with 25 of the smuggled. He had seven Matriculas in his possession, each bearing his picture and each in a different name.

In addition to concerns about the reliability and security of consular identification cards, some observers have also argued that foreign government efforts to gain local acceptance of those cards violates our national sovereignty. They assert that foreign governments should not be allowed to lobby U.S. States and localities to accept the cards, because the purpose of that lobbying is to undermine our Federal immigration laws and our national immigration policies.

They also argue that because States, localities and the Federal Government do not have access to consular information, the duty of verifying that a document is valid is improperly taken away from U.S. Authorities and given to agents of foreign powers who reside in the United States. This places U.S. Law enforcement at the mercy of those foreign governments, whose interests, particularly with respect to illegal aliens, may not be the same as ours.

On a related note, many question whether it is proper for cities and towns in the United States to accept documents that are not regulated by the U.S. Government or the States.

In this regard, I note the Supreme Court has held that, quote, for reasons long recognized as valid, the responsibility for regulating the relationship between the United States and our alien visitors has been committed to the political branches of the Federal Government, end quote.

Congress has plenary authority over substantive immigration decisions under the article 1, section 8 clause of the Constitution giving Congress the power, quote, to establish a uniform rule of naturalization, end quote.

Given this grant of power, Congress plainly must have the ability and the opportunity to regulate any document that would allow an alien to reside in the United States.

Because there is no method for regulating issuance of consular identification cards, critics of those cards assert that there is no way to ensure that issuance procedures for the cards are followed and that cards are not improperly issued in exchange for bribes.

In light of the aforementioned concerns, a growing number of localities have opted not to accept consular identification card. In May, the State of Colorado restricted public acceptance of the documents; and the American Association of Motor Vehicle Administrators issued a resolution stating that it was, quote, premature to recommend the use of any foreign consular ID, end quote, in issuing a driver's license or State ID.

Because of the serious nature of the concerns that have been raised about the security and reliability of consular identification cards and the sovereignty and national security implications posed by domestic acceptance of those cards, the Subcommittee has decided to open an investigation into both the issuance and acceptance of the cards. This hearing is a critical part of that investigation.

In conclusion, I note that foreign governments have issued increasing numbers of consular identification cards in the U.S. At the same time, agents of foreign powers have expanded their attempts to seek local acceptance of those documents. Given these facts, it is incumbent upon this Subcommittee to fully explore the impact of these foreign governments' efforts on U.S. Law enforcement and on our national security and sovereignty.

I turn now to my colleague, the Ranking Member, Ms. Jackson Lee, for any opening statements she would like to make.

Ms. JACKSON LEE. Thank you, Mr. Chairman, for this hearing, as well for some of the points that I believe I heard in the course of your testimony, terminology such as local uses, State uses, and domestic acceptance. So I thank you for the opportunity to explore this in the detailed way in which we should.

I would ask at this time to be allowed to offer my opening statement and to be able to include it in its entirety in the record as I proceed.

Mr. HOSTETTLER. Without objection.

Ms. JACKSON LEE. Let me emphasize our purpose for being here in this Committee. As I understand it, this is a Committee that deals with the immigration policies of the Nation; and I am proud to serve on it. I am also proud to note that the 18th Congressional District in Houston, TX, is the host to the Mexican consulate office; and I have spent a lot of hours with the Consul General there, watching the proceedings and the services that are granted to those members of our community.

Mr. Chairman, I want to also acknowledge and thank you publicly for the fact that we will, in the next week, hold a hearing on the smuggling of illegal immigrants into this Nation, obviously, with a look to the northern border as well as to the southern border.

But I am likewise a member of the community that suffered a great loss with a number of individuals who died in the very tragic incident that occurred about 3 or 4 weeks ago. Many of the family members of those deceased were, of course, from the Houston area. We suffered greatly, enormous impact on families burying loved ones and memorials and also stories about those individuals who have come here simply for an opportunity.

I use that as a backdrop; and might I use just another backdrop, anecdotal story?

Mr. Chairman, I say this—we have not had a chance to discuss this—but I note a report that has just come out by Amnesty International discussing the treatment of children of immigrants who are detained.

In our legislation last year, my colleague and myself, Congresswoman Lofgren, moved the handling of nonadult children who are in nonimmigrant status to be handled by HHS, Health and Human Services. I think it would be very helpful for this Committee, because of the very dire comments being made by this report, which I would be happy to share with you, that we would also like to explore how the children are being treated at this point, and maybe we can have a conversation; and I only say that because we have been working together. I think these hearings are instructive.

With that as a backdrop, however, and knowing what our role is here, again I want to emphasize that I believe that the issue is whether or not these documents are used to equate or connote immigrant status, whether in fact they bestow upon anyone an adjusted immigrant status. I think that is the question; and as we proceed in our hearings I hope that these are the questions that will be answered. I don't believe—and if I pronounce it correctly—the Matricula Consular card has become or should become an immigrant issue.

The Matricula is not issued as an immigration document, and it has no immigration purpose. The Government of Mexico has been issuing Matriculas at their consulates around the world for more than 130 years. They are getting prettier. The consulars do this to create an official record of its citizens in our countries.

Matricula is legal proof of registration with the consulate so that you can be helped, your families can be helped. The consulate in Mexico was—in Houston, rather—was particularly helpful during this tragic time when families were able to come and send messages back home on the status of their loved ones. This registration facilitates access to protection and consular services, because a certificate is evidence of Mexican nationality.

When we had tragic incidents with an unfortunate confrontation with the police, a tragedy of police brutality, the consular was able to reach the family because of the knowledge of the individual who died. Last year alone more than a million of these cards were issued to Mexican citizens living in the United States. It does not provide immigrant status of any kind. It cannot be used for travel, employment, or driving in the United States or in Mexico. The Matricula only attests that a Mexican consular has verified the individual's identity.

Now, we do know that there have been some State jurisdictions that are very kind—but that is a State issue—and they have their own guidelines in which to determine how they want to use those cards. Again, local uses, State uses, domestic acceptance have nothing to do with grant of immigration status.

The Matricula, however, does have some nonconsular uses. For instance, because it is an identification card, it provides Mexican nationals in the United States with access to banking services. Is that not better, Mr. Chairman, than moneys that can be held in places where these individuals become victims because they know their money is under a mattress or somewhere else? Isn't it better to have the banking institutions of America to be able to have these resources and, of course, to track whether or not any of these accounts are being used for illegal activities?

That is an asset to us. That helps law enforcement.

Without an acceptable identification card, many Mexican nationals in this country cannot open checking or savings accounts or use any other banking services. In 2002, Latino immigrants sent more than $30 billion to their families in Latin America. The cost of making such transfers is much higher if the person making it has to use a money-transmitting business such as Western Union or Moneygram instead of a regulated financial institution such as a bank or credit union.

No insult to Western Union or Moneygram. Keep going. But I can't imagine banks in America turning down $30 billion of interest that they can gain while having these accounts.

Moreover, the banks and credit unions want the Latino banking business. United States banks plan to spend at least $8.5 billion through 2005 to attract Hispanic customers.

The availability of banking service is a safety issue, too. Latinos are more likely to be victims of violent crime than any other racial or ethnic group. Much of this crime relates to the perception of criminals that because Latinos do not have bank accounts they carry large amounts of cash. As a result of this problem, police departments across the country support the use of the Matricula to enable Latinos to use mainstream financial institutions as a means of reducing crime and violence.

As I look at the various witnesses, I am delighted to see Congressman Gutierrez. I know that he has long worked on these issues, particularly this card; and I would be very interested to hear his assessment of whether we go forward with this or we go backwards in our effort to either regulate or eliminate the opportunity.

In an attempt to assist efforts to destroy the financial network that supports al Qaeda and other terrorist organizations, I believe the Committee on Financial Services enacted legislation to reform money-laundering laws. The enacted provisions were incorporated into the USA PATRIOT Act, and clearly these bank accounts would be a great asset to distinguish the bad guys from the good guys.

Customer identification provisions in this Act have a direct impact on the use of the Matricula as a legitimate form of identification to allow consumers to open bank accounts. Specifically, 326 of title III adds a new subsection that requires the Secretary to prescribe regulations setting forth minimum standards for financial institutions that relate to identification and verification of any person who applies to open an account. These regulations, Mr. Chairman, permit banks to accept identification cards issued by foreign governments. The regulations went into effect, but anti-immigrant groups and some State and Federal officials had expressed opposition, but they went into effect June 9, 2003.

My good friend, Mr. Gallegly, has introduced a bill that would make it more difficult for these Mexican citizens of the United States to use these cards. In his bill, the Identification Integrity Act, H.R. 687, would prohibit the Federal Government from accepting identification documents issued by foreign governments.

I believe frankly, that this is a State Department issue. The issue deals with the consular offices. Yes, we do deal with the State Department as it relates to visas, but I believe we need to be sure that these documents, as the legislation wants to do, as issued by a foreign government, are not to be utilized like they are, which is the right thing to do. We are suggesting—or he is suggesting that the passport should be the only purpose.

I raise concerns over this and hope that, as we proceed, we will find out that we have many classes of aliens applying for relief who are not required to be in possession of a valid passport and typically will not have one in any event. So these aliens who have different statuses should not be precluded from having some sort of identification. I hope that, as we proceed with this, we will find that there is a better way to address any concerns that my good friend has.

Therefore, we need to understand that many of those who have ID cards come from places who are Canadian nationals and have many other statuses. So I hope that as we move toward this hearing we will be sincere in our intent to get information. We will find out that some cures are better than the illness and that we will hope and realize that bank accounts that can be traced are better than those who cannot be and that taking the documentation does not grant any sort of immigration status to anyone who does not have the status originally through the proper documentation.

With that, Mr. Chairman, I thank you very much for your indulgence and kindness. I look forward to this hearing.

Mr. HOSTETTLER. I thank my colleague for her opening statement.

Without objection, all opening statements can be entered into the record. But is there a Member that would like to make an oral statement at the opening?

The gentleman from Utah.

Mr. CANNON. Thank you, Mr. Chairman.

I appreciate the opportunity to have this hearing today. For 130 years, the Government of Mexico has issued consular ID cards to its nationals traveling and living abroad. In recent years, the Mexican Government has made an effort to issue identification cards, called the Matricula Consular, to many of its citizens who have immigrated from Mexico to the United States.

The statistics indicate that more than 800 law enforcement agencies and 74 banks now accept the consular ID for identification purposes. I doubt that anyone would argue that Mexico has the right to issue identity cards to its citizens, just as I doubt that anyone would argue, I think, that Government agencies of the United States have the right to determine whether to accept these cards as proof of identification or not.

The real issue before us today is whether the Federal Government should prohibit, restrict or encourage rules of these cards which are used by both legally documented and illegal immigrants. I believe we should start with the assumption that we should accept the consular ID cards as proof of identification under certain conditions.

I would propose that we ask the Department of State to work with their counterparts in other governments that are now issuing consular ID cards under certain conditions. One condition can be that the foreign consulates share their registration lists with U.S. Government officials, and another condition can be that important information contained on the consular ID cards is shared with the United States Government. Another condition could be an agreement on the standards for issuing certain types of IDs and the records relied upon to issue them. I suggest that we work in a collaborative environment to share our security concerns and work together toward more secure borders.

I am open to the debate whether this information is best shared with agencies within the Federal Government or with those in State and local governments. But I believe this is sound policy that will benefit our country as well as those individuals receiving those cards.

I have taken time to visit with Government officials from Mexico about the security safeguards that they now implement in their identity cards. Since this panel of witnesses does not include any representatives from the countries now issuing consular ID cards or officials from the State Department who deal with the consular issues, I would encourage the Chairman and each Member of the Committee to check these things out personally.

I have firsthand—or have seen firsthand that these identification cards contain modern security safeguards that are designed to prevent falsification and to ensure that law enforcement officials from both Mexico and the United States are able to determine their authenticity. In many cases, these identification cards have move security enhancements than official American documents. Each card bears a photo of the applicant, taken at the consulate, a legal address, signature and a serial number. This information can provide law enforcement officials with a readily recognizable and traceable ID.

After the tragedy of September 11, the public attention on our Nation's borders and national security has become even more focused. The more we can do to enhance the identification of immigrants and visitors traveling within our borders, the safer our society becomes. This is especially true in cases involving illegal immigrants, where law enforcement has little other information to help them in solving crimes and tracking illegal activities.

In addition to enhancing our national security, consular ID cards can deliver substantial economic benefits to both the holder of the card and to U.S. Economy in general. The card can be especially important as a means to open a bank account. I propose you examine the convenience of a bank account, something most of us here take for granted. When you open a bank account, you can carry an ATM card and not large quantities of cash. You can save money safely for an emergency or a rainy day, in a place where it can gain interest. Establishing a bank account can allow an immigrant to qualify for a loan, enabling him to purchase a car or a home, or it can provide an immigrant with a chance to invest further in the community in which he lives.

I don't think anything would affect our economy more directly and more quickly than allowing people who are here as immigrants, legal and otherwise, to buy homes. That could literally double the new number of new homes we build a year in America.

Banks eliminate the need for costly wire transfers or other cash-based systems that can charge incredibly high rates. In addition, unbanked cash is an open invitation to crimes. Rates of muggings and burglaries are higher in societies where cash is carried. Bank accounts can also reduce the worries and anxieties of migrant farm workers who move seasonally from State to State.

The economic benefits to our own business and communities are obvious. Local banks gain more business. The savings rate in our country is improved, crime is reduced, and immigrants are more likely to make big-ticket purchases that bolster the local economy.

Throughout our Nation's history, we have succeeded in integrating immigrants into the economic fabric of our community. Some critics of the consular ID cards have objected that they grant amnesty to illegal immigrants at a time when we should be cracking down on them because of worries how they are connected to terrorism. But these cards pose no threat, no risk to our anti-terrorist efforts. Rather, the absence of identification poses a real threat.

These cards can simplify the identification of immigrants and facilitate their contact with Americans and our institutions. They should be considered a benefit to public safety, not a liability. Indeed, it seems that many law enforcement officials and agencies, over 800 as of today, are among the most vocal proponents of the use and promulgation of these cards.

Contrary to what critics argue, the consular ID card does not change this Nation's laws relating to immigration or the amnesty of illegal aliens. This debate is not simply a domestic issue. The Mexican immigrant community in the United States is vital to the success of the Mexican economy, which in turn has a big impact on our own economic well-being.

Mexico is our second largest trading partner that buys as many of our exports as China, Great Britain, Germany and Italy combined. Besides opening a great deal of economic activity which is currently being conducted in the shadows, the consular ID cards offer us the opportunity to work with Mexico on refining immigration policies in ways that advance our mutual interests.

I would like to see the United States prohibit some uses of the Matricula card while encouraging others, but, to do so, we will have to engage the Mexican Government in a realistic dialogue on these subjects. As we continue to improve our border security, we must simultaneously seek to increase legitimate flow of investment and trade and new immigrants that are so essential to our economy and our standing in the world.

September 11 has not changed that need. We should move beyond reforms that merely increase law enforcement's power. We need to bring greater coherence and strategy to the patchwork of laws we call our immigration policies, so those who want to harm America will have fewer opportunities to do so but those who seek opportunity and freedom will have more ways to contribute to our society.

I hope we can overcome this reluctance to reform, but in the meantime that we can take a realistic look at the practices of the Mexican Government in issuing consular IDs, which may actually make our communities safer and produce more positive economic results.

Thank you, Mr. Chairman. I yield back my time.

Mr. HOSTETTLER. Thank the gentleman from Utah.

The gentlelady from California, Ms. Sánchez.

Ms. SÁNCHEZ. Thank you, Chairman Hostettler and Ranking Member Jackson Lee, for holding this important hearing. I want to thank the witnesses, too, for coming here today to share their insights on the consular identification cards.

In recent months, concerns have been raised about the use of consular identification cards, and it is interesting to me that these concerns are surfacing now, since such cards have been used for many years.

Mexico, for example, has issued consular identification cards since 1871. In fact, consular registration of Mexican nationals assists Mexican consulates in complying with the functions recognized by the Vienna Convention on Consular Relations. In addition, as a sovereign nation, Mexico is entitled to issue such identification cards to foreign nationals. This was made clear by recent statements made by Asa Hutchinson, the Under Secretary of Border and Transportation Security.

Consular identification cards are accepted by banks, financial institutions and police officers in order to prove the bearer's identity. At least 80 banks in over 100 cities and hundreds of police departments accept the Mexican consular ID. In fact, the consular identification card is more fraud-proof than any passport or U.S.-Government-issued ID.

Contrary to what has been said, these cards do not legalize the status of any immigrant; and they cannot be used to obtain any immigration or citizenship benefit, including work authorization or the right to vote.

Mexican consulates explain this to every applicant. Despite these facts, some Members of Congress have begun arguing that these cards should not be accepted in the United States. This approach, if taken, may be more than just unnecessary, it could be detrimental to U.S. Interests and national security.

As a party to the Vienna Convention on Consular Relations, the United States is under an obligation to comply with the nondiscrimination provisions of that Convention. Those provisions call for parity and reciprocity among parties to the Convention. The Convention specifies that better or worse treatment will not be considered discriminatory as long as the same favorable or restrictive treatment is also applied to U.S. Citizens in the, quote, unquote sending state. In other words, whatever treatment we give Mexican consuls, the same treatment will be applied to U.S. Consuls in Mexico.

So if we use high barriers to Mexican nationals who want to live, do business or travel in the U.S., then we can expect that those same high barriers will be used against U.S. Citizens in Mexico. This kind of practice unnecessarily creates difficulties for U.S. Citizens and businesses.

At the same time, I do recognize that there are concerns related to the use of the Matricula Consular. Some people worry that these cards are not in fact sufficiently fraud-proof. Others worry that accepting these cards will make life easier and more enticing for immigrants who come here illegally. And a third concern is that accepting these cards from Mexico now will set a precedent we may not want to continue when other less friendly nations try to use similar cards.

I look forward to hearing from the witnesses, and I am hopeful that all of us will come to agree on the value of consular identification cards and the foolishness of banning their use in this country.

I thank you and yield back the balance of my time.

Mr. HOSTETTLER. I thank the gentlelady.

The Chair recognizes the gentleman from California, Mr. Gallegly.

Mr. GALLEGLY. I thank the gentleman.

I would like to have unanimous consent to have a written opening statement placed into the record subsequent to the meeting.

Mr. GALLEGLY. I would just like to make a very brief opening statement.

I was just handed a document that was placed on the table in violation of Committee rules by an organization that represents itself as the National Council of La Raza National Immigration Law Center. There may be—if there is someone here that has been putting this document out in violation of rules, I would ask that they please not do that if they do have any respect for the law.

I did take the liberty, though, to read one sentence in the document that they passed out, saying how harmful this would be to legal immigrants.

I have asked many people over recent months: Who has a need for this document other than an illegal immigrant? Not a legal immigrant, but illegal immigrants and international terrorists or a criminal seeking another form of identification? And to date I don't have any explanation.

If someone is a legal resident of the United States, they have any other number of forms of identification, and they don't need this form of identification.

I think in all of my years that I have been on this Committee—and this is my ninth term in Washington, I have been on this Committee for 10 or 12 years—I don't see any issue that is as potentially dangerous to the sovereignty, and it invites tremendous opportunity for terrorism in this country with this form of documentation. We have no control over the issuance.

I would just like to say that if there is any form—anything that is positive about the issuance of this document that law enforcement would use, it would be an indication that anyone using this document as a sole source of identification is illegally in this country.

I yield back.

Mr. HOSTETTLER. I thank the gentleman.

The Chair now recognizes the gentleman from California, Mr. Berman.

Mr. BERMAN. Thank you, Mr. Chairman.

I understand you are having a hearing next week. If it would be permissible, with the exception of one sentence, I would like to have an opportunity to give or submit an opening statement at that hearing, rather than today.

Mr. HOSTETTLER. Without objection.

Mr. BERMAN. I hope on this issue ideology does not triumph over common sense as we look at this question.

Mr. HOSTETTLER. Thank you.

The Chair now recognizes the gentleman from Texas, Mr. Smith.

Mr. SMITH. Thank you, Mr. Chairman.

Mr. Chairman, I have seldom seen an issue that we have considered as Members of Congress, I think, where there is such a fundamental difference on opinion on an agreed point. Because all of those who would argue in favor of the use of this consular identification card are basically arguing or saying that they are in favor of it because they want to make it easier for illegal immigrants to stay in America.

Those of us who oppose the card are opposed to it for that exact same reason, because it does make it easier for those who have broken our immigration laws to remain in the country.

So it is not very often do you get that clear-cut, fundamental difference of opinion, I don't think.

When I say it makes it easier for people to stay in the country, clearly that argues for common sense. Because when you make it easier for individuals to have bank accounts, when you make it easier for people to obtain driver's licenses and so forth, not only are you making it easier for them to stay in the country, but you are actually encouraging illegal immigration. Because the message that is sent is, come into the country, even if it is illegally, and we are going to make life easier for you once you get here. I think that that is the exact opposite message that we as Members of Congress and that the Federal Government should be sending.

The second point, Mr. Chairman, is that I just don't think it is credible for anyone to argue that these are secure documents, these consular identification cards. There is no check made on their validity. There is no check made with any database in Mexico to make sure these individuals are the people that they say that they are.

To say that they are tamperproof and that they can be duplicated, of course, ignores the real issue, which is either the use of underlying fraudulent documentation or the ability of individuals to get multiple consular identification cards. And the fact that they are tamperproof says nothing at all about how secure they are underneath that veneer of tamperproof.

The other point to make, I think Mr. Chairman, is that—and one of our witnesses in a few minutes is going to make the point that the major banks in Mexico themselves do not use the consular identification card in any way, shape or form as a legitimate card for the bank accounts of Mexican citizens. What in the world does that say that the United States banks are now being told that it is okay to use this identification card when the banks in Mexico themselves don't use this identification card? I mean, clearly this is the world turned upside down.

I hope our Treasury Department, which initially had given an indication to the U.S. Banks that it is okay to use this card, will frankly listen to the White House concerns about homeland security. They may even want to call the White House, because to use this card does undermine our homeland security and, therefore, potentially in the future endangers the lives of American citizens.

Mr. BERMAN. Will the gentleman yield?

Mr. SMITH. Mr. Berman, I will be happy to yield if I have some time, but I also recognize that the individual has his own time as well.

Mr. BERMAN. I just gave it up, unfortunately. Can I reclaim my time?

Mr. SMITH. I will be happy to yield.

Mr. BERMAN. One specific point I just want to disagree or quibble with. It may be that many people support this card because they want to make it easier for otherwise undocumented people to function in this country, but it is not correct to say that the only reason people want this card is for that purpose.

The Los Angeles Police Department believes that a card that shows the address of the individual, one, encourages people to report crime, secondly, makes it easier for them, particularly if there is a language barrier, to record the address of a complaining witness or a witness to criminal events or a victim of crime than it otherwise would be.

I could go on and on with respect to different agencies' interests which has nothing to do with wanting to make it easier but allows them simply to perform their functions and their governmental functions more effectively as well as private.

Mr. SMITH. Thank you. Let me reclaim my time to respond.

I am glad to hear the gentleman from California admit that a lot of individuals do use the argument that they are for the card because it makes it easier for people to stay in the country. Yes, there may be other reasons that the gentleman just gave, a couple of examples.

By and large, we are still talking—I don't know that the gentleman would want to correct this—that at least 90 percent of the people who are using these cards are more than likely in the country illegally, and therefore we are helping a mass of individuals stay in the country, making it easier for them to stay in the country, and also sending the message that encourages, I think, illegal immigration.

I will yield back, Mr. Chairman.

Mr. HOSTETTLER. The gentleman yields back his time.

At this point, I would like to introduce our panel of witnesses and thank you for your forbearance. This is a very important topic, and Members have varied opinions on the topic.

First of all, Representative Luis Gutierrez is a five-term Member of the United States House of Representatives. He represents Illinois' Fourth District. Representative Gutierrez is Chairman of the Congressional Hispanic Caucus' Task Force on Immigration and before his election to Congress worked as a teacher, social worker and community activist. Representative Gutierrez also previously served as an alderman in the City of Chicago, a position to which he was elected in 1986. He is a graduate of Northeastern Illinois University.

Senator John Andrews is the President of the Colorado Senate. He has represented Arapahoe County in the Colorado Senate since 1998. Senator Andrews serves on the Education, Finance, Judiciary and Public Policy Committee in the Colorado Senate. In addition to his legislative work, Senator Andrews runs a communications company and teaches humanities at the Colorado School of Minds. He also provides daily commentary on public television and publishes a monthly journal called Andrews America. Senator Andrews is a graduate of Principia College and served as a submarine officer in the United States Navy.

Marti Dinerstein is the President of Immigration Matters, a public policy firm which facilitates debate on U.S. Immigration issues. She is a fellow at the Center for Immigration Studies and has published various works in the field of immigration policy. Ms. Dinerstein has over 30 years of experience in communications, marketing, management, and consulting. She has also served on numerous nonprofit and private sector boards. She is a graduate of the Columbia University Graduate School of Business and Ohio State University.

Craig Nelsen is Executive Director of Friends of Immigration Law Enforcement, an organization for attorneys, law enforcement officers, legislators and academics concerned about the enforcement of our Nation's immigration laws. Prior to joining Friends of Immigration Law Enforcement, Mr. Nelsen served as Director of Project USA. He has been a restaurateur in New York and taught English as a second language in China. Mr. Nelsen attended New York University and St. John's College in Santa Fe, NM.

Thank the panelists once again for being here. Unanimous consent, without objection, you all may present your written testimony to the record; and you each have 5 minutes to deliver an oral testimony.

Ms. JACKSON LEE. Mr. Chairman, if you can yield for a comment, I want to let the witnesses know that there are two hearings going on that I am involved in—the Select Committee on Homeland Security, as we speak—and so I may be exiting. If I am exiting, it is just to attend that for a moment. Hopefully I will be able to return. Thank you very much. Thank you, Mr. Chairman.

Mr. HOSTETTLER. Very good.

Representative Gutierrez, you have the floor.

STATEMENT OF THE HONORABLE LUIS V. GUTIERREZ, A REPRESENTATIVE IN CONGRESS FROM THE STATE OF ILLINOIS

Mr. GUTIERREZ. Well, thank you and good afternoon, Mr. Chairman and Ranking Member Jackson Lee and Members of the Subcommittee. It is with great pleasure that I appear before the Subcommittee today to speak about an issue of great importance to me and the community that I serve.

Let me make some general statements, as I know that many people have raised many of the issues that are in my opening remarks.

Number one, I think it makes it safer for people to live in the United States of America. It makes it safer for me to know that my neighbor can call the police if somebody is robbing my home, if somebody makes attempts against my person. It makes the community more whole. So it does make it safer to live in a community. The fact is, and I think all of the Members of the Committee know, that we have, some say 5, some say 7, others scream 10 million undocumented workers in the United States of America. That is a fact.

In the absence, Mr. Chairman, of a program, a piece of legislation, the will and the resources of this Government of ours to deport in a systematic manner 10 million possibly undocumented workers in this country, then I think we have a response also to say, what are we going to do with them while they are here?

Because if we do not have a response and we do not show the will and the purpose to deport them, which there is none, Mr. Chairman, as I have been able to see as of yet, then we are simply co-conspirators in their exploitation; and we should work to make sure that they live in safer, more humane conditions.

The fact is that Mexico is a partner of our Nation in the war against terrorism. None of those that entered the country illegally and attacked this country on September 11 came through Mexico.

Yes, we know that the ID card, the Matricula ID card is tamperproof. It is much more tamperproof than the Illinois driver's license. But, Mr. Chairman, we could bring you testimony of many criminals, many criminals in the State of Illinois and throughout the States of this Nation that carry more than one driver's license with the same photo, with different names, and different addresses.

If we are not to accept the Matricula Consular, is the next step that we are going to take is not to accept a passport issued by the Mexican government or a passport issued by any other sovereign nation? The fact is that sovereignty is what it is.

When an American national travels abroad, that government, that nation expects us to check into the validity of that person, who he is, where he was born, and properly identify that person.

In Mexico, you don't expect to get a Mexican ID for an American national. You expect to have a passport issued by the Government of the United States of America. And, Mr. Chairman, they could very well be having those same hearings on American passports and bringing in testimony of people who have invalid drivers' licenses or illegitimately gotten drivers' licenses or other forms of ID.

Yeah, they are here. They are working. They are working at the worst jobs, the lowest-paid, most-exploited situations in our country.

You know, all of the Members of the panel, we have all slept in a hotel room and we know who made the bed and who cleaned the bathroom before we slept in that beautifully made bed and that clean bathroom. We have all eaten from a dish, and we know who is washing the dishes from which we eat from. We have all walked on beautifully waxed and polished floors, and we know who cleaned those floors. As a matter of fact, can anybody here say they haven't eaten a grape, an apple, an orange?

Seventy percent of all of the agricultural workers in the State of Washington are undocumented workers. If we say to them, we are not going to allow you to send the money back to your loved ones in Mexico—because, let's face it, that is one of the things that Matricula Consulars allow people to do.

But one of the Members of the Subcommittee says that we are kind of forcing the banks to use this. Let me assure you, Mr. Chairman, I doubt that you can get any CEO or anyone from Bank of America or any other of the dozen banks in this country—they are forcing them to spend tens of millions to garner the assets of these individuals into their financial institutions. It makes good sense for them to be in these financial institutions for issues of homeland security.

Why not have people establish a bank account, have that ID, know where they live and know what they do with their money? I think that helps. I think that helps.

I think this issue really is one that is kind of underlying the debate we should be having in this country; and that is, what do we do in the Nation that needs the work of immigrants, that has in the past used the work of immigrants, and that those immigrants have helped to foster the great society that we live in today?

Mexico is our partner. Listen, those millions and millions of undocumented workers, do you know what they do? They go to grocery stores, and they buy food. They rent homes. They buy cars. They create hundreds of thousands of jobs for other American citizens. And, Mr. Chairman, they send that money back to their moms and dads and their brothers and their wives back in Mexico, because that is what they do as immigrants, send the money back, billions of dollars.

Because Mexico is our second best trading partner, guess what that money means in the hands of those Mexican nationals back in Mexico? Jobs for those people who live in the United States of America. Because they purchase our goods back in Mexico. So we can look at this from a financial point of view. We can look at this from a homeland security point of view. We can look at it from a safety point of view.

The fact is that over 800 police departments accept the Matricula Consular. They like the Matricula. It gives them something to deal with.

I know we will have a lot more issues to deal with, Mr. Chairman. I want to thank you for allowing me to come before the Committee. I know that Mr. Gallegly and Mr. Smith and Mr. Berman and Ms. Sánchez and Ms. Jackson Lee and Mr. Cannon, all of us together, can come together with a reasonable response that takes into consideration any fears and trepidations people may have. I think that should be the goal; and I will look forward to working with you, Mr. Chairman, and the Ranking Member and all of the Members of the Committee.

Thank you so much.

Mr. HOSTETTLER. Thank you, Representative.

[The prepared statement of Mr. Gutierrez follows:]

PREPARED STATEMENT OF THE HONORABLE LUIS V. GUTIERREZ, A REPRESENTATIVE IN CONGRESS FROM THE STATE OF ILLINOIS

Good afternoon, Chairman Hostettler, Ranking Member Jackson Lee and members of the Subcommittee. It is with great pleasure that I appear before this subcommittee today to speak about an issue of great importance to me and to the community I serve.

It is my hope that over the course of this hearing, this subcommittee will be able to shine a light on the importance of the Matrícula Consular, debunk the misconceptions surrounding the program and put to rest some of the mischaracterizations of its purpose.

To start, let me talk for a minute about what the Matrícula Consular is—and also what it isn't.

A Matrícula Consular is a laminated, tamper-proof photo ID that is distributed by Mexican consulates to their nationals living abroad. The consulates have been issuing this form of identification since 1871. In Chicago, where I live, nearly 170,000 Matrículas were issued last year and more than one million were issued nationwide.

The main purpose of the Matrícula is to establish a registry and provide a document that proves the identity of Mexican nationals.

The Matrícula does not connote any legal status other than Mexican citizenship and it cannot be used for travel, employment, or for driving in the United States or Mexico. In fact, the Matrícula only attests that a Mexican consulate has verified an individual's identity and their home address in the United States.

And contrary to what critics may say, qualifying for a Matrícula is not an easy process. To obtain a Matrícula, an individual must present:

- A Mexican birth certificate;
- Another official identity document, such as a Mexican voter registration card or driver's license;
- And something that proves the individual's permanent address in the United States, such as a utility bill.

And in an effort to further enhance security features, the Integral Program for the Improvement of the Consular Services started issuing a new higher security Consular ID in March of 2002. The new initiative is called the Matrícula Consular de Alta Seguridad, or high-tech ID Card.

The new ID card incorporates holograms and other embedded designs to make it more tamper proof.

For millions of people, obtaining a Matrícula represents the first step toward participating in our financial system and for accessing basic services that are available to others in the United States,

such as opening a bank account; purchasing basic utilities, such as phone and television services; gaining access to rental housing; for entering federal buildings; and for enrolling children in schools.

In recent years, municipalities and businesses from Los Angeles to Waukegan have begun accepting the Matrícula. Currently, more than 400 cities accept the Matrícula as a proper form of identification. Today, more than 80 financial institutions accept the Matrícula to open bank accounts, approximately 825 police departments recognize it as legal identification and 13 states acknowledge it as a means to acquire a drivers' license.

The Matrícula card has become an important tool for opening financial institutions to the unbanked. As a senior member of the House Financial Services Committee, I know that having fair access to financial services is not simply a convenience—it is crucial.

When people are denied banking opportunities, they are also denied the confidence that comes with placing their hard-earned wages in financial institutions where their money will be safe and where they can earn interest and establish credit records.

It is a win-win situation. The financial institutions can tap new customers. And the customers can gain access to fundamental financial services that were previously unattainable.

According to a recent General Accounting Office study, which I requested with the Chair of the Subcommittee, where I serve as the Ranking Member, found that approximately 55.8 million U.S. adults are currently unbanked. That means that 28 percent of all U.S. adults today do not have a bank account.

In addition, a recent study conducted by Bendixen & Associates found that 42 percent of Latin American immigrants in the United States do not have a basic bank account.

The acceptance of the Matrícula strikes at the heart of this problem. Being able to open a bank account helps protect individuals from unregulated check-cashers who often charge between 8 and 10 percent interest for every $100 being cashed.

Research shows that transfer costs for remittances are lowest when they are sent through regulated financial institutions, such as banks and credit unions. For Mexicans, who last year alone sent more than $10 billion home, having an account at a regulated institution represents the opportunity to wire more money back home for their families that need it to pay for daily expenses such as food, medicines and education.

The Matrícula Consular also means more discretionary income that can be spent in local communities and neighborhoods throughout the United States. For Mexico, which receives more than one third of its remittances from the United States, wire transfers represent a key source of domestic income.

For thousands of people, the inability to enter the banking system results in a higher cost of borrowing, a lack of access to home mortgages, an inability to invest in businesses and problems paying bills in an efficient and timely manner.

In an age of e-banking and 401(k) plans, many immigrants live in an almost ancient and archaic financial system, either getting paid in cash or crowding check-cashing stores every payday to convert checks into cash.

This translates into immigrants being increasingly susceptible to crime and theft. In other words, come payday, many of the region's Hispanic enclaves become a mugger's paradise, a community flooded with vulnerable residents walking around with large sums of cash.

Therefore, the Matrícula Consular represents a strong sense of security for those who no longer have to carry their paychecks around with them. Each payday, instead of keeping money under their mattresses, they are able to put it in a bank. And instead of carrying $10,000 with them when they travel to Mexico, they send it through a wire transfer. At the same time, these individuals are building their credit record and are able to save more money for the future.

For financial institutions, the Matrícula Consular means a thriving untapped market of potential customers who could serve as a vital base of business growth that our country so desperately needs.

In addition to its benefits to our financial markets and the economy, the Matrícula Consular also can play an important role in another pressing issue: Homeland Security.

The program helps law enforcement officials by creating an improved system of accountability, where people aren't afraid to come out of the shadows and report crimes.

Personal accountability. Economic vitality. Financial stability. Homeland Security.

These are just four of the reasons why acceptance of the Matrícula Consular is so important.

Thank you again, Chairman Hostettler and Ranking Member Jackson Lee, for the opportunity to present this testimony today.

Mr. HOSTETTLER. Senator Andrews.

STATEMENT OF SENATOR JOHN ANDREWS, PRESIDENT OF THE COLORADO STATE SENATE

Mr. ANDREWS. Thank you, Mr. Chairman and Members of the Committee. I am glad for the opportunity to bring you a perspective from the Colorado General Assembly on this important issue and to tell you what we have done about it legislatively just this year.

There is a lot of concern in Colorado about foreign governments issuing identity documents to their citizens in this country, not that the issuance itself occurs, but our concern is that it seems to be occurring in a manner intentionally erasing the distinction between who is here legally and who is here illegally.

We are concerned that such documents aren't secure in that they don't necessarily prove the bearer is who he says he is. We are concerned they aren't verifiable in that they don't always check out that the bearer is in compliance with U.S. Immigration law, as has been stated already.

When accepted by Government agencies—and let's leave aside banks, money transmitters, utilities and others in the private sector. When accepted by Government agencies, these documents, I believe, raise three grave public policy concerns:

First, they do undermine homeland security, because they help the bearer blend into American life, even if he may have entered this country with intent to do us harm.

Second, they undermine fiscal integrity for our State and local governments, because they give the bearer access in some cases to taxpayer resources that were intended only for the use of legal residents only.

And, third, most importantly, such documents can undermine the rule of law itself. They provide a shortcut for individuals who entered this country in disregard of our laws to enjoy the same status and benefits as individuals who took the trouble to obey our laws.

We in Colorado just believe that is wrong, Mr. Chairman. Widespread governmental acceptance of those nonsecure and nonverifiable foreign ID cards sends the message that Congress isn't serious when it enacts laws to control our borders. Maybe we were just kidding.

If the State of Colorado or the City and County of Denver allows its agencies to accept such documents, we send the message that Federal law doesn't concern us. Secure borders, oh, those are somebody else's problem.

Because the Colorado General Assembly believes that secure borders are everyone's problem, this year we became the first State legislature to close the door on nonsecure, nonverifiable foreign ID cards for use with governmental agencies.

Again, private sector off to one side, not part of our bill. Our bill is Colorado House Bill 1224, the Secure and Verifiable Identity Act. It was signed into law a month ago by Governor Bill Owens, after months of debate in the Colorado General Assembly.

Here is what the bill does: It provides that, for identification purposes, State and local agencies in Colorado can only accept secure and verifiable documents. It defines those as documents issued by a State or Federal jurisdiction in this country or issued by some foreign jurisdiction and officially recognized by the United States Government. The best example of this is a passport.

One Member of the Committee suggested we are on a slippery slope to where foreign passports can be disallowed. I don't imagine any such circumstance. The bill doesn't refer specifically to the Matricula Consular or to any foreign ID card. It just excludes them by its definition of what is secure, what is verifiable.

For teeth, the bill provides that any official who knowingly violates will forfeit his governmental immunity from lawsuit and liability damages, and that is a strong motivator for compliance.

There is an exception for peace officers in the normal performance of their duties. This is important. My son is a police officer. I know how important it is to law enforcement. I am with you on that, Congressman Gutierrez.

But provided that the law enforcement officer who accepts a nonsecure and nonverifiable card such as the Matricula enters all of the information in the criminal justice record, including fingerprints if possible.

When the bill was in conference, we added a provision that would have reported the data for Matricula cards collected by law enforcement officers to the INS every 60 days. We were shocked that INS officials told Colorado law enforcement, don't bother, we don't want it. That almost led to the bill being killed in conference, until we took that provision out.

So, to sum up, Mr. Chairman, these ID cards that ignore the distinction between legal and illegal immigrants have been issued by the tens of thousands by just one consular office of one country, the Mexican consulate in Denver; and a number of other countries are doing the same thing from dozens of offices all over the United States. Twenty countries are now reportedly about to get into this, all of the way from Poland to Argentina.

In the case of the Mexican consulate in Denver, we know of one man who easily obtained three Matricula cards, each bearing his picture, issued in three different names. We know there is no attempt to prove an applicant's legal residency in this country before he or she can get the card.

We know of improper lobbying activities on the part of one consular employee in Denver that led to a formal letter of complaint from our governor.

[3 p.m.]

Mr. ANDREWS. These nonsecured, nonverifiable identity cards are a bad situation, Mr. Chairman, Members of the Committee. It is getting more serious every day. Our House bill 1224 is one response. I hope Congress will frame similar reasonable legislation, not to say no to all the cards but to make sure we are making a bright line between legal and illegal immigrants.

[The prepared statement of Mr. Andrews follows:]

PREPARED STATEMENT OF JOHN ANDREWS

We in Colorado are deeply concerned about foreign governments issuing identity documents to their citizens in this country in a manner that tends to blur the distinction between who is here legally and who is here illegally.

Such documents are not *secure*, in terms of proving that a particular individual is who he says he is. They are not verifiable, in terms of checking out that the bearer is in compliance with US immigration law.

When accepted by federal, state, or local government agencies for official purposes, such documents have a negative impact on *homeland security*, because they help the bearer blend into American life even if he may have entered this country with intent to do us harm.

They have a negative impact on *fiscal integrity*, because they give the bearer access to taxpayer resources which in many cases are intended for the use of legal residents only.

Most importantly, such documents have a negative impact on the rule of law, because they provide a short cut for individuals who have entered this country in disobedience to our laws, to gain the identical status and benefits as individuals who took the trouble to obey our laws. That's wrong.

Widespread acceptance of these non-secure, non-verifiable foreign ID cards sends the message that Congress is not serious when it enacts laws to control our borders. It says maybe we were just kidding, we didn't mean it, because our government agencies are willing to look the other way.

In the case of a state like Colorado or a city like Denver, if we allow our officials to accept such cards, it says that federal law is of no concern to us—secure borders are someone else's problem.

The Colorado General Assembly doesn't believe that, Mr. Chairman. We believe that secure borders and are everyone's problem. This year we became the first state legislature to close the door on non-secure, non-verifiable foreign ID cards. What we did should become a model for legislation by many other states and ultimately by this Congress.

Colorado House Bill 1224, the Secure and Verifiable Identity Document Act, was introduced this January by Rep. Don Lee in the House and sponsored by me in the Senate. It passed both houses on May 1 and was signed into law by Gov. Bill Owens on May 22.

The bill provides that for identification purposes, state and local agencies shall accept only secure and verifiable documents—which it defines as documents issued by a state or federal jurisdiction in this country, or issued by some foreign jurisdiction and formally recognized by the United States government—such as a foreign passport. The bill makes no specific reference to the matricula consular or similar foreign ID cards—it simply excludes them by the above definition.

The bill provides that any official who knowingly violates it will forfeit his governmental immunity. An exception is made for peace officers in the performance of their duties, provided that when accepting a matricula or other non-secure ID card, they enter all information into the criminal justice record, including fingerprints if possible.

This provision led to a disturbing episode while the bill was in conference in April 2003. We wanted to write as strong a law as possible, without impeding the work of law enforcement. My son is a police officer, and I know how they hate needless paperwork. But the conference committee did add a federal reporting requirement, so that matricula card data would be forwarded in bulk from local police or sheriffs to the US Immigration and Naturalization Service every 60 days.

Law enforcement lobbyists then set out to kill the bill unless that requirement was eliminated. They said the INS did not want the data, had no use for it, nowhere to even keep it. Mr. Chairman, I was shocked by this. I was offended. I really expected better from our federal immigration authorities, two years after 9/11. But I had no choice but to remove the INS reporting requirement from the bill in order to save it.

ID cards that ignore the distinction between legal and illegal immigrants have been issued by the tens of thousands by just one consular office of one country, the Mexican Consulate in Denver. Mexico has over 40 other offices across the United States, doing the same thing.

At least five other countries are now reportedly issuing or preparing to issue similar cards—ranging all the way from Poland to Peru—as well as Guatemala, Honduras, and El Salvador.

In the case of the Mexican Consulate in Denver, we know of one man who easily obtained three matricula cards, each bearing his picture but issued in three different names. We know that no attempt is made to prove an applicant's legal residency in this country before the card is issued. We know of improper lobbying activities on the part of a consular employee, leading to a formal letter of complaint from the governor of our state.

These non-secure, non-verifiable ID cards are a bad situation, Mr. Chairman—a serious problem that is getting more serious every day. Colorado's House Bill 1224 is one step toward correcting the problem. I urge the committee to draft federal legislation along the same lines. We owe that to the American people.

See full text of Colorado House Bill 1224 attached, or online at: *http://www.leg.state.co.us*

ATTACHMENT

COLORADO GENERAL ASSEMBLY

HOUSE BILL 03-1224

BY REPRESENTATIVE(S) Lee, Schultheis, Harvey, Briggs, Brophy, Cadman, Clapp, Crane, Fairbank, Fritz, Hall, Hefley, King, Lundberg, May M., McCluskey, Mitchell, Rhodes, Rose, Sinclair, Spence, Spradley, Stafford, Stengel, White, Wiens, and Hoppe;

also SENATOR(S) Andrews, May R., Chlouber, Arnold, Cairns, Dyer, Entz, Hillman, Johnson S., Jones, Kester, McElhany, Owen, Taylor, and Teck.

CONCERNING A PROHIBITION AGAINST THE ACCEPTANCE BY PUBLIC ENTITIES OF IDENTITY DOCUMENTS THAT ARE NOT SECURE.

Be it enacted by the General Assembly of the State of Colorado:

SECTION 1. Title 24, Colorado Revised Statutes, is amended BY THE ADDITION OF A NEW ARTICLE to read:

ARTICLE 72.1 Secure and Verifiable Identity Documents

24-72.1-101. Short title. THIS ARTICLE SHALL BE KNOWN AND MAY BE CITED AS THE "SECURE AND VERIFIABLE IDENTITY DOCUMENT ACT".

24-72.1-102. Definitions. AS USED IN THIS ARTICLE, UNLESS THE CONTEXT OTHERWISE REQUIRES:

(1) "CHILDREN" MEANS CHILDREN AS DEFINED BY 42 U.S.C. SEC. 1786 (b).

(2) "INFANTS" MEANS INFANTS AS DEFINED BY 42 U.S.C. SEC. 1786 (b).

(3) "PUBLIC ENTITY" MEANS AN AGENCY, DEPARTMENT, BOARD, DIVISION, BUREAU, COMMISSION, COUNCIL, OR POLITICAL SUBDIVISION OF THE STATE.

(4) "PUBLIC OFFICIAL" MEANS AN ELECTED OR APPOINTED OFFICIAL, AN EMPLOYEE, OR AN AGENT OF A PUBLIC ENTITY.

Continued...

(5) "SECURE AND VERIFIABLE DOCUMENT" MEANS A DOCUMENT ISSUED BY A STATE OR FEDERAL JURISDICTION OR RECOGNIZED BY THE UNITED STATES GOVERNMENT AND THAT IS VERIFIABLE BY FEDERAL OR STATE LAW ENFORCEMENT, INTELLIGENCE, OR HOMELAND SECURITY AGENCIES.

24-72.1-103. Identity documents - verifiable. (1) A PUBLIC ENTITY THAT PROVIDES SERVICES SHALL NOT ACCEPT, RELY UPON, OR UTILIZE AN IDENTIFICATION DOCUMENT TO PROVIDE SERVICES UNLESS IT IS A SECURE AND VERIFIABLE DOCUMENT.

(2) A PUBLIC ENTITY THAT IS ISSUING AN IDENTIFICATION CARD, LICENSE, PERMIT, OR OFFICIAL DOCUMENT SHALL NOT AUTHORIZE ACCEPTANCE OF AN IDENTIFICATION DOCUMENT, NOR SHALL A PUBLIC OFFICIAL ACTING IN AN OFFICIAL CAPACITY ACCEPT AN IDENTIFICATION DOCUMENT BEFORE ISSUING SUCH DOCUMENTS, UNLESS SUCH IDENTIFICATION DOCUMENT IS A SECURE AND VERIFIABLE DOCUMENT.

24-72.1-104. Records. INFORMATION GATHERED PURSUANT TO SECTION 24-72.1-105 (2) (a) SHALL BE A PUBLIC RECORD ACCESSED PURSUANT TO SECTION 24-72-306 UNLESS THE SUBJECT OF THE INFORMATION IS A JUVENILE OR THE INFORMATION CONCERNS AN ONGOING CRIMINAL INVESTIGATION. SUCH RECORDS SHALL BE RETAINED FOR THREE YEARS, BUT.PAGE 3-HOUSE BILL 03-1224
MAY BE DISPOSED OF AFTER THREE YEARS.

24-72.1-105. Violations - immunity. (1) ACTIONS TAKEN IN KNOWING VIOLATION OF THIS ARTICLE SHALL NOT BE PROTECTED BY GOVERNMENTAL IMMUNITY PROVIDED TO PUBLIC EMPLOYEES BY ARTICLE 10 OF THIS TITLE.

(2) A PEACE OFFICER WHO, IN THE PERFORMANCE OF THE OFFICER'S DUTIES, UTILIZES IDENTIFICATION THAT IS NOT SECURE AND VERIFIABLE SHALL NOT FORFEIT GOVERNMENTAL IMMUNITY PURSUANT TO THIS SECTION IF SUCH OFFICER:

(a) GATHERS ALL INFORMATION FROM SUCH IDENTIFICATION; AND

(b) IF FEASIBLE, ACCORDING TO ANY APPLICABLE LAW ENFORCEMENT AGENCY GUIDELINES, GATHERS FINGERPRINT INFORMATION FROM SUCH PERSON AND STORES SUCH FINGERPRINTS FOR AT LEAST ONE YEAR AS A CRIMINAL JUSTICE RECORD.

Continued...

24-72.1-106. Applicability. THIS ARTICLE SHALL NOT APPLY TO A PERSON REPORTING A CRIME; A PUBLIC ENTITY OR OFFICIAL ACCEPTING A CRIME REPORT, CONDUCTING A CRIMINAL INVESTIGATION, ACCEPTING AN APPLICATION FOR THE PROVISION OF SERVICES OR PROVIDING SERVICES TO INFANTS AND CHILDREN BORN IN THE UNITED STATES PURSUANT TO 42 U.S.C. SEC. 1786, OR PROVIDING EMERGENCY MEDICAL SERVICE; A PEACE OFFICER IN THE PERFORMANCE OF THE OFFICER'S DUTIES AND WITHIN THE SCOPE OF THE OFFICER'S EMPLOYMENT IF SUCH OFFICER COMPLIES WITH SECTION 24-72.1-105 (2); OR INSTANCES WHEN A FEDERAL LAW MANDATES ACCEPTANCE OF A DOCUMENT.

SECTION 2. 18-5-102, Colorado Revised Statutes, is amended BY THE ADDITION OF A NEW SUBSECTION to read:

]18-5-102. Forgery. (3) UTTERING A FORGED DOCUMENT TO A PEACE OFFICER SHALL CREATE A PRESUMPTION THAT THE PERSON INTENDED TO DEFRAUD SUCH PEACE OFFICER.

SECTION 3. Applicability. This act shall apply to acts committed on or after the effective date of this act.

SECTION 4. Safety clause. The general assembly hereby finds, determines, and declares that this act is necessary for the immediate preservation of the public peace, health, and safety.

Lola Spradley SPEAKER OF THE HOUSE OF REPRESENTATIVES	John Andrews PRESIDENT OF THE SENATE
Judith Rodrigue CHIEF CLERK OF THE HOUSE OF REPRESENTATIVES	Mona Heustis SECRETARY OF THE SENATE

APPROVED_______________________________
Bill Owens
GOVERNOR OF THE STATE OF COLORADO

Mr. HOSTETTLER. I thank you, Senator Andrews, and I can tell you that the Chair is very disconcerted by the knowledge that in attempting to work with Federal authorities on immigration policy with regard to consular ID cards, you were essentially rebuffed. It will be a subject of an inquiry that I will have of the new bureau. I thank you for that information.

Ms. Dinerstein.

STATEMENT OF MARTI DINERSTEIN, PRESIDENT, IMMIGRATION MATTERS

Ms. DINERSTEIN. Thank you. Mr. Chairman, Ranking Member Jackson Lee and Members of the Subcommittee, I am pleased to appear before you to discuss whether Government entities and businesses should treat the consular card issued by foreign governments as valid identification within the United States. I strongly believe that to do so only undermines U.S. Immigration law—I am sorry, not only undermines immigration law but is also a potential threat to our homeland security.

The events of 9/11 showed all too clearly that our core identification documents need to be more secure to ensure that only people lawfully residing in the U.S. have access to them. However, positive developments in that regard are being undercut by an identity card, the Matricula Consular being issued by the government of Mexico. Mexico has done this for many years and its purposes have been totally benign. It has wanted it for consular registration, and no host government, including the U.S., had any problem with it. But recently Mexico decided to imbue additional benefits to the Matricula cards for the benefit of their citizens residing here illegally, and they wish it to be accepted by U.S. authorities for the express purpose of providing a very illegal benefit.

For Mexico to win widespread acceptance of the Matricula Consular as a substitute for U.S.-issued identification, it had to convince Government authorities that it is a secure identity card. So the face of the Matricula was redesigned to make it bilingual and to include a local U.S. address. Several features to deter counterfeiting were also embedded.

However, my research revealed that the Matricula is not a secure identity document. The goal of a secured identity document is one person, one identity, one card. The Matricula does not meet the latter two standards. To be truly secure, so-called breeder documents used to obtain an ID must be matched against some other data that corroborates the information.

A Mexican birth certificate is the principal document being used to obtain a Matricula. Press reports indicate that it and other documents are being cross-checked against computerized records in Mexico. They are not. The manner in which consular cards are being issued basically guarantees that no authentication will take place. Matriculas are issued on a same day basis, often from remote locations without the kind of sophisticated communications needed to authenticate breeder documents in an online, real-time environment.

The Matricula also fails to meet the standard to ensure that no—that one person is issued no more than one card, since no system is yet in place to access data in all 47 Mexican consulates that issue Matriculas.

But even if these significant security shortcomings were to be addressed in future years, there is one profound problem that will never go away. Only Mexico has access to the breeder documents used to obtain the Matricula and some supplementary information that they require that is not displayed on the card. This renders U.S. law enforcement impotent to conduct a thorough background investigation if a Mexican national whose only identification is a Matricula card commits a serious crime while in America.

Mexico has engaged in a grass roots lobbying campaign that has borne fruit. As the Chairman mentioned, this month Mexico announced that the Matricula is accepted by 402 localities, 32 counties, 122 financial institutions and 908 law enforcement offices. Mexico's aggressive lobbying has become a direct challenge to U.S. sovereignty. It changes America's de facto immigration policy, a right reserved only to Congress.

Predictably, the success of Mexico's efforts has had the effect of prompting other countries to follow suit. The governments of El Salvador, Guatemala, Honduras, Nicaragua, Poland and Peru have begun or are considering issuing cards of their own. More countries could follow, including some that the U.S. believes have been harboring terrorists. It is in these governments' interest for their nationals residing here illegally to remain and to continue remitting money back to their home countries often where it is sorely needed. It is in America's interest to control our borders and enforce our immigration laws.

Accepting a consular identity card from any country further erodes our ability and incentive to control which foreign nationals can enter and live here permanently. The acceptance of consular identification cards has profound implications for U.S. immigration policy and our homeland security.

[The prepared statement of Ms. Dinerstein follows:]

PREPARED STATEMENT OF MARTI DINERSTEIN

Good afternoon, Chairman Hostettler, Ranking Member Jackson Lee and members of the Subcommittee. I'm pleased to appear before this subcommittee to speak about an issue with important ramifications for homeland security and U.S. immigration policy.

SECURE IDENTIFICATION DOCUMENTS ARE ESSENTIAL TO HOMELAND SECURITY.

Before 9/11, America was in many ways an innocent nation. We expedited visas to those who wished to study here, made tourist and work visas readily available and welcomed those who wished to emigrate permanently. Indeed, we even were heading toward a "don't ask, don't tell" policy, where people in the country illegally were tacitly permitted to remain to make a better life for themselves and their families.

Post 9/11, we realized that we had been too permissive in our open-handed visa policy, negligent about monitoring the timely departure of visa holders and culpable in failing to protect our borders end enforce our immigration laws.

We also received a wake-up call that something must be done to protect America's core identity documents. The American people were shocked to learn that 18 of the 19 terrorists possessed either state-issued or counterfeit driver's licenses or ID cards, and all 19 had obtained Social Security numbers—some real, some fake. Possession of these documents permitted the hijackers, at least three of whom were here illegally on 9/11, to seamlessly meld into our society and freely move throughout the country.

Many states tightened the procedures by which foreign nationals obtain driver's licenses and ID cards and some moved to make legal residence one of the requirements for a license. Congress was quick to call the INS, State Department and Social Security Administration to task and press for immediate programs to rectify gaping holes in our issuance of identification documents.

Indeed, the USA PATRIOT Act of 2001, passed overwhelmingly by Congress, specifically addressed two areas of weakness with respect to America's identity documents.

Concerned that some of the terrorists had obtained commercial driver's licenses to transport hazardous materials, Congress mandated that no commercial license be issued without a check of the relevant criminal history databases and, in the case of an alien, a determination of his or her legal status in the United States.

Similarly, Congress directed the Treasury Department, in consultation with regulatory and other agencies, to study and provide recommendations for enhancing the ability of domestic financial institutions to verify the identity of foreign nationals.

Ironically, however, these positive developments are being undercut by an identity card issued by the government of Mexico, the specific intent of which is to gain privileges and benefits previously reserved for citizens and legal immigrants for an estimated five million Mexicans residing illegally in the U.S.

MEXICO'S CONSULAR ID CARD IS NOT SECURE AND VERIFIABLE.

Mexico has issued the matricula consular since 1870 to its nationals living abroad in case they had need of consular assistance. It's purpose and use was totally benign and of no concern to any host country, including the United States.

But after 9/11, our tolerance for permitting illegal aliens to reside in the U.S. abated considerably, coupled with a new-found determination to increase the reliability of U.S.-issued identification documents. This environment made it likely that life would become more difficult for millions of Mexican citizens residing here illegally. But, Mexico needs them to continue to live and work here and send a large portion of their earnings back home. Remittances to Mexico totaled $10 billion in 2002—money that has become essential to its faltering economy.

So Mexico decided to try to win widespread acceptance of the matricula consular as a substitute for U.S.-issued identification. To accomplish this it had to convince local, state and federal government agencies and U.S. business entities that the matricula is a secure identity document.

The face of the matricula was redesigned to make it bilingual and to include a local U.S. address. Recognizing that America wanted more secure identity documents, Mexico added several features to prevent counterfeiting. However, my research revealed that while those counterfeiting safeguards certainly improve the card's reliability, the matricula is not a secure identity document.

The goal of a secure ID card is one person, one identity, one card. The matricula does not meet the latter two standards.

"BREEDER" DOCUMENTS USED TO OBTAIN THE CONSULAR ID ARE NOT AUTHENTICATED.

To be truly secure, so-called breeder documents used to obtain an ID must be matched against some other data that corroborates the information.

A Mexican birth certificate is the principal document being used to obtain a matricula. Press reports indicate that it or other documents are being crosschecked against computerized records in Mexico. They are not.

The breeder documents are not being electronically scanned at the Mexican consulates that issue matriculas. Instead, paper files are kept. So, there is no computerized data to crosscheck anything with in Mexico.

Also, the manner in which the Mexican consular cards are issued basically guarantees that no authentication will take place. Matriculas are issued on a same-day basis, often from remote locations with no sophisticated communications equipment. For example, in April, the Chicago-based Mexican consulate issued 1,500 matriculas in only two days at the offices of the Wisconsin Hispanic Scholarship Foundation.

To authenticate breeder documents in an on-line, real time environment, the following would be needed:

- dedicated data lines and multiple layers of communications security
- almost instantaneous confirmation or declination of the documents
- sophisticated interface programming
- communications technology and support at each consulate

The price tag would easily be in the tens of millions of dollars. What is really happening is that Mexico is relying on staff members in the 47 consulate offices to visually authenticate the documents.

SAFEGUARDS NOT IN PLACE TO PREVENT MULTIPLE ISSUANCE OF MATRICULA TO ONE INDIVIDUAL.

Without safeguards to prevent multiple issuance, the matricula also fails to meet the standard to insure only one card for one person.

Concurrent with the issuance of each new matricula, a digital file of the photograph, signature and data elements is created. That file needs to be transmitted either to a central database in Mexico or on some networked basis to all the other 47 consulates to insure that no more than one card has been issued to that one person.

In its discussions with law enforcement and motor vehicle officials, Mexico has indicated it was building this network. But it it's not ready yet. Everyone seems to think it will become a reality and it's just a matter of time. But in this case, timing is everything.

Well over one million matriculas issued before 2002 are still valid and in circulation. They have no security features whatsoever. Mexico issued over one million of the improved matriculas in 2002, with no system in place to authenticate breeder documents or safeguard against duplicate issuance.

Fraud is occurring. To use just one example, the INS in Denver arrested a man who was carrying three different matriculas. All had his photograph, but three different names.

UNDERLYING IDENTITY DATA OF MATRICULA HOLDERS BELONGS TO MEXICO, NOT THE U.S.

Beyond normal concerns related to issuance of any secure and verifiable identification card is the troubling problem that all of the data collected to issue the matricula is owned and controlled by Mexico.

There is the possibility of graft within Mexico's 47 consulate offices. No country is immune from corrupt employees who sell identity documents for cash. But in Mexico corruption is endemic and is common throughout the government. Low-paid consular staff might succumb to bribes and provide matriculas to OTMs (Other Than Mexicans) engaged in drug or human smuggling or terror financing activities. These employees would be covered by diplomatic immunity.

Finally, there is the profound problem that only Mexico has access to the breeder documents used to obtain the matrticula and some supplementary information Mexico requires that is not displayed on the card itself. This renders U.S. law enforcement agencies impotent to conduct a thorough background investigation if a Mexican national whose only identification is a matricula card commits a serious crime while in America. Contrast this to the situation after the 9/11 terrorist attacks when the U.S. was able to assemble significant information about the hijackers because each had to provide information on a U.S. visa and their entrance and exits from the country were recorded by customs officials.

MATRICULA BLURS THE DISTINCTION BETWEEN LEGAL AND ILLEGAL IMMIGRANTS.

Mexico's strategy is to win acceptance for the matricula through a grassroots lobbying campaign at the local and state level. These efforts have borne fruit. This month Mexico announced that the matricula is now accepted by 402 localities, 32 counties, 122 financial institutions and 908 law enforcement offices.

Whenever challenged about the propriety of these lobbying activities, Mexico repeatedly emphasizes that a matricula is simply an identity card and does not change anyone's immigration status. Thankfully, that is true—but it comes close to achieving the functional equivalent.

The matricula is changing the lives of undocumented Mexicans, making it far more likely that they can remain here undetected and receive a type of immunity—not just from their illegal presence but for crimes committed on American soil. In localities where the matricula is accepted, it:

- has reduced the chances that illegal Mexican aliens will be arrested, jailed or deported
- given them entree to mainstream banking services
- provided access to city and state services and privileges, including in-state tuition rates denied to military families posted temporarily in a state.

- in some states gained them access to exactly the same driver's licenses as those carried by American citizens.

Mexico did not confer those privileges—local governments and entities within the United States did.

MATRICULA HAS BECOME A BADGE OF PROTECTION FOR MEXICAN ILLEGALS.

Local police in communities with a large number of Mexican illegal aliens have been willing to accept the matricula because some identification is better than none. The ground rules seem to be that no arrests will be made for minor infractions. This means that no background checks are run. No fingerprints are taken. No criminal databases are checked.

For Mexican citizens who posses one, the matricula has become a shield that hides any past criminal activity. But criminality is rampant in Mexico and, inevitably crosses our porous border. This is particularly true for drug traffickers, but also for money launderers and human smugglers, who have recently been linked to organized crime in Mexico. Given the free pass that local police are giving to matricula holders, it is highly likely that Mexican criminals, irrespective of their legal status, obtain one from their consulate office.

Mexican illegals also routinely commit crimes related to their illegal status. These include fraudulently obtaining U.S. birth certificates, Social Security numbers and driver's licenses; engaging in sham marriages and other strategems to obtain legal status; using fake U.S. immigration documents to receive government benefits; repeatedly crossing our border without permission, etc.

Some local police believe it is not their job to enforce federal immigration law. But for the police to ignore federal immigration law is tantamount to subverting it. Foreign residents living here lawfully have U.S.-issued documents. If in accepting the matricula, an identity document needed only by illegal aliens, local police are failing to conduct background checks, they are abdicating their law enforcement responsibilities and putting their community at risk.

This point was called into stark relief last month when Eugene, Oregon police stopped a Mexican national for a traffic infraction. A background check revealed that he had a criminal history including arrests and convictions for drugs, burglary, kidnapping and assault. He also was on the Bureau of Immigration and Custom Enforcement's "most wanted" criminal aliens list, having absconded after being ordered deported. Presumably, he would not have been captured by any of the 908 local law enforcement offices that are "accepting" the matricula.

A DRIVER'S LICENSE SERVES AS OUR DOMESTIC PASSPORT.

All illegal aliens prize a license because it is the most widely accepted identity document in America.

It is an unfortunate reality that in many communities, a substantial percentage of the population is Mexican illegals. This makes it difficult for elected local and state officials to ignore entreaties that illegals need driver's licenses to get to work in order to support their families. It is a topic that has occupied many state capitals in the last two years. Twelve states currently accept the matricula as identification to obtain a license. But efforts are unceasing to increase that number.

In a positive sign, in May the American Association of Motor Vehicle Administrators, with representatives from all 50 states, after careful study made a decision that it was "premature" to accept the matricula as part of its list of documents recommended for use by Department of Motor Vehicle employees.

It is concerned that the matricula lacks standardized issuance procedures, uniform security features and a secure database for verification purposes. In addition, AAMVA endorsed a standard that no foreign documents other than passports, in conjunction with proper immigration documents, be used to validate legal presence.

Contrast the responsible stand of AAMVA to protect the security of driver's licenses with that of a U.S. government agency—the Internal Revenue Service. Most states that accept the matricula as ID for a driver's license do so because the state also allows the Individual Taxpayer Identification Number (ITIN) to serve as a substitute for a Social Security number.

IRS KNOWS THE ITIN IS UNVERIFIED BUT HAS NOT STOPPED ITS USAGE AS IDENTIFICATION.

As background, in 1996 the IRS, a division of the Treasury Department, began issuing ITINS as a way to encourage illegals, who are not eligible for Social Security cards, to comply with U.S. tax laws. In its publications, website and forms, the IRS makes clear that the ITIN is "for tax purposes" only. Perhaps because of its perceived limited purpose as a tax tracking number, the IRS made little or no effort to authenticate the documents presented by foreign nationals to obtain the ITIN.

This laxness led to a stampede of U.S. illegal residents from nations all around the world applying for ITINs. The IRS has issued 6 million ITINs since 1996, but, strangely, only 2 million were used for the purpose of filing U.S. tax returns. It is assumed that individuals who receive an ITIN and do not file taxes are using it as official U.S. government identification to obtain bank accounts, government services and—ominously—driver's licenses.

Belatedly, at the end of 2002 both the Treasury Department and the IRS threw up strong warning signals that the ITIN cannot—or should not—be accepted as an identification document. Treasury said in its report to Congress on the USA PATRIOT Act that the "the IRS does not employ rigorous identification verification procedures." Similarly, the IRS announced that as of April 15, 2003 it would require more identity documentation from ITIN applicants, including proof of their alien status.

In response to a question this week, an IRS spokesman said: "The ITIN was created solely for tax administration purposes. The ITIN was never intended to be a supplemental identification document for purposes other than filing a tax return." However, the IRS has issued no public statement confirming that the foreign documents used to obtain an ITIN are not authenticated and, therefore, the ITIN is not a reliable identification document. Such a statement would lead state motor vehicle bureaus to exclude the ITIN from their list of acceptable documents. It is highly unlikely that illegal residents would be able to obtain a driver's license in any state based solely on possession of a foreign government-issued consular card.

THE TREASURY DEPARTMENT HAS TACITLY ENCOURAGED BANKS TO ACCEPT THE MATRICULA.

A relatively small number—122 out of over 9,000 federally-insured financial institutions—are accepting matriculas to open accounts. Even this small number is a remarkable occurrence, as all legitimate financial institutions are regulated and must meet guidelines set by their regulators to "know your customer."

It appears that banks are accepting the matricula consular because Mexico requested the State and Treasury Departments' help to help find ways to reduce the cost of remitting money to Mexico. It also was interested in U.S. financial institutions undertaking a program to "bank the unbanked." Since Mexican illegals possess none of the usually accepted ID documents, the Treasury Department gave its tacit approval for financial institutions to accept the matricula instead.

In fact, it did so in a report to Congress dealing with the secure identification requirments mandated by the USA PATRIOT Act, where it said the "proposed regulations do not discourage bank acceptance of the "matricula consular" identity card that is being issued by the Mexican government to immigrants."

This is ironic as Mexican banks do not hold the matricula in high regard as an identity document. No major bank headquarters in Mexico lists the "matricula consular" among the several official identification documents they accept to start accounts. In fact, according to a Mexican government press release, as of the end of 2002, the matricula was being accepted as an identity document for any purpose in only 10 of Mexico's 33 states.

Especially in the context of the PATRIOT Act and our focus on homeland security, it is difficult to comprehend why Treasury would give comfort to an identity card being offered by a single foreign government, as it could be predicted that other foreign governments would demand the same treatment.

ACCEPTANCE OF FOREIGN GOVERNMENT CONSULAR CARDS HAS PROFOUND IMPLICATIONS FOR U.S. IMMIGRATION POLICY AND HOMELAND SECURITY.

The proliferation and acceptance of foreign government consular cards as a substitute for U.S.-issued identification endangers our homeland security. In addition to Mexico, the governments of Guatemala, Honduras, Poland, Peru and El Salvador have begun or are considering issuing cards of their own. More countries could follow, including some that the U.S. believes have been harboring terrorists.

Public opinion polls for decades have shown that while the American public supports legal immigration, it is opposed to illegal immigration. Obviously, the events of 9/11 only strengthened the intensity of these opinions.

The reason why government want acceptance of their consular cards is to make it easier for their foreign nationals residing illegally in the U.S. to "come out of the shadows." It is in these governments' interest for their illegals to remain in the U.S. and remit money back to their home countries.

It is in America's interest to control our borders and enforce our immigration laws. Accepting a less than secure identity card from any country further erodes our ability and incentive to control which foreign nationals can enter and live permanently in the U.S. It has profound implications for U.S. immigration policy and our homeland security.

ATTACHMENT

Center for Immigration Studies

Backgrounder

January 2003

IDs for Illegals

The 'Matricula Consular' Advances Mexico's Immigration Agenda

By Marti Dinerstein

In the wake of the 9/11 terrorist attacks, a migration deal with Mexico was tabled while attention turned to homeland security. So the Mexican government abruptly changed its White House strategy and substituted a grass-roots approach that would focus at the local level, seek small successes, and build momentum for congressional action. The linchpin for this new strategy was to be the "matricula consular," an official identity card issued by the Mexican government, which it wanted to be officially recognized within the United States.

This *Backgrounder* is the first detailed examination of the matricula issue. Among the findings:

- The matricula consular is useful in the United States only for illegal aliens, since legal immigrants, by definition, have U.S. government-issued documents.
- The Mexican government has launched an aggressive grassroots lobbying campaign to win acceptance for its matricula card from state and local jurisdictions and from banks, especially in areas where Mexican illegal aliens are concentrated.
- The objective of this lobbying effort is to achieve quasi-legal status for Mexican illegals in the United States without waiting for action from Washington.
- The matricula itself, however, is useful to illegal aliens only insofar as U.S. institutions are willing to collaborate with Mexico's efforts to circumvent U.S. immigration law.
- While many jurisdictions have resisted pressure from the Mexican government, others have not; the matricula is now accepted by 800 local law enforcement agencies and 74 banks, as well as by 13 states for purposes of obtaining a driver's license.
- Not only does the matricula subvert U.S. immigration law, it is not even a secure identity document. Mexico is not authenticating the documents used to obtain the matricula against computerized data files in Mexico.
- Safeguards are not in place to prevent multiple issuance of matriculas to the same individual; in fact, the INS has already reported finding multiple cards in different names issued to the same person.
- The matricula is becoming a shield that hides criminal activity for two reasons: first, the holder's identity was not verified when the card was issued, and second, police in jurisdictions that accept the matricula are less likely to run background checks on card holders picked up for minor infractions.
- The U.S. Treasury Department has given its approval to banks to accept the matricula for opening bank accounts.
- The acceptance of Mexico's matricula consular sets a precedent, making it almost impossible to reject similar cards presented by illegal aliens from other countries, including those which have sent terrorists to the United States in the past.

Marti Dinerstein (mdinerstein@earthlink.net) is President of Immigration Matters, a public policy analysis firm in New York, and is a Fellow at the Center for Immigration Studies. She is the author of two recent Backgrounders: *"America's Identity Crisis: Document Fraud is Pervasive and Pernicious" and "Giving Cover to Illegal Aliens: IRS Tax ID Numbers Subvert Immigration Law."*

Mexico's voter registration card contains a fingerprint and would have been counter-productive to Mexico's aim of avoiding deportation of its citizens. Anyone caught crossing the border without permission is fingerprinted and penalties rise for repeat offenders.

Early in September 2001, the Mexican government had every expectation that it would soon achieve its principal foreign policy goal — a comprehensive migration agreement with the United States that would create new guest worker programs, exempt Mexico from visa limits, and "regularize" the immigration status of the estimated three to five million Mexicans already living in the United States illegally.

After 9/11, public and congressional opposition in the United States to an illegal-alien amnesty hardened and made such a deal impossible. In its place, Mexico sought piecemeal changes, centered on gaining acceptance in the United States for the "matricula consular." But Mexico's new approach has become a direct challenge to U.S. sovereignty — by aggressively lobbying state and local governments, Mexico is changing America's de facto immigration policy in lieu of congressional action. And it has been doing so while the U.S. government watched — or even gave its tacit consent.

Rebirth of the Matricula

The issue of secure identification became a national concern in the United States after it was discovered that all 19 9/11 hijackers had valid or fake Social Security numbers and 18 of the 19 had authentic or phony driver's licenses or motor vehicle ID cards. There was a public outcry and steps were taken to tighten the eligibility requirements for both Social Security cards and driver's licenses. It has became common operating procedure for ID to be required in order to enter certain buildings, gain access to secure areas at airports, and attend high-profile public activities, like New Year's Eve in Times Square. Life became even more difficult for the undocumented, the majority of whom are Mexicans.

Wanting to ensure that its nationals could illegally remain in the United States with as little hassle as possible, the Fox government turned its attention to providing them with Mexican identification that would be accepted by U.S. authorities.

Simply providing passports was not a viable option. The United States requires Mexican citizens to obtain a visa before entering the country, a nicety ignored by people who cross our borders without permission. Possession of a Mexican passport without a visa would only highlight their illegal status.

Another option could have been Mexico's voter registration card, which is regarded as a secure identity document. It was revamped at great expense in the 1990s to stem endemic corruption in the Mexican electoral system. But that card, too, was a non-starter. It contains a fingerprint and, thus, would have been counter-productive to Mexico's aim of avoiding deportation of its citizens. Anyone caught crossing the border without permission is fingerprinted and penalties rise for repeat offenders. Knowing this, Mexican illegals often use fake identities, not wanting to have their legal name in INS arrest files. But if fingerprints match, a false identity doesn't cut it. Identity theft is a felony and subjects an offender to deportation.

So the Mexican government turned to the matricula consular, a logical choice, since it was created in 1870 specifically to help Mexican citizens living abroad get help from their local consulate if needed. In its simplest form the matricula card is an official Mexican government document that certifies the name and age of the bearer. Well over one million matriculas were already in circulation in the United States before the September 2001 terrorist attacks. Even though those cards contain no security features, they remain valid, according to a consulate official in New York.[1]

In an audacious political maneuver, Mexico decided to try to turn the matricula consular into a vehicle to achieve quasi-legal status for its undocumented population in the United States. Its strategy was two-pronged. First, it needed to convince U.S. authorities that the matricula was secure identification. Second, it planned an aggressive grassroots lobbying campaign to win acceptance for it at the local and state level, especially in areas where large numbers of Mexicans resided and were, in fact, members of the community.

New matricula contains useful information and offers protection against counterfeiting. The new matricula card was first introduced in major metropolitan areas in March 2002 and gradually was made available in consulate areas throughout the United States. It is wallet-sized, making it easy to carry on a daily basis. It is generally valid for five years and is bargain-priced at $28. The card contains the name, date and place of birth, a current photograph, and the holder's signature. A new feature is inclusion of a U.S. address, which is information banks require and the police also want, even if someone is simply reporting a crime. A current address also is required to obtain local social services and access to community facilities.

Another new addition is the telephone number of the local Mexican consulate office, which is provided for two reasons. First, it is a way that local officials can verify the card's authenticity. Second, it is a reminder to the police that a Mexican national in trouble has a right to call his or her consulate office for assistance.

In designing the new card, Mexico put emphasis on features to prevent counterfeiting. Some of them are visible, like the patterned green security paper and an "advantage seal" that in natural light changes color from green to brown and is superimposed over the bearer's photograph.

Other anti-forging features are visible only in florescent or infrared light and others require a high-tech decoder to be seen. "At one angle, the decoder reveals the bearer's name over the phograph. From other angles, the decoder reveals the bearer's birth date and the letters 'SRE,' initials of the Secretaria de Relaciones Exteriores, the Mexican agency responsible for issuing the card."[2]

The Mexican government calls the new matricula card the "high security consular ID." This phrase is used in conjunction with descriptions of its anti-forgery technology.

The counterfeiting safeguards certainly add to the matricula's reliability, but they are not a substitute for other security measures, some of which Mexico has used to promote the matricula but has not yet delivered.

Matricula not Secure

Mexico is not authenticating breeder documents. For an identity card to be secure, the "breeder" documents provided must be authenticated to guard against identity fraud. Safeguards must also be in place to ensure that the goal of one person, one identity, one card is met.

This issue is particularly complicated for the Mexican government, which is fully aware that its nationals commit document and identity fraud to remain in the United States. Previously, this issue was not of concern to them; but now, the Mexican government is warning its citizens against this practice.[3]

To guard against fraud, Mexico requires that applicants for the matricula appear in person to have their photograph taken and to submit identity documents and proof of residence in the geographic region served by the consulate issuing the card.

An original or certified copy of a Mexican birth certificate is required. Another piece of photo identification, preferably from Mexico, is also required. Consular officials say the documents they accept include a voter registration card, a military service card, or a valid passport. In the absence of a photo ID from Mexico, consular officials are granted discretion in deciding what U.S. documents to accept. Media reports have mentioned employer ID cards, motor vehicle department ID cards, and student ID cards. Concern has been expressed that the standards for issuing matriculas differ considerably from consulate to consulate.

For the matricula card to be secure, these "breeder" documents must be authenticated. And Mexico has said it was doing so.[4] However, local consulates do not, and probably cannot, verify the authenticity of these documents against computerized data files in Mexico. An official at the Mexican Embassy in Washington said that it relies on the expertise of the staff in the 47 consulates to visually authenticate the documents.

The breeder documents presented by those applying for a matricula card are not electronically scanned. Instead, hard copies are made of the documents, which are kept in physical files at the appropriate consulate. So as a practical matter, the consulates have no computerized data to transmit, even if they were linked to databases in Mexico against which the matricula applicants' information could be checked.

Issued on same-day basis, even in remote locations. Given the sheer volume of the matriculas being issued and the physical conditions under which this is accomplished, it is easy to understand why the process is not highly automated. The "new and improved" matricula has been a runaway best seller with undocumented Mexicans living in the United States. On some days the demand exceeds the ability of the consular staffs to process all of the people waiting in long lines.

This is particularly true when mobile offices are set up to accommodate people who live in rural areas distant from the nearest consulate office. These visits are publicized within the local Mexican community and word-of-mouth travels fast. The venues for the mobile consulates are not fancy, ranging from an adult education school in Brentwood, Calif., to a tent outside the Cardinal Savings Bank in Woodstock,

Ill., to the El Rincon Vaquero trading post in West Columbia, S.C. All matriculas – even from these remote locations – are issued on a same-day basis.

For a consulate to transmit personal information about matricula applicants on an on-line, real-time basis to a confidential database maintained in Mexico would (or should) require dedicated data lines and multiple layers of communications security. It would also require that the consulate receive back almost instantaneous confirmation of the validity of the applicant's documents. For that to happen, sophisticated, costly, and time-consuming interface programming would be needed, as well as investments in communications technology and support at each consulate. The price tag would easily be in the tens of millions of dollars.

Those realities raise troubling questions and doubts about Mexico's candor when explaining the extent — and limits — of the matricula as a secure ID document.

Safeguards not in place to prevent multiple issuance of matriculas to same individual. Mexico had to absorb a multi-million dollar start-up investment for new equipment and technology before its 47 consulates could issue the improved matricula. That investment was required for the redesign of the card, for digital cameras to photograph each matricula applicant on-site, for technology to prevent counterfeiting, and for the equipment that actually produces the cards.

Concurrent with the issuance of each matricula, a digital file of the photograph, signature, and data elements is created. Such a file could be electronically transmitted to Mexico and matched against databases in all 47 consulates to ensure that no more than one card is issued to any individual. In its discussions with law enforcement, banking, and motor vehicle officials to gain acceptance for the matricula, Mexico has referenced this database as another security layer.

There is one big problem, however. The network is not yet operational. Estimates of when it will be available range from several months to several years. Most U.S. officials seem to feel that Mexico is serious about providing it, if for no other reason than it needs it for its own purposes. The issue seems to be a matter of timing, not intent.

But as the saying goes, timing is everything. Well over one million older matriculas, which have no security features and the data from which cannot be converted into electronic format, are still in circulation. The Mexican government announced it issued over one million matriculas in 2002. Thus, with estimates of Mexico's illegal population in the United States ranging from three to five million people, a significant percentage of that population possess matriculas that do not meet a generally accepted definition of secure identification.

The absence of a computer network linking the 47 consulates is a serious security flaw. Possessing multiple copies of a genuine photo ID document touted as having "high security" would provide excellent cover to a host of unsavory characters.

Fraud is occurring. "One guy we arrested recently had three different matriculas with three different names. It was his picture, issued through the consulate," said an INS official in Denver. "Our one worry is that this gives someone whose intentions are bad one genuine piece of identification."[5]

Some Washington officials are quietly worried about graft within the 47 consulate offices. No country is immune from corrupt employees who sell identity documents for cash. But in Mexico corruption is endemic and is common throughout the government. Rumor has it that some employees simply pocket the $28 matricula fee, paid in cash with no audit trail. Others worry that low-paid consular staff might succumb to bribes and provide matriculas to OTMs (Other Than Mexicans) engaged in drug or human smuggling or terror financing activities. These employees would be covered by diplomatic immunity.

A good reason to believe that the consular network will become a reality is that Mexico has its own reasons to prevent fraud in its issuance of the matricula. In the past, Mexico has had to guess how many of its citizens live in the United States. And it had no clue who they were or where they lived. Compiling an accurate registry of these names serves Mexico's economic, political, and foreign policy objectives.

Mexicans Push Matricula Acceptance

It's obvious why the matricula is so popular with Mexican illegals. It is transforming their quality of life in America. It sells itself. Mexican officials and illegal immigrant advocates repeat over and over like a mantra that the matricula does not confer legal status. They trivialize the benefits it confers, referencing library cards, video rentals, and utility services. Yet, in less than a year, the matricula has come a long way toward achieving what Mexico hoped it would — quasi-legal status for its undocumented population in areas where the matricula is widely accepted.

In localities where it is accepted as valid identification, the matricula consular has reduced the chances that illegal Mexican aliens will be arrested and deported, given them entree to mainstream banking services, provided access to city and state services – and in 13 states gained them exactly the same driver's licenses as those carried by American citizens. (See sidebar.)

The matricula is just a laminated piece of paper. Its value derives from the fact that U.S. police departments, banks, local governments, and state motor vehicle bureaus voluntarily have agreed to accept it, no questions asked.

This is due to the brilliant propaganda campaign, conceived by Mexico's foreign ministry and executed by its 47 consulate offices, the largest diplomatic presence in the United States. Their plan is to gain widespread acceptance for the card throughout the United States. This involves consulate personnel traveling from city to town within their geographic region, calling on the mayor, police chief, local bank officials, motor vehicle bureaus, state legislators, etc., and urging them to accept the matriucla as official identification. They speak at official meetings, court prominent community leaders, meet with the editorial boards of newspapers, and seize every opportunity given for media coverage.

Each small success is celebrated and announced to the local media. A scorecard is maintained in Washington and disseminated to the local consulate offices. Thus, a "win" with a local police chief in California can be cited by the consulate office in Georgia as evidence of the growing momentum to accept the matricula throughout the United States.

The results of this lobbying effort have been impressive. On December 30, the Mexican Foreign Ministry announced that in 2002 it had issued 1,040,934 matricula consulars to Mexicans in the United States. Approximately 64 percent were issued by 10 Mexican consulate offices in three border states — Arizona, California, and Texas — and in Chicago, which has the second largest Mexican population after Los Angeles. To date, 74 banks accept the matricula as identification to open accounts. According to the Mexican government, the matricula also is accepted as official ID by more than 800 U.S. police departments and by 13 states to obtain a driver's license.[6]

Matricula Shields Criminals

At one level, it is hard to understand why 800 police forces would accept the matricula as acceptable ID, but it has a certain logic. In selling the matricula to the police, Mexican officials emphasize its security features, public safety, and human dignity. They make the point that illegal Mexican aliens in the community would be more likely to report crimes to the police if they did not fear doing so could lead to their deportation.

These arguments resonate with local police, whose principal job is to protect their community. The police department in Austin, Texas, was among the first to accept the matricula.[7] It did so because its own records indicated that Mexicans assumed to be illegal

Matricula ID Transforms Life for Illegal Aliens

Can Legally Obtain Most Requested ID Card in the United States

- Receive same driver's license as citizens (in 13 states)

Reduced Risk of Arrest and Deportation

- Police less likely to arrest; instead cite and release for minor violations
- Lower chance of being fingerprinted
- Reduced risk of background checks for past criminal acts
- Lessen chance of crosscheck with INS for repeated border crossings

Access to Banking Services, Credit Cards, and Home Mortgages

- Open bank accounts
- Obtain ATM cards for relatives living in Mexico
- Leverage bank account to obtain credit cards
- Obtain home mortgages by building credit history
- Bank accounts lead to issuance of official U.S. ID number from the IRS

Obtain City and State Services

- Get hospital ID for medical services
- Register for local health department services
- Obtain marriage license
- Apply for birth or death certificate
- Enter government buildings
- Receive resident discounts for city parks, etc.

Diminished Difficulty of Living in the United States

- Rent or buy homes and apartments (protection under fair housing laws)
- Qualify for subsidized housing
- Obtain telephone and utility services
- Board airplanes

> **It is a certainty that criminals, irrespective of their legal status, are in line when the consulate mobile offices arrive in their localities. Why not? The only requirement to receive the matricula is Mexican citizenship.**

were subject to a disproportionately high level of crime, particularly robberies.

Matricula reduces risk of arrest, jail, and deportation. Police need to see identification even for minor infractions. If an individual has none, he or she must be taken to a police station and booked. It is a time-consuming process and causes ill will within the community when, arguably, the offense is not a serious one. Immigrant advocates shrilly remind the media that local police are not responsible for enforcing federal immigration law. And some local police agree with this assertion. The assistant chief of police in Austin "acknowledged that some citizens have criticized the authorities' acceptance of the card. However, he noted, enforcing immigration law is a federal responsibility.[8]

But for the police to ignore federal immigration law is tantamount to subverting it. And that is exactly what has been happening since the Mexican government launched its full-court press to get local law enforcement officials to accept the matricula on a pari passu basis with U.S.-issued identification or valid passports.

In some localities, an illegal Mexican alien in possession of a matricula is being cited and released. Without a matricula, he or she would be taken to a police station, fingerprinted, and a background check run. Police would examine any papers in the suspect's possession to determine the person's identity. If their search gave them reason to believe the person was in possession of fraudulent documents, he or she would be charged with that crime, as well as the one that had brought them to the attention of the police in the first place. The individual's name and fingerprints would be run through criminal databases, which now include the INS list of over 300,000 aliens who absconded after being served with deportation notices. A large number of them are from Mexico.

While local police do not routinely notify the INS when an illegal alien is arrested, they apparently do so if a serious crime has been committed. Thus, they seem to be comfortable selectively enforcing federal immigration law.[9]

But in an increasing number of U.S. cities, towns, and villages, none of these activities are taking place. For any Mexican citizen who possesses one, and particularly for those here illegally, the matricula has become a shield that hides past or current criminal activity.

Matricula available to hard-core criminals, no questions asked. Given the free pass that local police are giving to matricula holders, it is a certainty that criminals, irrespective of their legal status, are in line when the consulate mobile offices arrive in their localities. Why not? The only requirement to receive the matricula is Mexican citizenship. No criminal background checks are run. It is an identity document, nothing else. But local law enforcement officials in the U.S., trying to cope with an influx of illegal Mexican aliens into their communities, have turned it into a sort of protection badge.

Criminality is rampant in Mexico and, inevitably, crosses our porous border. This is particularly true with drug smugglers. It is an unfortunate fact of life that illegal drugs are grown and manufactured in Mexico, trafficked by Mexicans, but used by Americans.

Within the last decade, Mexican drug traffickers have become major wholesalers throughout the United States of marijuana, heroin, cocaine, methamphetamine, and ecstasy. Their distribution hubs are expanding away from just border communities. According to a Drug Enforcement Administration official, "The southwest border isn't along the Rio Grande anymore. It's in Atlanta and North Carolina and Chicago and even Yonkers and New Rochelle."[10]

They like to work close to towns that provide easy highway access to big cities and where poor immigrant residents can be recruited as couriers. These "towns offer the cover of hard-working immigrants and a pool of potential recruits among the out of luck and unemployed. . . . From bases on the West Coast, Mexican traffickers have moved across the Northwest and Midwest, hiding among fruit pickers in Washington, resort workers in Colorado, and construction workers in Minnesota. . . .The Mexican traffickers are notably low profile, and police officers say the immigrant workers on whom they prey are similarly discreet."[11]

The vast majority of illegal Mexican aliens are not perceived to be "criminals," although they commit criminal acts like crossing our border without permission, engaging in identity theft, and using fake, stolen, or borrowed Social Security numbers to find work. While Americans who commit those crimes would be arrested and prosecuted, there is great reluctance to do so in communities with large illegal populations because it could result in their deportation.

The matricula is compounding this problem and giving both illegals and local law enforcement a way to ignore this troubling reality.

Mexico Lobbies Banks

Some Mexican illegals view a banking relationship as the most important tangible value of the matricula consular. For those who work off the books, it provides peace of mind to know they no longer are easy marks for thieves who prey on people who fear going to the police. For others, it makes cashing paychecks easier. Not only does it reduce the cost of sending money to their homes in Mexico, it provides these families with an ATM card, so they can withdraw only enough cash to meet their needs and keep the rest secure in a bank.

At first blush it seems almost impossible to believe that some of the largest and most prestigious banks in the country are knowingly offering accounts to Mexican illegal aliens. The reasons are complicated and encompass outreach to assist a minority community, perceived profits to be made from accessing a fast-growing new market, and even a way to increase the dollars remitted to Mexico, in the expectation that some will be allocated to economic development projects. But the most important reason is that neither banking regulators nor the U.S. Treasury Department have objected to opening banking accounts for Mexican illegals who use the matricula as their identification. In fact, a good case can be made that regulators and the Treasury Department have tacitly encouraged banks to do so.

The irony is that Mexican banks do not hold the matricula in high regard as an identity document. No major bank headquarters in Mexico lists the "matricula consular" among the several official identification documents they accept to start accounts. Perhaps recognizing that this revelation could be embarrassing, on July 1, 2002, the Mexican Ministry of Interior instructed regional offices of the National Migration Institute that full recognition and validity be authorized for the matricula consular for identification purpose and for entry into Mexico. As of December 30, 2002, the document was being accepted in 10 of Mexico's 33 states.[12]

Remittances and economic development projects important to Mexico. According to the Inter-American Development Bank, money sent home to Latin America and Caribbean countries from their nationals quadrupled in the last decade to $23 billion in 2001.[13] Given current migration patterns, this growth is expected to continue throughout the decade. This remittance phenomenon, combined with a concurrent decrease in U.S. foreign aid, has led the State and Treasury Departments to work jointly with the international development aid community to find ways to redirect some of the money to promote economic development in these impoverished nations.

This is a high priority for President Fox. Echoing concerns shared by the World Bank and the Inter-American Development Bank, he has lamented "that an overwhelming majority of immigrant dollars sent to Mexico were used to provide for the day-to-day survival of the poorest families. Little is saved. Even less is invested in projects that could stimulate economic growth. . . . Mr. Fox has expanded government programs that match, peso for peso, the money that immigrants send for public works projects in their home communities."[14]

Mexico received $9.3 billion in remittances in 2001 but claims its citizens sent even more. The cost of money transfers gobbled up from 10 to 20 percent of the total amount remitted. The international economic aid community reasoned that large U.S. commercial banks could help decrease these high remittance-processing costs.

When Mexico approached large U.S. banks to discuss lowering the cost of remittances and accepting the matricula consular to open accounts tailored to poor Mexicans, it met a receptive audience at some institutions. It is likely that executives in retail banking would have noticed the Census projections that Hispanics would soon overtake blacks as the largest minority group in America and would welcome the opportunity to tap into a large new market. Similarly, since the late 1970s, U.S. regulators have required evidence that banks have made an effort to serve poor, minority communities within their market areas. This community development activity usually reports to the executive responsible for assuring that the bank receives satisfactory ratings from its regulators.

And some of those regulators, most notably the Federal Deposit Insurance Corporation and local Federal Reserve banks, perhaps responding to the unprecedented level of immigration in the 1990s, were concurrently sponsoring seminars about "financial literacy" for the "unbanked" in poor minority communities. The promised new "high security" matricula would provide an opportunity to open bank accounts for the largest immigrant group in the United

States. Of course, since Mexicans legally in the United States already possessed the appropriate documentation to establish bank accounts, it was understood that only undocumented Mexicans would need the matricula. The timing was also fortunate because the Internal Revenue Service had started to issue the Individual Taxpayer Identification Number, which could serve as the second ID usually required by banks to fulfill their "know your customer" obligations.

Internal Revenue Service gives Mexican illegals second ID needed to open bank accounts. In 1996 the IRS, a division of the Treasury Department, began issuing Individual Taxpayer Identification Numbers to foreign nationals who were not eligible to receive a Social Security card as a way to encourage compliance with U.S. tax laws. A policy decision was made to make the ITIN available to illegal immigrants based on their "substantial presence" in the United States. In its publications, website, and forms, the IRS makes clear that the ITIN is "for tax purposes only." Perhaps because of its stated limited purpose, the IRS made little or no effort to authenticate the documents presented by foreign nationals to obtain the ITIN. Perhaps it did not feel it was necessary to do so, because the agency was knowingly giving them to illegal aliens.

This laxness led to a stampede of illegals from nations all around the world applying for ITINs. As of October 2002, over 5.5 million ITINs had been issued. But, strangely, only 1.5 million tax returns actually were filed using the ITIN number. It is assumed that the people who applied for the ITIN and do not file taxes are using it as official U.S. government identification to obtain driver's licenses, bank accounts, and government services. It is not known if ITINs are easily available to citizens of countries that harbor terrorists or to resident aliens appearing on the FBI's criminal database or to the more than 300,000 aliens who absconded after being served with deportation notices.[15]

The ITIN has been linked in media stories to the burgeoning popularity of the matricula. Banks need an official U.S. tax number to open an interest bearing account and, by definition, illegal aliens are not legally entitled to a Social Security number. So Mexican consulate staffs have been suggesting the ITIN as an acceptable alternative and, apparently, neither the banks nor the IRS raised objections. However, within the last three months, both the Treasury Department and IRS have thrown up strong warning signals that the ITIN cannot (or should not) be accepted as an identification document.

In its October 21, 2002, report to Congress, the Treasury Department said "the IRS does not employ rigorous identification verification procedures. For example, a foreign national can apply for an ITIN by mail or through an authorized ITIN Acceptance Agent, which is a person or entity authorized by the IRS to take applications."[16]

Similarly, on December 17, 2002, the IRS announced that henceforth applicants must submit documents proving their alien status and identity.[17] It is unclear exactly how or if the IRS plans to use this information. It has a policy of shielding illegal immigrants from exposure to the INS, which has seemed to continue even though the USA Patriot Act explicitly calls for greater information sharing among government agencies, law enforcement, and the intelligence community.[18]

U.S. Treasury gives banks comfort to accept the matricula. A key factor influencing the banking community to accept the matricula is its belief that the U.S. Treasury Department has given its approval.[19] "Under section 326(b) of the USA Patriot Act, Congress directed that Treasury, in consultation with the federal functional regulators and other relevant agencies, study and provide recommendations for enhancing the ability of domestic financial institutions to verify the identity of foreign nationals."[20]

In its report to Congress, Treasury spelled out what type of information a financial institution may require from a non-U.S. person seeking to open an account: "The regulations state that financial institutions may accept one or more of the following: a U.S. taxpayer identification number; a passport number and country of issuance; an alien identification card number, *or the number and country of issuance of any other government-issued document evidencing nationality or residence and bearing a photograph or similar safeguard*." (Italics added.)[21]

That sentence was followed by footnote 17. It was a shocker. "Thus, the proposed regulations do not discourage bank acceptance of the 'matricula consular' identity card that is being issued by the Mexican government to immigrants."

The intent of the USA Patriot Act of 2001, passed overwhelmingly by Congress in response to the 9/11 terrorist attacks, was to strengthen our homeland security. It addressed the issue of secure identification because the hijackers had obtained both Social Security numbers and driver's licenses. Especially in this context, it is difficult to comprehend why Treasury went out of its way to give approval to an identity card being offered by a single foreign government whose contiguous border is a matter of acute concern to the United States and whose nationals represent the majority of illegals within the United States.

Matricula Leads to a Drivers License

As we saw with the hijackers, illegal aliens of all nationalities prize a state-issued driver's license above all other identity documents because it serves as a domestic passport. It is the most widely accepted identity document in America and gains you access to places, services, and transportation. Once a Mexican has a driver's license, he or she could throw away their matricula. It would no longer be needed.

After 9/11, it was generally recognized that current state driver's license laws, regulations, and procedures are rife with loopholes and subject to political pressure. A number of states immediately took action to close administrative loopholes and introduce legislation to more tightly control the conditions under which foreign nationals illegally in the United States can obtain driver's licenses. Some states still openly subvert federal immigration law and issue licenses to illegal aliens. Their justification usually is a pragmatic one. Illegals are going to drive anyway to get to work, and it improves public safety if they pass a driver's test, know the rules of the road, and obtain insurance.

In trying to grapple with this issue, some state legislatures have suggested a compromise. Licenses would be issued to undocumented individuals but the front of the license would bear a message similar to "For driving purposes only." This resulted in torrents of criticism from immigrants and their advocates, charges of discrimination and racism and the pronouncement that driving is a basic human right. The bottom line is that illegal aliens want a driver's license precisely because it masks their illegal status.

Two states with large undocumented populations resist lobbying and just say "No." Although there is some dispute as to the actual number of states accepting the matricula as proof of identity to obtain a driver's license, Mexico says 13 states are doing so. Consulate officials are actively lobbying other states to either alter motor vehicle department regulations regarding acceptable identity documents for undocumented aliens or pass legislation that would explicitly permit acceptance of the matricula.

The new, improved matricula became available to residents of New York, New Jersey, and Connecticut in March 2002. The news was announced by the regional Mexican consul who said "The ideal would be if the matriculation card could gain points to obtain a driver's license in the tri-state area. . . . We are holding talks now with representatives from the departments of transportation of the three states."[22]

But New York's Department of Motor Vehicles refused to add the matricula to its list of approved identity documents to obtain a driver's license. "In other cities the validity of the Mexican ID card has prompted heated debates over whether recognition would amount to legitimization of illegal immigrants. New York politicians, however, rarely raise issues relating to the legal or illegal status of immigrants. Instead, the conversations in city and state offices over the Mexican ID have focused on the heightened concerns over security and identity fraud since the terrorist attacks."[23]

Similarly, in a year he was standing for re-election in the state with the largest Mexican population, California Governor Gray Davis showed political courage by vetoing legislation that would have granted licenses to illegal immigrants. He did so despite the fact that the legislation had been significantly revised to address concerns he had raised; "The bills would have allowed illegal immigrants to obtain licenses if they passed all driving tests, underwent criminal background checks, were applying for legal residency and could prove they were employed and had lived in California for at least 15 months in the last three years."[24] The governor's veto message said, "the tragedy of September 11 made it abundantly clear that the driver's license is more than just a license to drive; it is one of the primary documents we use to identify ourselves."[25]

While this veto outraged many in the Hispanic community, not all opposed the governor's decision. Not only did the California Hispanic Chamber of Commerce subsequently endorse him for re-election, its president said her group had "similar concerns as to what the governor expressed. We agree with what he did." And others, such as the chairman of the Latino Journal's editorial board, expressed disappointment but said that it "wasn't a make-or-break issue" for his group.[26]

Integrity of driver's licenses is a security matter. States historically have protected their right to issue driver's licenses, and any federal attempt to interfere has been fiercely opposed. The Mexican government seems to understand this and is actively lobbying state legislatures to grant special dispensation to matricula cardholders from "proof of legal residence" requirements. This activity endangers homeland

Accepting a less than secure identity card from Mexico would be the functional equivalent of a quasi-amnesty for approximately 50 percent of our illegal population without any national debate on the merits and implications of that action.

security because today the state driver's license, with all its weaknesses, is the most accepted American identity document. It is a prime example of the almost non-existent interior enforcement of our immigration laws that states would even consider issuing it to illegal aliens.

The American Association of Motor Vehicle Administrators (AAMVA) is helping states develop national standards with respect to driver's licenses' appearance, data content, and security requirements. Cards would be made more tamper-proof and consideration is being given to including a biometric identifier, such as a fingerprint or retinal scan. There would also be a uniform set of standards regarding the documents needed to prove identity, residency, and legal status of non-citizens. Identity documents would be verified electronically with appropriate federal agencies. Similarly, to ensure that no individual holds more than one valid driver's license at a time, a computer link would give states access to each other's driver databases.[27]

Several congressional bills were introduced in 2002 that addressed different aspects of the integrity of America's identity documents. They didn't move out of committee, so there was no public debate on the merits. Past congressional efforts to tighten document security in part by linking databases have been fiercely opposed by a coalition of civil libertarians, data privacy groups, states rights advocates, and libertarians concerned with government intrusion. Current sentiment seems to lean toward letting state motor vehicle departments, AAMVA, and organizations such as the National Governors Association and the National Conference of State Legislatures try to reach consensus on uniform issuance and card security standards. If that is accomplished, the next issue would be how best to implement those standards. One option would be federal legislation.

The specter of the Mexican government heavily lobbying state motor vehicle departments and state legislatures to accept the matricula as a valid identity document is energizing those discussions.

Institutionalized Illegality

No one disputes that Mexico has a right to issue the matricula consular and maintain a registry of its citizens living in other nations. What is in dispute is the wisdom of American institutions and governmental entities accepting as official identification a foreign government's document, the purpose of which is to make it easier for their nationals to reside in the United States illegally. This issue extends beyond the immediate example of Mexico and the matricula and must be considered in terms of precedent-setting policy for treatment of other foreign governments who wish to do the same for their illegal populations.

Within the last month, these concerns have been raised by members of Congress in letters sent to the Secretary of State and the Treasury Department and by the Governor of Colorado, who asked a Mexican consul general to explain her office's lobbying efforts on behalf of the matricula. Similarly, concerned citizens' organizations have become more vocal at the local level, explaining U.S. immigration law as regards illegal aliens and pointing out legal risks localities may run by subverting those laws.

The reason why we find ourselves addressing the far-reaching implications of the matricula issue is an almost total lack of interior enforcement of our immigration laws. This has resulted in an illegal population of nine million people — 40 percent are visa overstayers and 60 percent crossed our borders without permission. Of the latter group, the vast majority are Mexicans.

The matricula issue has starkly highlighted the dangers inherent in this benign neglect. Immigrant advocates, politicians, and businesses seeking cheap labor have been successful in blurring the distinction between legal and illegal immigration. But it is a distinction the American people find easy to make, as evidenced by numerous public opinion polls spanning many years.

Accepting a less than secure identity card from Mexico would be the functional equivalent of a quasi-amnesty for approximately 50 percent of our illegal population without any national debate on the merits and implications of that action.

Accepting a less than secure identity card from any country further erodes our ability and incentive to control which foreign nationals can enter and live permanently in the U.S. It has profound implications for future immigration policy and evolving policies regarding homeland security.

End Notes

[1] "New ID Helps Mexicans Come Out of the Shadows," *El Diario,* March 20, 2002.

[2] Olson, David, "Matricular consular helps new residents prove identity, obtain services, *The News and Observer* (Raleigh, NC), August 12, 2002.

[3] Giovine, Patricia, "Gov't urges migrants to stop using fake identities," *Agencia EFE,* November 21, 2002.

[4] "Migrants to U.S. are a major resource for Mexico," *The New York Times,* March 25, 2002; Sachs, Susan, "Citing security, New York rejects Mexican ID cards," *The New York Times,* December 28, 2002.

[5] Riley, Michael, "Mexican ID cards caught in growing debate," *Denver Post,* October 10, 2002.

[6] "Mas de un million 40 mil matriculas consulares expedidas en Estados Unidos en 2002," *Secretaria de Relaciones Exteriores,* Comunicado de prensa No. 282/02, 30 de diciembre de 2002.

[7] Sheridan, Mary Beth, "An entry card for immigrants," *The Washington Post,* July 26, 2002; pg. B1.

[8] "An entry card for immigrants," op.cit.

[9] Iwasaki, John, "Mexicans in the U.S. get that second piece of I.D," *The Seattle Post-Intelligencer,* December 7, 2002.

[10] Golden, Tim, "Mexican Drug Dealers Turning U.S. Towns Into Major Depots," *The New York Times,* November 16, 2002.

[11] "Mexican Drug Dealers Turning U.S. Towns into Major Depots," op.cit.

[12] "Mas de un million 40 mil matriculas consulares expedidas en estados unidos en 2002," op. cit.

[13] Gamboa, Suzanne, "Report: Migrants Sent Home $23B," *Star Tribune,* November 22, 2002.

[14] Thompson, Ginger, "Migrants to U.S. are a major resource for Mexico," *The New York Times,* March 25, 2002.

[15] Dinerstein, Marti, "Giving Cover to Illegal Aliens: IRS Tax ID Numbers Subvert Immigration Law," CIS *Backgrounder,* November 2002. http://www.cis.org/articles/2002/back1202/html

[16] http://www.ustreas.gov/press/releases/reports/sec326breport.final.pdf

[17] "IRS makes changes to individual taxpayer identification number (ITIN) application," *Internal Revenue Service,* News Release, IR-02-139 (17 Dec 2002.

[18] "Giving Cover to Illegal Aliens: IRS Tax ID Numbers Subvert Immigration Law," op.cit.

[19] Gori, Graham, "A card allows U.S. banks to aid Mexican immigrants," *The New York Times,* July 6, 2002.

[20] "Treasury Department Issues USA PATRIOT Act Report to Congress," *Office of Public Affairs, Treasury Department,* PO-3567, October 22, 2002.

[21] http://www.ustreas.gov/press/releases/reports/sec326breport.final.pdf

[22] "New ID Helps Mexicans Come out of the Shadows," op.cit.

[23] "Citing Security, New York Rejects Mexican ID Cards," op.cit.

[24] Vogel, Nancy and Dan Morain, "No Licenses for Illegal Immigrants: Davis vetoes measure despite vows of support, citing national security, as he faces deadline for legislation in his first term," *The Los Angeles Times,* October 1, 2002.

[25] http://www.governor.ca.gov/govsite/msdocs/press_release/L02_246_AB_60_and_SB_804_veto_message.doc

[26] Talev, Margaret and Kevin Yamamura, "Davis defends driver's license veto," *The Sacramento Bee,* October 19, 2002. http://www.sacbee.com/content/politics/story/4856842p-5870062c.html

[27] Dinerstein, Marti, "America's Identity Crisis: Document Fraud is Pervasive and Pernicious," CIS *Backgrounder,* April 2002. http://www.cis.org/articles/2002/back302.html

Backgrounder

IDs for Illegals
The 'Matricula Consular' Advances Mexico's Immigration Agenda

By Marti Dinerstein

In the wake of the 9/11 terrorist attacks, a migration deal with Mexico was tabled while attention turned to homeland security. So the Mexican government abruptly changed its White House strategy and substituted a grass-roots approach that would focus at the local level, seek small successes, and build momentum for congressional action. The lynchpin for this new strategy was to be the "matricula consular," an official identity card issued by the Mexican government, which it wanted to be officially recognized within the United States.

This *Backgrounder* is the first detailed examination of the matricula issue. Among the findings:

- The matricula consular is useful in the United States only for illegal aliens, since legal immigrants, by definition, have U.S. government-issued documents.
- The Mexican government has launched an aggressive grassroots lobbying campaign to win acceptance for its matricula card from state and local jurisdictions and from banks, especially in areas where Mexican illegal aliens are concentrated.
- The objective of this lobbying effort is to achieve quasi-legal status for Mexican illegals in the United States without waiting for action from Washington.
- The matricula itself, however, is useful to illegal aliens only insofar as U.S. institutions are willing to collaborate with Mexico's efforts to circumvent U.S. immigration law.

3-03

Center for Immigration Studies
1522 K Street N.W. Suite 820
Washington, DC 20005-1202
(202) 466-8185
center@cis.org
www.cis.org

NON-PROFIT
U.S. POSTAGE
PAID
PERMIT #6117
WASHINGTON, DC

Mr. HOSTETTLER. Thank you Ms. Dinerstein.
Mr. Nelsen.

STATEMENT OF CRAIG NELSEN, DIRECTOR, FRIENDS OF IMMIGRATION LAW ENFORCEMENT

Mr. NELSEN. Thank you, Mr. Chairman and Members of the Subcommittee. I want to thank you for this opportunity to summarize the very serious legal and political reasons why no U.S. Institution should accept any consular ID cards, including the Mexican Matricula Consular, issued by foreign governments to their nationals illegally residing in the United States.

First, since the Constitution gives absolute power to Congress over all immigration matters. It is unconstitutional for any local or State entity to put itself above Congressional prerogatives by adopting its own Matricula policy.

Second, under section 274 of the Immigration and Nationality Act it is a Federal crime to encourage an alien to reside illegally in the United States. Most Americans would agree that a local or private policy that explicitly recognizes an identification card carried by illegal aliens, especially for the disbursement of public services or for financial gain, obviously encourages such alien to remain illegally in the United States.

Third, it is our opinion that a public entity exposes itself to civil liability suits if it adopts a policy to accept a card. Imagine a scenario in which an illegal alien is stopped by a police officer in a city or State that recognizes the Matricula Consular. Say the alien presents the card, the officer accepts it and then by policy releases the alien back into the general public rather than turning him or her over to the proper authorities. If the illegal alien then commits a violent crime against an American citizen or a legal resident, the victim of the crime may have grounds to sue the city or State for knowingly and with reckless disregard contributing to a dangerous situation.

Aside from these serious legal concerns, acceptance of the Matricula card is politically objectionable because it reinforces widespread flouting of U.S. Immigration laws. In a world in which there are nearly 5 billion people living in countries poorer than Mexico, the United States must become serious about enforcing our laws on immigration. If U.S. Institutions are allowed to accept Mexican IDs from illegal aliens, it is not hard to predict that other countries will soon follow Mexico's lead, and some already are. American policymakers need to think carefully about where this slippery slope is leading us.

I was once an open borders advocate. In my twenties I even wrote an article published in a newspaper in New York in which I called for open borders. I also owned restaurants in Manhattan's East Village and I saw nothing wrong if some of the workers crossed the border illegally. But my experiences in the restaurant industry in New York City and during a 2-year stint living in China convinced me that my open borders were shortsighted, selfish and naive. I came to recognize the slippery slope down which our country is heading.

I became so concerned that I did more than just talk. I got out of the restaurant business, started an immigration reform organization to try to help raise awareness of the long-term consequences of open borders immigration.

Polls show that that awareness has been raised. A recent Roper poll found that 85 percent of Americans want local police to enforce immigration laws. Seventy-five percent of Americans believe persons who open bank accounts should be required to show legal presence in the United States. It is therefore unbelievable that, contrary to the overwhelming desire of the American people, 800 or more police departments and a large segment of the banking industry now accept the Matricula Consular from illegal aliens.

Proposed Treasury regulations recently issued are another affront to the American people. The regulations, if they are allowed to stand, will permit U.S. Banking corporations to put profits above the public good, and using foreign consular IDs to open accounts continues to help illegal aliens remain in the United States. If these regulations go into full effect, we will be faced with the remarkable spectacle of having a Government in which one agency, the Department of Homeland Security, is charged with deporting illegal aliens while another, the Treasury Department, is allowing them to open bank accounts.

Mexico makes the outrageous claim that the Matricula card is more secure than American IDs even though there is no way any American law enforcement officer or bank officer can verify any of the information found on the Mexican ID card.

On the other hand, by the end of this year, every State in the Union will have implemented on its driver's licenses and State IDs the Intelli-Check system, a process by which American law enforcement officers can instantly verify the validity of any identification card issued by any other State.

In other words, while States are moving rapidly to tighten identification procedures in the wake of 9/11, there is a rush by some policymakers and corporate profiteers to actually loosen identification standards.

In closing, while Mexico and Nicaragua, Syria, Pakistan and China and every other country in the world have the right to issue whatever cards they want to their nationals, there is no reason that the U.S. Government should recognize them. In fact, recognition of illegal alien ID cards by U.S. Entities is legally impermissible, is a threat to national security, and is irresponsible public policy.

Thank you.

[The prepared statement of Mr. Nelsen follows:]

PREPARED STATEMENT OF CRAIG NELSEN

Mr. Chairman, members of the subcommittee:

Thank you for this opportunity to address the very important issue of whether U.S. institutions should be accepting or recognizing identification cards issued by foreign governments to their nationals illegally residing in the United States.

It is the opinion of Friends of Immigration Law Enforcement that no American public entity or government agency should accept any foreign— or consular-issued ID card for the purpose of disbursing public services normally reserved to American citizens, or those legally present in the country. Nor should any private institution establish any commercial relationship with foreign nationals based in whole or in part on the information contained on such cards.

The reasons U.S. institutions should not accept foreign consular or similar ID cards fall into two categories: First, there are serious legal objections to their acceptance; second, there are serious political objections to their acceptance. While these legal and political objections hold true for all foreign-issued ID cards, hereafter, I will speak specifically of the Mexican *matricula consular* card, because Mexico has been by far the most aggressive foreign nation in issuing the card to its nationals living illegally in the United States, and in pressuring local U.S. governments to accept its ID card as a way to provide illegal aliens access to public services.

There are three legal objections to any policy that sanctions acceptance by U.S. institutions of the *matricula consular* in the United States: Such a policy is a violation of the Constitution, it is a statutory offense, and it exposes public entities and private institutions to civil liability risks.

First, since the Constitution gives absolute power to Congress over all immigration matters, it is unconstitutional for any local or state entity to put itself above Congressional prerogatives by adopting its own *matricula* policy.

Second, by Section 274 of the Immigration and Nationality Act, it is a federal crime to encourage an illegal alien to reside illegally in the United States. We think most Americans would agree that a local or private policy that explicitly recognizes an identification card carried by illegal aliens—especially for the disbursement of public services, or for financial gain—manifestly violates that law.

Third, it is our opinion that a public entity exposes itself to civil liability suits if it adopts a policy to accept the card. Imagine a scenario in which, say, an illegal alien is stopped by a police officer in a city or state that by policy recognizes the Mexican illegal alien ID card. Imagine that the alien presents the card, but, rather than delivered to the proper immigration authorities, is subsequently released back into the general public. Imagine the illegal alien then commits a violent crime against a resident of that jurisdiction. We believe the victim of the crime will have grounds to sue the city or state for knowingly, and with reckless disregard for the illegal status of the criminal, contributing to a dangerous situation. We believe a jury would probably award damages to such a plaintiff.

In the case of a bank, or other commercial enterprise that profits by accepting a *matricula* card, the enterprise is liable under the Racketeer and Corrupt Organizations Act (RICO) for damages caused to the bank's competitors by the illegal activity. A violation of the INA is a predicate offense under RICO. Continuing acceptance of the card establishes a pattern of racketeering activity. To succeed in a RICO suit, a plaintiff competitor must show that an injury was suffered and that the criminal activity was the cause of the injury. A competitor of a bank accepting the matricula ID will be able to make such a showing. By unlawfully accepting the matricula ID, a bank is gaining additional customers and revenue not available to the law-abiding competitor. Since, under proposed new Treasury regulations, it will be easy to document the number of customers that open accounts with a matricula ID alone, the damages to the competitor will not be too speculative to determine. This documentation will also show causation, since it will indicate the amount of illegal business gained at the expense of competitors.

Furthermore, aside from these serious legal concerns, acceptance of the *matricula* card is simply irresponsible policy because it reinforces widespread flouting of U.S. immigration laws, since, as has been openly admitted by all sides, only illegal aliens have need of the card.

In a world in which there are nearly five billion people living in countries poorer than Mexico, the United States simply must become serious about enforcing immigration laws. Rather than encouraging foreign nationals to remain illegally in the United States, we should be humanely, but firmly, helping them return to their home countries.

If illegal aliens from Mexico are allowed to use Mexican-issued ID cards in the United States, it is not hard to predict that other countries will soon follow Mexico's example. Indeed, we have included in our packet for today's hearing a copy of a memo from the government of Nicaragua to our State Department asking State to help Nicaragua set up its own *matricula* policy. The Nicaraguan memo explicitly states that it is of no concern to the government of Nicaragua whether those receiving the card are illegal aliens. In other words, Nicaragua is asking our government to help Nicaraguans break our laws. American policy-makers need to think carefully about where this slippery slope is leading us. If U.S. entities accept Mexican ID cards from Mexican nationals illegally in the United States, why not Nicaragua? Or Peru, for that matter? Or Iraq? Or China? Or Saudi Arabia? We Americans need to ask ourselves what, ultimately, we are to become as a nation: A huge, overcrowded, balkanized aggregate of strangers? A free-for-all of foreigners? A huge, cheap labor camp divided into large, unassimilated communities *literally* identifying with foreign, often hostile, nations?

Mexico deserves special censure for the aggressive way in which it has pushed local governments into accepting its illegal alien ID card. Mexico, like the United States, is a signatory to the Vienna Convention on Consular Relations, and as such, has promised not to interfere with the internal political affairs of the United States. But, Mexico has openly boasted that its well-coordinated campaign to achieve widespread acceptance in the United States of the *matricula* card was a "bottom up" way to do an "end run" around the Congress of the United States, subvert the laws of the American people, and achieve a massive *de facto* amnesty for millions of their citizens illegally residing in the United States.

We Americans want our immigration laws enforced. A recent Roper Poll found that nearly 9 out of 10 Americans want local police to enforce immigration laws. Seventy-five percent of us believe persons who open bank accounts in the United States should be required to show legal presence. It is unbelievable that, contrary to the overwhelming desire of the American people, 800 police departments in the United States now accept foreign issued ID cards from illegal aliens, rather than enforce immigration law, and our banking industry is rushing to open bank accounts for them.

Proposed Treasury regulations recently issued are another affront to the American people. The regulations, if they are allowed to stand, will permit U.S. banking corporations to put profit above the public good and open bank accounts for illegal aliens. If these regulations go into full effect, we will be faced with the remarkable spectacle of having a government in which one agency, the Department of Homeland Security, is charged with deporting illegal aliens, while another, the Treasury Department, is allowing them to open bank accounts.

Furthermore, as was demonstrated all too clearly on September 11, 2001, inattention to U.S. immigration laws can have devastating consequences. It is simply a betrayal of the public trust for any Federal agency, or public official, to take any action that makes it easier for foreign nationals, terrorists, or "garden variety" criminals to operate more easily in the United States.

In closing, while Mexico, Nicaragua, Syria, China, and Pakistan have every right to issue whatever cards they want to their nationals, there is no reason the U.S. government needs to recognize them. In fact, recognition of illegal alien ID cards by U.S. entities is both legally impermissible, and extremely reckless and irresponsible public policy.

ATTACHMENT 1

LEGAL OBJECTIONS TO ACCEPTANCE BY U.S. INSTITUTIONS OF THE *MATRICULA CONSULAR* AND OTHER FOREIGN-ISSUED CONSULAR IDENTIFICATION CARDS

Micah King
Friends of Immigration Law Enforcement
Washington, DC
June 16, 2003

INDEX

AUTHORITIES CITED

CASES:

STATUTES:

MISCELLANEOUS:

Oct.10, 2002.

RESTATEMENT (SECOND) OF TORTS § 286 (1965)
6, 7

U.S. Const. Art. VI, cl. 2
12

Vienna Convention on Consular Relations, Apr. 24, 1963, 21 U.S.T. 77,
Article 5(d)
14
Article 55(1)
15

QUESTIONS PRESENTED

I. Whether banks and public entities can be held criminally liable under the Immigration and Nationality Act for "aiding and abetting illegal immigration" by accepting the *matricula consular* ID card, an unreliable form of identification needed only by illegal aliens.

II. Whether banks and public entities that accept the *matricula consular* can be held civilly liable for injuries sustained by U.S. citizens caused by the illegal aliens who unlawfully remain in this country due to the benefits provided by the *matricula* ID.

III. Whether banks can be held liable under the Racketeer Influenced and Corrupt Organizations Act (RICO) for gaining financially from criminal violations of the Immigration and Nationality Act at the expense of law-abiding competitors.

IV. Whether state and local officials and U.S. citizens may establish policies permitting acceptance of the *matricula* ID even though, constitutionally, the federal government has plenary power over immigration policy.

V. Whether acceptance of the *matricula* ID is required by the provisions of the Vienna Convention on Consular Relations or by the international law principle of reciprocity.

STATEMENT OF FACTS

The *matricula consular* is an identification card similar in appearance to a state-issued driver's license that contains a person's name, address, photo, date and place of birth, and identification number. Mexican consular offices located in the United States issue the card. All that is required to obtain the card is presentment of a Mexican birth certificate, $29, and, Mexico now claims, a second photo ID. The consulates do not conduct any criminal background check of the applicant, nor do the consulates maintain a central database of issued cards.

While the card does contain various safeguards to prevent fraudulent duplication, the card is easy to obtain fraudulently. In fact, the card is so easy to obtain fraudulently that border patrol agents say the card is unreliable, and that they routinely find illegal aliens carrying more than one card containing the alien's picture but different fictitious names. See, e.g., Michael Riley, Mexican ID Cards Caught in Growing Debate, Denver Post, Oct.10, 2002. Also, since the consulates do not maintain a central database of issued cards, neither Mexican nor U.S. officials have the ability to see whether the applicant has previously obtained a card from another consular office.

In addition to the card's unreliability, its use is unnecessary by all but illegal aliens. Permanent residents and visitors are issued identification papers, such as a green card, visa, or other U.S.-issued stamp or document. In fact, Miriam Fonseca, the Consular Affairs Director for Nicaragua, when asking the U.S. State Department to assist in creating a Nicaraguan consular ID program, "conceded that legal Nicaraguan residents already have identification documents and only illegal residents are likely to benefit from the program." Memorandum from the American Embassy in Managua, Nicaragua, to Colin Powell, Secretary of State (May 3, 2003) (on file).

SUMMARY OF ARGUMENT

Acceptance of the *matricula consular* by public and private entities for identification purposes exposes those entities to criminal and civil liability. Entities that do establish policies permitting acceptance of the *matricula* violate federal statutes pertaining to immigration. Additionally, these policies illegally infringe on the federal government's plenary power over immigration policy and are thus preempted due to the supremacy clause. Furthermore, no treaty to which the United States is a signatory, n6r any principle of international law, requires the federal or state governments to accept the *matricula* ID.

Acceptance of the *matricula consular* by both public and private entities is a criminal violation of 8 U.S.C. 1324. The statute makes it a crime to knowingly "encourage or induce an alien to come to, enter, or reside in the United States." Entities that accept the *matricula consular* do "encourage" and "induce" illegal aliens to reside in the United States because those entities confer benefits to illegal aliens that allow them to stand equally with U.S. citizens. The requisite mental state of "knowingly" encouraging or inducing is met by virtue of the fact that only illegal aliens must rely on the *matricula* ID because U.S. citizens, legal immigrants, and visitors have access to identification documents provided by the U.S. government. Thus, an entity accepting the card from a person who has no other form of valid identification would have constructive knowledge that the person is likely to be an illegal alien, and that such acceptance violates 8 U.S.C. 1324.

In addition to criminal liability, these entities may be held civilly liable for damages caused by illegal aliens who remain in this country as a result of the card's acceptance. Acceptance of the *matricula* ID, a violation of 8 U.S.C. 1324, is a breach of duty to the American public, so a plaintiff need only prove causation to get the case to a jury. If the *matricula* ID is not accepted, then illegal aliens will have a more difficult time remaining in this country undetected. By accepting the card, entities encourage these illegal aliens to remain. Thus, in some cases, acceptance of the card will be a "but for" cause of the continued unlawful presence of the illegal alien. In such a case, if that alien then injures a U.S. citizen, the entity that encouraged the alien's illegal presence could be held liable.

Since acceptance of the *matricula consular* is a violation of 8 U.S.C. § 1324, a bank accepting the card is liable under the Racketeer and Corrupt Organizations Act (RICO) for damages caused to the bank's competitors by the illegal activity. A violation of the INA is a predicate offense under RICO. Continuing acceptance of the card establishes a pattern of racketeering activity. To succeed in a RICO suit, a plaintiff competitor must show that an injury was suffered and that the criminal activity was the cause of the injury. A competitor of a bank accepting the *matricula* ID will be able to make such a showing. By unlawfully accepting the *matricula* ID, a bank is gaining additional customers and revenue not available to the law-abiding competitor. Since, under proposed new Treasury regulations, it will be easy to document the number of customers that open accounts with a *matricula* ID alone, the damages to the competitor will not be too speculative to determine. This documentation will also show causation, since it will indicate the amount of illegal business gained at the expense of competitors.

Even if liability is not established, both public and private entities are precluded from establishing policies permitting acceptance of the *matricula consular* because the federal government has plenary power over immigration policy by virtue of the commerce clause. While local and state governments can establish policies that mirror federal immigration policy, they are precluded from undermining the federal government's authority. The Department of Homeland Security, the executive department charged with formulating and enforcing immigration policy, is opposed to acceptance of the *matricula* ID. Thus, any policy by public and private entities that authorizes acceptance of the card undermines or conflicts with, rather than mirrors, federal policy, and is, therefore, unconstitutional.

While treaties can require federal and state governments to enact certain policies, no existing treaty or principle of international law requires acceptance of the *matricula consular* by any U.S. entity. The Vienna Convention on Consular Relations, to which both the United States and Mexico are signatories, is inapplicable to the issue of internal domestic acceptance of consular ID cards. While this convention does govern a sovereign's ability to issue passports or other travel documents, it does not require a signatory to accept any foreign-issued identification document, especially one issued with insufficient anti-fraud and security protections. Likewise, any fear of reciprocal action from Mexico in response to the decision by the United States not to accept the *matricula* is unfounded.

While the *matricula consular* is the focus of the following argument, the arguments contained herein apply equally to any consular-issued identification card.

ARGUMENT

I. ACCEPTANCE OF THE *MATRICULA CONSULAR* BY PUBLIC AND PRIVATE ENTITIES IS A CRIMINAL VIOLATION OF THE IMMIGRATION AND NATIONALITY ACT.

Anyone who accepts the *matricula* "encourages or induces an alien to come to, enter, or reside in the United States, knowing or in reckless disregard of the fact that such coming to, entry, or residence is or will be in violation of law," a criminal violation of the Immigration and Nationality Act (INA). 8 U.S.C. § 1324(a)(1)(A)(iv) (2003). By accepting the *matricula consular*, public and private entities are encouraging illegal aliens already in the United States to remain. As such, violators face prison terms of up to five years, or ten years if the violation was committed for financial gain. 8 U.S.C. § 1324(a)(1)(B) (2003).

The Fourth Circuit has held that the INA applies to actions directed at aliens already in this country or those contemplating illegal entry. U.S. v. Oloyede, 982 F.2d 133, 136 (4th Cir. 1992). The Fourth Circuit also held that "'encouraging' is not limited to bringing in, transporting or concealing illegal aliens. Rather, 'encouraging' relates to actions taken to convince the illegal alien to come to this country or to stay in this country." Id. at 137. In Oloyede, the defendant was found guilty of violating the INA for providing false identification documents to illegal aliens residing in the United States. The Court stated that the defendant's actions did "encourage" illegal immigration because the aliens were provided with all the benefits of citizenship, including no fear of deportation and the ability to gain work. Id.

Similarly, acceptance of the *matricula* by U.S. institutions provides the benefits of citizenship to illegal aliens. Some banks allow illegal aliens to open checking accounts upon presentment of the *matricula*. This permits illegal aliens to obtain the benefits of the U.S. banking system. Some municipalities allow illegal aliens to establish identity by presenting the card when stopped by police. This allows illegal aliens to escape detention and deportation, which they might have faced otherwise because they would have had no identity documents on their persons. Some states and municipalities allow illegal aliens to access public services with the *matricula consular* card, services for which illegal aliens may be ineligible. Because the *matricula* provides the same benefits of citizenship as those produced by the defendant's actions in Oloyede, acceptance of the *matricula* encourages those illegal aliens present in the United States to remain.

Those accepting the *matricula* raise the confidence of illegal aliens present in the United States that they can remain with impunity. The Seventh Circuit upheld a jury instruction that used Black's Law Dictionary to define "encourage" as "to give courage to; to inspirit; to embolden; to raise confidence." U.S. v. He, 245 F.3d 954, 960 (7th Cir. 2001). Acceptance of the *matricula* raises the confidence of illegal aliens and emboldens them to remain unlawfully in the United States because the card gives them access to most of the benefits of U.S. citizenship.

Supporters of U.S. acceptance of the *matricula* incorrectly assert that no INA violation can be sustained because the knowledge requirement is not present. They argue that since the card does not indicate the immigration status of the presenter, the person accepting the card does not know that the presenter is an illegal alien. However, as previously mentioned, only illegal aliens have need of the *matricula* as a form of identification; thus, the person accepting the card would have constructive knowledge that the presenter is an illegal alien due to the fact that the *matricula* is being relied upon for identification.

II. PUBLIC AND PRIVATE ENTITIES MAY BE HELD CIVILLY LIABLE FOR INJURIES TO U.S. CITIZENS CAUSED BY ILLEGAL ALIENS WHO REMAIN IN THE U.S. ILLEGALLY DUE TO ACCEPTANCE OF THE *MATRICULA CONSULAR*.

U.S. citizens who suffer injury at the hands of illegal aliens may be able to sustain a negligence claim against those entities that encouraged the alien's unlawful presence through acceptance of the *matricula*. Generally, to prove negligence, a plaintiff must show that: 1) a duty of care was owed by defendant to plaintiff; (2) the defendant's conduct fell below the applicable standard of care, which amounts to a breach of that duty; (3) the defendant's conduct was an actual and proximate cause of plaintiff's injury; and (4) the plaintiff did suffer actual loss or injury. E.g., Robinson v. May Dept. Stores

Co., 246 F.Supp.2d 440, 445 (E.D. Pa. 2003).

The INA imposes upon all U.S. citizens the duty to refrain from encouraging illegal immigration. A criminal statute can be used to establish the appropriate standard of care if the statute is found to protect from the particular harm caused by the defendant the class of persons to which the plaintiff belongs. RESTATEMENT (SECOND) OF TORTS: EXCUSED VIOLATIONS § 286 (1965). "In enacting the Immigration Act [INA], Congress intended to encourage aliens to enter this country in an orderly fashion, within the guidelines of immigration procedures." U.S. v. Anaya, 509 F.Supp. 289, 298 (D.C. Fla. 1980). A major component of immigration procedures is a criminal background check of the immigrant, which is conducted to protect the American population from dangerous immigrants by making them inadmissible. 8 U.S.C. § 1182 (a)(2)(i) (2003). Thus, the INA is partly designed to protect U.S. citizens from the criminal behavior of foreign nationals attempting to enter the United States. Moreover, aliens with serious criminal records are deportable. 8 U.S.C. § 1227 (a)(2) (2003). Therefore, the provisions of the INA can be used by the plaintiff, a U.S. citizen, or person legally present in the country, to establish the appropriate standard of care owed by the defendant.

Entities that accept the *matricula* breach their duty to U.S. citizens. As mentioned, acceptance of the *matricula* is a violation of the INA; this indicates that a4n entity accepting the card has breached its legal duty to the plaintiff, a U.S. citizen or legal permanent resident. The defendant may assert that acceptance of the *matricula* is an exercise of reasonable care, thus the statutory violation should be excused. However, this excuse is valid only if the defendant is "unable after reasonable diligence or care to comply." RESTATEMENT (SECOND) OF TORTS: EXCUSED VIOLATIONS § 286 (1965). Compliance with the INA is not difficult; simply requiring applicants for services to produce U.S.-issued documents satisfies the statute, so acceptance of the *matricula* cannot amount to a reasonable attempt to comply. This is analogous to a driver who chooses to exceed the posted speed limit; adherence to the limit is not difficult, and the failure to do so is merely a choice, not a legal excuse. Thus, the unexcused statutory violation satisfies the element of breach of duty.

With duty and breach of duty established as a matter of law, the facts of each particular case will determine whether causation is present. There will be many instances where this element may be met. One example is where a local or state police officer stops an individual and that individual produces a *matricula* to establish identity. If the officer accepts the card alone as evidence of identity, then the illegal alien is not detained. If the officer requires the illegal alien to produce another form of identification, and the alien cannot do so, then he or she normally would be detained until identity and immigration status can be determined. Aliens determined to be here illegally then can be turned over to federal authorities for removal. Thus, an officer that accepts the card prevents what is mandated by law - deportation. This acceptance is a "but for" cause of the illegal alien's continued unlawful presence - but for the acceptance of the card, the illegal alien would no longer be in the United States. Therefore, if the alien later injures or kills a U.S. citizen or legal permanent resident, the officer's acceptance of the card is a cause of the injury or wrongful death.

The public entity that, by policy, permitted the officer to accept the card may claim that it is immune from suit under discretionary function immunity. This doctrine precludes suits against a government or government official for public policy decisions made by a government entity that has the authority to do so. However, this immunity will not apply in these negligence cases. A government has no discretion to disregard a legal duty it has under tort law. Miller v. Grants Pass Irr. Dist., 686 P.2d 324, 330 (Or. 1984). In Miller, the Court held that immunity did not apply to a decision by the government not to post warning signs at a dam because the government had a tort duty to warn. Id. As noted, public entities have a duty to adhere to the INA, and failure to so adhere is a breach of duty under tort law. Public entities have no discretion to enact policies that disregard the duty established in the INA; so discretionary function immunity does not apply to a decision to accept the *matricula.*

Another example where causation may be found is a case in which a bank allows an illegal alien to open an account using a *matricula*. If that illegal alien then uses the account to launder money or fund criminal activity, then the bank's actions would be a cause of the crime. Though the bank may argue that criminal activity is not foreseeable, a court will likely find that allowing an illegal alien to open an account by accepting an unreliable form of identification was a substantial factor of the resulting injury. Courts typically use the substantial factor test when numerous events combine to cause the injury. E.g., Maneth v. Tucker, 34 S.W.3d 755, 758 (Ark. Ct. App. 2000). Had the bank refused to allow the illegal alien to open the account with the *matricula* alone, then the criminal activity would likely have been prevented, thus acceptance of the card is a substantial factor of the criminal behavior.

For the foregoing reasons, many plaintiffs will likely be able to survive motions to dismiss and get such negligence claims to a jury. Since duty and breach of duty are established in all cases by virtue of the INA violation, the plaintiff must only assert causation and injury to bring the case to trial. This is even more likely given that, in any motion for summary judgment or dismissal, all facts are viewed in a light most favorable to the plaintiff, and the burden rests on the defendant to prove that there are no genuine issues of material fact. E.g., Celotex Corp. v. Catrett, 477 U.S. 317 (1986). While it is unclear what findings a jury will make in these cases, many jurors will likely be sympathetic to a U.S. citizen who is killed or injured by an illegal alien, especially when that illegal alien is present in the country due to the illegal policies of a bank, a state, or a municipality.

III. BANKS ACCEPTING THE *MATRICULA CONSULAR* CAN BE HELD LIABLE UNDER THE RICO ACT FOR GAINING FINANCIALLY FROM CRIMINAL ACTIVITY AT THE EXPENSE OF COMPETITORS.

A bank that lawfully abides by the INA and refuses to accept the *matricula* from illegal aliens attempting to open an account has standing under 18 U.S.C. § 1961, the Racketeer Influenced and Corrupt Organizations (RICO) Act, to sue a competitor bank that illegally accepts the *matricula*. By accepting the *matricula* on more than one occasion, the defendant bank engages in a pattern of racketeering activity. The plaintiff bank suffers lost market share and competitive disadvantage as a direct result of the defendant bank's illegal activity. Additionally, the potential barriers to this kind of suit, such as improper plaintiff, lack of causation, or risk of multiple liability, do not apply here.

Banks that permit illegal aliens to open accounts by presenting the *matricula* gain financially from illegal activity, a clear violation of RICO. "Under RICO, 'any person injured in his business or property by reason of a violation of section 1962 of this chapter may sue therefore in any appropriate United States district court' for civil damages." Mendoza v. Zirkle Fruit Co., 301 F.3d 1163, 1168 (9th Cir. 2002). A competitor bank that does not accept the *matricula* may be able to plead and prove a RICO violation.

As noted above, acceptance of the *matricula* is a violation of the INA, so a bank that accepts the card violates Section 1962 of the RICO Act. The RICO Act states, "'racketeering activity' means any act which is indictable under the Immigration and Nationality Act, Section 274 [8 USCS § 1324]." 18 U.S.C. § 1961(1)(F) (2003). Since acceptance of the *matricula* is a violation of the INA, its unlawful acceptance by banks is "racketeering activity." The RICO Act is violated if the defendant engages in a pattern of racketeering activity, defined as "at least two acts of racketeering activity." 18 U.S.C. § 1961(5) (2003). Thus, a bank that has accepted the matricula for financial gain on more than one occasion violates Section 1962.

The plaintiff bank that abides by the INA and refuses to accept the *matricula* suffers injury to its business in the form of relatively diminished market share and competitive disadvantage due to the illegal actions of the defendant. The plaintiff has standing to recover if the injury was caused by the defendant's illegal actions, "a requirement the Supreme Court has interpreted to encompass proximate as well as factual causation." Mendoza, 301 F.3d. at 1168. In Mendoza, the Ninth Circuit enumerated three factors used to determine whether causation exists: 1) whether there are more direct victims of the defendant's wrongful conduct that should bring suit, 2) whether the plaintiff's damages will be difficult to ascertain, and 3) whether the court will have difficulty apportioning damages in a way that lessens the risk of multiple recoveries. Id. at 1169. An analysis of these factors indicates that the plaintiff bank will have standing.

There is no other victim of the defendant's unlawful conduct that is better able to bring a RICO suit than a competitor bank. In Mendoza, documented workers sued a competitor fruit grower for depressing wages by hiring undocumented workers in violation of the INA. The Ninth Circuit held that the documented workers were the direct victims because the defendant's "alleged scheme here was intended to give the growers a contract advantage at the expense of the documented workers, a direct rather than a pass-through injury." Id. at 1170. An INA-violating defendant bank causes direct injury to a plaintiff bank because the defendant gains a competitive advantage by having more money available for loans and investments, illegally strengthening its market position at the expense of the plaintiff. Furthermore, no victim suffers a more direct injury than the plaintiff bank, and there is no other victim better able to bring suit. Thus, a competitor bank is the proper entity to bring suit.

The plaintiff bank's damages will not be difficult to ascertain. In Mendoza, the Ninth Circuit disagreed with the District Court's determination that damages would be too speculative. Id. at 1171. While the District Court argued that numerous factors could have contributed to the suppression of wages, the Court of Appeals stated that the plaintiff should have the opportunity at trial to present expert testimony to establish its claim that the defendant's illegal actions caused the suppression. "It is inappropriate at this stage to substitute speculation for the complaint's allegations of causation." Id. Thus, as long as the plaintiff alleges direct causation and asserts how the damage occurred, the defendant will not be able to dismiss prior to trial.

The plaintiff bank will be able to prove direct causation and establish damages. The defendant bank's unlawful conduct is a "but for" cause of the injury - but for the defendant's illegal acceptance of the *matricula*, accounts would not have been opened by illegal aliens, so the defendant would not have gained an unfair competitive advantage. This unfair advantage directly injures law-abiding banks in the market. Damages will not be difficult to ascertain because the number and value of the illegal accounts can be documented, and simple calculations will show what profits and income the defendant bank made as a result of those accounts.

The court will not have a difficult time fashioning an appropriate remedy. The Second Circuit clarified this factor as being concerned with compensation paid to both first tier and second tier plaintiffs when damages paid only to first tier plaintiffs would "cure the harm to the second tier plaintiffs." Commercial Cleaning Servs. v. Colin Serv.

Sys., Inc., 271 F.3d 374, 383 (2nd Cir. 2001). In Commercial Cleaning, the Second Circuit held that the plaintiff, who claimed lost business due to the defendant's ability to underbid contracts as a result of hiring undocumented workers, was the only plaintiff injured, so there was no risk of "second-tier" plaintiffs. Id. at 384. Similarly, the plaintiff bank in the present case is the only direct victim, so there is no concern over multiple recoveries. The fact that multiple banks may be injured and seek compensation is not relevant because "compensating [them] would not overcompensate any plaintiff," which is the main concern of this part of the analysis. Id. Thus, there is no risk of overcompensation to any single plaintiff, so there is no concern with judicial administration.

A successful plaintiff in a RICO suit is entitled to recover "threefold the damages he sustains and the cost of the suit, including a reasonable attorney's fee." 18 U.S.C. § 1964(c) (2003). Additionally, the defendant may be forced to divest itself of part or all of its enterprise and may be enjoined from engaging in any "future investments or activities" the court sees fit. 18 U.S.C. § 1964(a) (2003). The Attorney General of the United States also has the ability to bring criminal charges against the defendant, where the court can impose a sentence of up to twenty years in prison and fine the defendant up to twice the amount of the gross profits gained from the illegal activity. 18 U.S.C. § 1963(a) (2003).

IV. PUBLIC AND PRIVATE ENTITIES ARE PRECLUDED FROM ENACTING POLICIES PERMITTING ACCEPTANCE OF THE *MATRICULA* BECAUSE SUCH POLICIES INFRINGE ON THE FEDERAL GOVERNMENT'S PLENARY POWER TO SET IMMIGRATION POLICY.

The federal government has plenary power over immigration policy, and the supremacy clause of the U.S. Constitution precludes both public and private entities from enacting policies that conflict with federal immigration law. U.S. Const. Art. VI, cl. 2. "Our cases have long recognized the preeminent role of the Federal Government with respect to the regulation of aliens within our borders [citations omitted]. Federal authority to regulate the status of aliens derives from various sources, including the

Federal Government's power '[t]o establish [a] uniform Rule of Naturalization,' U.S. Const., Art. I § 8, cl. 4, its power '[t]o regulate Commerce with foreign Nations', Id. cl. 3, and its broad authority over foreign affairs." Toll v. Moreno, 458 U.S. 1, 10 (1982). "Under the Constitution the states are granted no such powers; they can neither add to nor take from the conditions lawfully imposed by Congress upon admission, naturalization and residence of aliens in the United States or the several states." Id. at 11. Thus, policies that permit acceptance of the *matricula* are unconstitutional because they alter the conditions of residence of illegal aliens.

In Toll, the Supreme Court held that a state policy denying in-state tuition status to children whose parents had nonimmigrant alien visas violated the supremacy clause. Id. at 17. The Court stated that since the federal government had enacted policies that governed the tax liabilities of this class of aliens, a state policy that established a penalty for the nonpayment of those taxes frustrated federal policy. Id. Policies permitting acceptance of the *matricula* also frustrate federal policy. By accepting the *matricula*, public and private entities alter the benefits and advantages that a particular class of aliens - illegal ones - can obtain. This frustrates the provisions of the INA that govern employment of illegal aliens, immigration procedures, and security precautions.

Supporters of the card argue that the federal government sanctions the use of the *matricula*, but this argument is invalid. The supporters rely on recent regulations proposed by the Treasury Department regarding the acceptance of the *matricula* to open bank accounts. First, these regulations do not support the use of the *matricula*; they merely fail to discourage its use. A footnote to the regulations states, "the final rule neither endorses nor prohibits bank acceptance...of identification documents issued by foreign governments." 31 C.F.R. § 103 n.25 (2003). Additionally, the *matricula* ID is not sufficient to meet the demands imposed by Treasury's new regulations. Treasury requires banks to establish customer identification procedures that "enable the bank to form a reasonable belief that it knows the true identity of each customer." 31 C.F.R. § 103.121(b)(2) (2003). As previously shown, the *matricula* ID is not a reliable form of identification; thus, a bank accepting the *matricula* ID cannot have a "reasonable belief" that the identity of the presenter is established. Furthermore, there is no way for bank officers or law enforcement officials to verify the document. Indeed, the *matricula* is so unreliable that banks in Mexico do not accept it to open accounts.

Regardless, the Treasury Department does not have authority over immigration policy - such power belongs to the Department of Homeland Security (DHS). "All authorities and functions of the Department of Homeland Security to administer and enforce the immigration laws are vested in the Secretary of Homeland Security." 8 C.F.R. 2.1 (2003). While DHS has not issued regulations governing use of the *matricula* specifically, it certainly has not authorized its use. Furthermore, DHS officials have indicated that they do not support acceptance of the *matricula*. On April 10, 2003, Asa Hutchinson, Undersecretary for Border and Transportation Security at DHS, testified to a House subcommittee that acceptance of the *matricula* ID makes it more difficult to enforce U.S. immigration laws when the ID "can be used to get benefits or services or access to facilities they would not otherwise have." He urged banks *not* to allow someone who is here illegally to reap a benefit they would not otherwise be entitled to by using the *matricula* ID. Department of Homeland Transition: Hearings Before the Subcomm. on Immigration, Borders and Claims of the House Comm. on the Judiciary, 108th Cong. 41-42 (2003).

Since federal law is frustrated by policies that permit acceptance of the *matricula*, the policies are unconstitutional under the supremacy clause.

V. NO TREATY TO WHICH THE U.S. IS A SIGNATORY, NOR ANY PRINCIPLE OF INTERNATIONAL LAW, REQUIRES THE U.S. OR U.S. INSTITUTIONS TO ACCEPT THE *MATRICULA CONSULAR*.

Supporters of U.S. acceptance of the *matricula* assert that the Vienna Convention on Consular Relations (VCCR) and the principle of reciprocity require the United States to accept the *matricula*, but this assertion is incorrect. While the United States is a signatory to the VCCR, its provisions do not require a receiving state to accept any and all identification documents issued by a foreign state with which it has diplomatic relations. Reciprocity does not apply to this situation, since the United States does not ask the Mexican government to recognize for the provision of services the consular ID card issued by the State Department.

The VCCR establishes rules of diplomatic relations primarily in the form of protections for the consular officers of a sending state. Most provisions of the convention protect consular officials from lawsuits, taxation, and immigration procedures, while a few describe some of the powers of a consular office. One power enumerated is the right of the consulates in a foreign country to issue "passports and travel documents to nationals of the sending State, and visas or appropriate documents to persons wishing to travel to the sending State." Vienna Convention on Consular Relations, Apr. 24, 1963, art. 5(d), 21 U.S.T. 77. While this certainly allows the consulate to issue the *matricula* to Mexican nationals and to accept it at its offices to assist Mexican nationals, no provision of the treaty requires the United States, or any U.S. entity, to accept it for identification purposes. In fact, the only requirement placed on the receiving state is to honor the aforementioned immunities granted to consular officials.

Furthermore, the VCCR is subject to the laws of the United States. "This proposition is embodied in the Vienna Convention itself, which provides that the rights expressed in the Convention 'shall be exercised in conformity with the laws and regulations of the receiving State [Article 36(2), 21 U.S. T., at 101].'" Breard v. Greene, 118 S.Ct. 1352, 1355 (1998). Since the Mexican government issues the *matricula* to Mexican nationals without regard to their legal status in the United States, Mexican consulates should not insist the United States accept or recognize an unreliable form of identification merely because Mexico has the right to issue the ID.

Neither can the consulates rely on the principle of reciprocity. Reciprocity is defined as "the mutual concession of advantage or privileges for purposes of commercial or diplomatic relations." BLACK'S LAW DICTIONARY 1276 (7th ed. 1999). Under international law, this principle is usually applied to the recognition of the judgment of foreign courts, where, for example, a U.S. court accepts the judgment of a foreign court so that decisions of U.S. courts will be accepted in the foreign state. E.g., Boos v. Berry, 108 S.Ct. 1157, 1165 (1988). Supporters of U.S. acceptance of the *matricula* argue that the U.S. must accept the *matricula* or Mexico will take reciprocal action by denying the rights of U.S. consular officials in Mexico. However, by refusing to accept the *matricula*, the United States is not refusing to honor any privilege that it asserts in Mexico.

The United States does not demand that Mexico accept a U.S. consular document for the provision of services to Americans illegally in Mexico, so Mexico cannot claim that U.S. acceptance of the *matricula* is a matter of reciprocity. Reciprocity would apply if, hypothetically, the United States refused to honor Mexican passports; Mexico would then be justified in refusing to honor U.S. passports.

Neither the VCCR nor reciprocity requires the United States to accept the *matricula*. Indeed, such a requirement would violate a fundamental principle of international law - state sovereignty. By demanding that the United States accept the *matricula*, Mexico is interfering with the right of the United States to protect its territory and people. As mentioned above, those charged with enforcing immigration law see the *matricula* as a threat to national security.

If there is any violation of international law occurring with respect to the *matricula consular*, the violation is being committed by the Mexican government. The VCCR states that diplomats and consular officials "have a duty not to interfere in the internal affairs of that [receiving] state." Vienna Convention on Consular Relations, Apr. 24, 1963, art. 55(1), 21 U.S.T. 77. As has been widely documented, Mexican diplomats have actively lobbied both public and private entities to accept the *matricula*; this is interference in the internal affairs of the United States in violation of the VCCR. Thus, rather than requiring the United States to accept the *matricula*, the VCCR requires Mexican diplomats to cease their unlawful interference in domestic U.S. political affairs.

CONCLUSION

Public and private entities that accept the *matricula consular*, an unreliable form of identification, expose themselves to criminal and civil liability and violate the U.S. Constitution. By accepting the *matricula*, those entities encourage and induce illegal immigration, a criminal violation of the INA. This violation not only warrants criminal penalties for those entities, it also may serve as a breach of duty for a negligence claim and a predicate offense under the RICO Act.

In addition to exposing themselves to liability, those entities enacting policies permitting acceptance of the *matricula* violate the U.S. Constitution. The federal government has plenary power over all aspects of immigration law. Policies permitting acceptance of the *matricula* conflict with federal immigration laws and undermine the federal government's ability to establish and enforce immigration policy; thus they are precluded by the supremacy clause.

The United States is not bound by any treaty or principle of international law to accept the *matricula*. The VCCR is not applicable. Since the United States does not request Mexico to accept an unreliable form of identification issued by U.S. consular offices in Mexico, Mexico cannot rest on the principle of reciprocity to pressure the United States to accept the *matricula*. Furthermore, international law prohibits Mexico from interfering in the internal affairs of the United States, and Mexican officials are currently doing just that by lobbying both public and private entities to accept the *matricula* in violation of U.S. law.

APPENDIX

U.S. Constitution

Art. VI, cl. 2:

> This Constitution, and the Laws of the United States which shall be made in Pursuance thereof; and all Treaties made, or which shall be made, under the Authority of the United States, shall be the supreme Law of the Land; and the Judges in every State shall be bound thereby, any Thing in the Constitution or Laws of any State to the Contrary notwithstanding.

Immigration and Nationality Act

8 U.S.C. § 1182 (a)(2)(A)(i)

(2) Criminal and related grounds

(A) Conviction of certain crimes

(i) In general

Except as provided in clause (ii), any alien convicted of, or who admits having committed, or who admits committing acts which constitute the essential elements of -

(I) a crime involving moral turpitude (other than a purely political offense) or an attempt or conspiracy to commit such a crime, or

(II) a violation of (or a conspiracy or attempt to violate) any law or regulation of a State, the United States, or a foreign country relating to a controlled substance (as defined in section 802 of title 21), is inadmissible.

8 U.S.C. § 1227 (a)(2)

(2) Criminal offenses

(A) General crimes

(i) Crimes of moral turpitude

Any alien who -

(I) is convicted of a crime involving moral turpitude committed within five years (or 10 years in the case of an alien provided lawful permanent resident status under section 1255(j) of this title) after the date of admission, and

(II) is convicted of a crime for which a sentence of one year or longer may be imposed, is deportable.

(ii) Multiple criminal convictions

Any alien who at any time after admission is convicted of two or more crimes involving moral turpitude, not arising out of a single scheme of criminal misconduct, regardless of whether confined therefor and regardless of whether the convictions were in a single trial, is deportable.

(iii) Aggravated felony

Any alien who is convicted of an aggravated felony at any time after admission is deportable.

(iv) High speed flight

Any alien who is convicted of a violation of section 758 of title 18 (relating to high speed flight from an immigration checkpoint) is deportable.

(v) Waiver authorized

Clauses (i), (ii), (iii), and (iv) shall not apply in the case of an alien with respect to a criminal conviction if the alien subsequent to the criminal conviction has been granted a full and unconditional pardon by the President of the United States or by the Governor of any of the several States.

(B) Controlled substances

(i) Conviction

Any alien who at any time after admission has been convicted of a violation of (or a conspiracy or attempt to violate) any law or regulation of a State, the United States, or a foreign country relating to a controlled substance (as defined in section 802 of title 21), other than a single offense involving possession for one's own use of 30 grams or less of marijuana, is deportable.

(ii) Drug abusers and addicts

Any alien who is, or at any time after admission has been, a drug abuser or addict is deportable.

(C) Certain firearm offenses

Any alien who at any time after admission is convicted under any law of purchasing, selling, offering for sale, exchanging, using, owning, possessing, or carrying, or of attempting or conspiring to purchase, sell, offer for sale, exchange, use, own, possess, or carry, any weapon, part, or accessory which is a firearm or destructive device (as defined in section 921(a) of title 18) in violation of any law is deportable.

(D) Miscellaneous crimes

Any alien who at any time has been convicted (the judgment on such conviction becoming final) of, or has been so convicted of a conspiracy or attempt to violate -

(i) any offense under chapter 37 (relating to espionage), chapter 105 (relating to sabotage), or chapter 115 (relating to treason and sedition) of title 18 for which a term of imprisonment of five or more years may be imposed;
(ii) any offense under section 871 or 960 of title 18;
(iii) a violation of any provision of the Military Selective Service Act (50 U.S.C. App. 451 et seq.) or the Trading With the Enemy Act (50 U.S.C. App. 1 et seq.); or
(iv) a violation of section 1185 or 1328 of this title, is deportable.

(E) Crimes of domestic violence, stalking, or violation of protection order, crimes against children and

(i) Domestic violence, stalking, and child abuse

Any alien who at any time after admission is convicted of a crime of domestic violence, a crime of stalking, or a crime of child abuse, child neglect, or child abandonment is deportable. For purposes of this clause, the term "crime of domestic violence" means any crime of violence (as defined in section 16 of title 18) against a person committed by a current or former spouse of the person, by an individual with whom the person shares a child in common, by an individual who is cohabiting with or has cohabited with the person as a spouse, by an individual similarly situated to a spouse of the person under the domestic or family violence laws of the jurisdiction where the offense occurs, or by any other individual against a person who is protected from that individual's acts under the domestic or family violence laws of the United States or any State, Indian tribal government, or unit of local government.

(ii) Violators of protection orders

Any alien who at any time after admission is enjoined under a protection order issued by a court and whom the court determines has engaged in conduct that violates the portion of a protection order that involves protection against credible threats of violence, repeated harassment, or bodily injury to the person or persons for whom the protection order was issued is deportable. For purposes of this clause, the term "protection order" means any injunction issued for the purpose of preventing violent or threatening acts of domestic violence, including temporary or final orders issued by civil or criminal courts (other than support or child custody orders or provisions) whether obtained by filing an independent action or as a pendente lite order in another proceeding.

Section 274(A), 8 U.S.C. § 1324(a) (1)

(a) Criminal penalties.

(1)

(A) Any person who-

(iv) encourages or induces an alien to come to, enter, or reside in the United States, knowing or in reckless disregard of the fact that such coming to, entry, or residence is or will be in violation of law shall be punished as provided in subparagraph (B).

(B) A person who violates subparagraph (A) shall, for each alien in respect to whom such a violation occurs-

(i) in the case of a violation of subparagraph (A)(i) or (v)(I) or in the case of a violation of subparagraph (A)(ii), (iii), or (iv) in which the offense was done for the purpose of commercial advantage or private financial gain, be fined under title 18, United States Code, imprisoned not more than 10 years, or both;

(ii) in the case of a violation of subparagraph (A) (ii), (iii), (iv), or (v)(II), be fined under title 18, United States Code, imprisoned not more than 5 years, or both;

(iii) in the case of a violation of subparagraph (A) (i), (ii), (iii), (iv), or (v) during and in relation to which the person causes serious bodily injury (as defined in section 1365 of title 18, United States Code) to, or places in jeopardy the life of, any person, be fined under title 18, United States Code, imprisoned not more than 20 years, or both; and

(iv) in the case of a violation of subparagraph (A) (i), (ii), (iii), (iv), or (v) resulting in the death of any person, be punished by death or imprisoned for any term of years or for life, fined under title 18, United States Code, or both

Racketeer Influenced and Corrupt Organizations Act

18 U.S.C. § 1961: Definitions:

As used in this chapter [18 USCS §§ 1961 et seq.]-

(1) "racketeering activity" means

(F) any act which is indictable under the Immigration and Nationality Act, section 274 [8 USCS § 1324] (relating to bringing in and harboring certain aliens), section 277 [8 USCS § 1327] (relating to aiding or assisting certain aliens to enter the United States), or section 278 [8 USCS § 1328] (relating to importation of alien for immoral purpose) if the act indictable under such section of such Act was committed for the purpose of financial gain

(5) "pattern of racketeering activity" requires at least two acts of racketeering activity, one of which occurred after the effective date of this chapter and the last of which occurred within ten years (excluding any period of imprisonment) after the commission of a prior act of racketeering activity.

18 U.S.C. § 1962: Prohibited activities:

(a) It shall be unlawful for any person who has received any income derived, directly or indirectly, from a pattern of racketeering activity or through collection of an unlawful debt in which such person has participated as a principal within the meaning of section 2, title 18, United States Code, to use or invest, directly or indirectly, any part of such income, or the proceeds of such income, in acquisition of any interest in, or the establishment or operation of, any enterprise which is engaged in, or the activities of which affect, interstate or foreign commerce. A purchase of securities on the open market for purposes of investment, and without the intention of controlling or participating in the control of the issuer, or of assisting another to do so, shall not be unlawful under this subsection if the securities of the issuer held by the purchaser, the members of his immediate family, and his or their accomplices in any pattern or racketeering activity or the collection of an unlawful debt after such purchase do not amount in the aggregate to one percent of the outstanding securities of any one class, and do not confer, either in law or in fact, the power to elect one or more directors of the issuer.
(b) It shall be unlawful for any person through a pattern of racketeering activity or through collection of an unlawful debt to acquire or maintain, directly or indirectly, any interest in or control of any enterprise which is engaged in, or the activities of which affect, interstate or foreign commerce.
(c) It shall be unlawful for any person employed by or associated with any enterprise engaged in, or the activities of which affect, interstate or foreign commerce, to conduct or participate, directly or indirectly, in the conduct of such enterprise's affairs through a pattern of racketeering activity or collection of unlawful debt.
(d) It shall be unlawful for any person to conspire to violate any of the provisions of subsection (a), (b), or (c) of this section.

18 U.S.C. § 1963: Criminal Penalties

(a) Whoever violates any provision of section 1962 of this chapter shall be fined under this title or imprisoned not more than 20 years (or for life if the violation is based on a racketeering activity for which the maximum penalty includes life imprisonment), or both, and shall forfeit to the United States, irrespective of any provision of State law-

(1) any interest the person has acquired or maintained in violation of section 1962;

(2) any-

(A) interest in;

(B) security of;
(C) claim against; or
(D) property or contractual right of any kind affording a source of influence over; any enterprise which the person has established, operated, controlled, conducted, or participated in the conduct of, in violation of section 1962; and

(3) any property constituting, or derived from, any proceeds which the person obtained, directly or indirectly, from racketeering activity or unlawful debt collection in violation of section 1962.

The court, in imposing sentence on such person shall order, in addition to any other sentence imposed pursuant to this section, that the person forfeit to the United States all property described in this subsection. In lieu of a fine otherwise authorized by this section, a defendant who derives profits or other proceeds from an offense may be fined not more than twice the gross profits or other proceeds.

18 U.S.C. § 1964: Civil Remedies

(a) The district courts of the United States shall have jurisdiction to prevent and restrain violations of section 1962 of this chapter by issuing appropriate orders, including, but not limited to: ordering any person to divest himself of any interest, direct or indirect, in any enterprise; imposing reasonable restrictions on the future activities or investments of any person, including, but not limited to, prohibiting any person from engaging in the same type of endeavor as the enterprise engaged in, the activities of which affect interstate or foreign commerce; or ordering dissolution or reorganization of any enterprise, making due provision for the rights of innocent persons.

(c) Any person injured in his business or property by reason of a violation of section 1962 of this chapter may sue therefore in any appropriate United States district court and shall recover threefold the damages he sustains and the cost of the suit, including a reasonable attorney's fee, except that no person may rely upon any conduct that would have been actionable as fraud in the purchase or sale of securities to establish a violation of section 1962. The exception contained in the preceding sentence does not apply to an action against any person that is criminally convicted in connection with the fraud, in which case the statute of limitations shall start to run on the date on which the conviction becomes final.

Vienna Convention on Consular Relations

Article 5(d), 21 U.S.T. 77: Consular Functions

Consular functions consist in:

> (d) issuing passports and travel documents to nationals of the sending State, and visas or appropriate documents to persons wishing to travel to the sending State

Article 55(1), 21 U.S.T. 77: Respect for the laws and regulations of the receiving State

> 1. Without prejudice to their privileges and immunities, it is the duty of all persons enjoying such privileges and immunities to respect the laws and regulations of the receiving State. They also have a duty not to interfere in the internal affairs of that State.

ATTACHMENT 2

Cable Text:
UTE9039
ACTION VO-01

INFO	LOG-00	NP-00	CA-01	CIAE-00	INL-00	DODE-00	WHA-00
	DS-00	OIGO-00	FBIE-00	UTED-00	VC-00	TEDE-00	INR-00
	IO-00	VCE-00	AC-01	NSAE-00	ACE-00	TEST-00	DSCC-00
	PRM-00	DRL-01	NFAT-00	SAS-00	/004W		

------------------60C2A7 062336Z /38

American Embassy

R 062222Z MAY 03
FM AMEMBASSY MANAGUA
TO SECSTATE WASHDC 5570
INFO WHA CENTRAL AMERICAN COLLECTIVE
AMEMBASSY MEXICO
HQ INS WASHINGTON DC

Secretary of State

UNCLAS MANAGUA 001324

E.O. 12958: N/A
TAGS: CVIS, KFRD, PGOV, PREL, SMIG
SUBJECT: GON SEEKS TO EMULATE MEXICO WITH CONSULAR ID CARDS

Summary and Action Request

1. The GON plans to implement a consular ID card program similar to the one begun by the Mexican Government for Mexican citizens in the U.S. The ID card, which would be issued by the GON to Nicaraguans living in the U.S., would be used to open bank accounts and obtain utility services from local governments. The program would be initially implemented as a pilot in Miami and eventually expanded to other cities with large Nicaraguan populations. The GON is negotiating with the company that produces the ID cards for the Mexican Government and the Nicaraguan ID card will have security features similar to its Mexican counterpart. The ID card would be made available to any Nicaraguan citizen, regardless of legal status in the U.S. Although the GON has definite ideas regarding the major outlines of the program, it has not worked out the details. Furthermore, the card could be issued to an applicant lacking any identity documents, provided he has two witnesses who can attest to the applicant's identity. Post requests guidance for discussions with the GON. See action request at para 7. End Summary.

Responding to Citizens' Requests

2. After reading in the local press that the GON was proposing a consular ID program similar to the one recently implemented by the Mexican Government for Mexican nationals in the United States, Emboffs met with Consular Affairs Director Miriam Fonseca April 28, 2003, to inquire about the plan. Fonseca told Emboffs that the consular ID program was a direct response to numerous requests from Nicaraguans in

the U.S., who allude to Mexico's success with such ID cards and seek similar benefits. The program is currently designed as a pilot to be implemented first in Miami, where the GON believes there are 150,000 Nicaraguan citizens, and eventually expanded to other cities with large Nicaraguan populations, such as Los Angeles. The Foreign Ministry had initially planned for the program to be operational in June but is now projecting inauguration late this year.

3. Fonseca believes that the cards will be accepted to open bank accounts, obtain utility services from the city, and possibly get driver's licenses. The GON plans to install a card-making machine in the consular office and to provide ID cards on the spot. No approval will be required from Managua. The cost to the GON is projected to be USD 6 per card, for which individuals will be charged USD 25 each. In early April, the Vice-Foreign Minister presented the proposal for approval to the Supreme Electoral Council (CSE), a GON agency in charge of providing voting ID cards to Nicaraguans domestically. To date, the CSE has not responded.

Features Comparable to Mexican ID Cards
----

4. The GON is currently in negotiations with the same company that produces consular ID cards for the Mexican Government. The cards would presumably carry the same security features as the Mexican ID cards, but Fonseca was unfamiliar with the specifics. Although the security features of the card may be substantial and the card may be difficult to falsify, it is the criteria for issuance of the card that is problematic. Under Nicaraguan law, a person can usually establish his identity without documents when accompanied by two adult witnesses who can attest to the person's identity. For example, a person can use "witnesses" to be able to vote without a voter ID card and to obtain a copy of a birth certificate. According to Fonseca, this same "witness" process will be applied to the issuance of consular ID cards.

Legal Status Not a GON Concern
----

5. In issuing a consular ID card, the GON will not inquire as to the individual's legal status in the U.S. According to Fonseca, that is not a GON concern. The consular office will issue a card provided that the individual can establish his Nicaraguan citizenship with "appropriate documents." However, Fonseca conceded that legal Nicaraguan residents already have identification documents and only illegal residents are likely to benefit from the program.

Comment
----

6. It is fairly evident that although the GON may have determined the major outlines of the program, it has yet to focus on the details. For example, exactly what documents will be required to be presented to obtain the ID card have yet to be determined. In addition, requirements regarding

UNCLASSIFIED

age and residency in the U.S. have not been considered. Control of the database, and whether there will be Managua oversight, is unresolved. More importantly, the GON's practice of establishing identity with two witnesses is unlikely to impress bank, city, county, or State officials. To date, the GON has consulted with none of the entities to whom individuals are likely to present the cards. End Comment.

Action Request

7. Because the consular ID program is in its early stages and the Consular Affairs Director and Foreign Minister seem open to Embassy input, the U.S. Government has an excellent opportunity to influence the implementation of the program. Post requests Department guidance on what to tell the GON on this issue.
MOORE

NNNN

End Cable Text

Mr. HOSTETTLER. Thank you, Mr. Nelsen. And I want to forewarn the panel that because we are probably going to run up against the next set of votes and the end of the legislative week that I will hold fairly tightly to the 5-minute rule, even for the Chair, if that is possible.

First of all, Ms. Dinerstein, to clarify the situation with regard to consular IDs, the reason why consular IDs exist is for a relationship between the foreign national and the consulate in the country in which that foreign national happens to be at that point; is that not correct?

Ms. DINERSTEIN. That is absolutely correct. They are issued by many, many countries and they do so, as was said, so they can keep track of their foreign nationals that are living in a foreign country in case the national runs into problems, gets sick, needs to be transported home, has an accident. It is to provide consular assistance. That is the traditional reason and only reason that they have been issued.

Mr. HOSTETTLER. And that is why the United States and other—foreign consulates in the United States do not have jurisdiction over the issue of those consular IDs is because of that very unique relationship, but restricted relationship and purpose for the consular ID card?

Ms. DINERSTEIN. That is correct. They have nothing to do with the United States.

Mr. HOSTETTLER. Now you state in your testimony that the fact that only Mexico has access to the breeder documents used to obtain the consular ID cards, and specifically the Matricula Consular for Mexico and supplementary information that Mexico requires that is not on the document itself, quote, this renders U.S. law enforcement, U.S. agencies impotent to conduct a thorough background investigation if a Mexican national whose only identification is a Matricula card commits a serious crime while in America, unquote.

What is the basis for your conclusion?

Ms. DINERSTEIN. There is information on a birth certificate and information which the Mexican government collects on its application for a Matricula that is not available to U.S. authorities. For instance, Mexico asks for a contact name in Mexico. So it is not unusual if foreign nationals commit a serious crime for them to flee the U.S. and return to their home country.

This is indeed what happened with the woman who was found to be the head of the smuggling ring. She returned to Honduras. If the local address was available to the U.S., they could then pursue additional lines of inquiry. They are being hampered because they do not have full access to that information.

Mr. HOSTETTLER. So it is difficult for law enforcement to get the necessary information from Mexican authorities?

Ms. DINERSTEIN. They would be dependent upon the cooperation of the Mexican consulate to give it to them.

Mr. HOSTETTLER. Of a crime that is committed in the United States?

Ms. DINERSTEIN. Of a crime that is committed in the United States, that is correct.

Mr. HOSTETTLER. Mr. Nelsen, if a suspect stopped in the United States were to present a Matricula for identification purposes, what would the officer have to do to verify that the Matricula is authentic?

Mr. NELSEN. If the local consulate agreed to verify the information that was contained on the consular card, he might have that. But the unfortunate problem with the Matricula Consular card and probably any other consular card is that there is no central database to which even Mexico has access by which authorities, Mexican or American, could verify the information. So he would have no way of knowing that the information is correct.

Mr. HOSTETTLER. And there is no requirement for the foreign consulate to divulge the information that the law enforcement community asks for?

Mr. NELSEN. None whatsoever. I heard the term reciprocity come up a few times in the debate today. With officially recognized IDs like passports, there are agreements that countries have to cooperate. The consular ID card is not a part of any agreement, specifically the Vienna Convention, which generally covers consular relations. People today that have been talking about reciprocity saying we have to recognize the consular card or else Mexico won't recognize our passports, they are really missing the point. What they are really saying is that if American officials were in Mexico demanding that Mexico provide services through an American consular ID card to American illegal aliens in Mexico, that would be a case of reciprocity. There is nothing like that that exists with the current situation.

Mr. HOSTETTLER. Senator Andrews, in your testimony you state that you, quote, know of improper lobbying activities on the part of a consular employee leading to a formal letter of complaint from the Governor of Colorado, end quote. For what nation's consulate did this employee work?

Mr. ANDREWS. Mr. Chairman, this refers to an incident this past January. I have the news story in front of me. This was the press spokesman for the Mexican consulate in Denver. And our legislature and our Governor generally have excellent relations with the Honorable Leticia Calzada, the Consul General, but in this case there was a gentleman by the name of Mario Hernandez, of whom it was reported by some legislators who asked that their names not be divulged that he approached them seeking to influence legislation on such matters as driver's licenses being issued to illegal aliens and in State tuition being extended to illegal aliens residing in Colorado. And it was considered serious enough that our Governor Bill Owens wrote a letter to the Consul General asking her to clarify whether Mr. Hernandez had acted improperly and to render a legal opinion as to whether he ought to be registering with our Secretary of State as well as our lobbyists do as well as our United States Department of State regulations that might have been called in question. The incident then faded away. I think it was one of those matters where the Consul's office and the Governor's office both agreed to let it drop, but the warning was made very clear.

Mr. HOSTETTLER. The Chair's time has expired. I recognize the gentlelady from Texas, Ms. Jackson Lee.

Ms. JACKSON LEE. Mr. Chairman, you mean what you say and you do what you say and I will do my very best. I thank you very much, Mr. Chairman. I wish the winds of cooperation between President Vincente Fox and the President were still blowing because if that were the case we wouldn't have these hearings because as far as I know in the summer of 2001 we were about to consummate a very good partnership, clearing up an enormous amount of undocumented aliens and as well creating the kind of cooperation which would have answered Ms. Dinerstein, Mr. Nelsen, Senator Andrews and would have kept a smile on Congressman Gutierrez's face, but we would have been able to track down those who are, if at all, attempting to do us harm and as well to find Honduran smugglers in Honduras or elsewhere. And I hope, Ms. Dinerstein, you have a chance to look at the legislation I will be filing on smashing the smuggling rings, and we might be able to work together.

We are here today because that was not done. And the one thing I would like to get on the record, even if my time expires, is that we should not make this a fight between the anxieties that we have in our western States between the undocumented individuals who happen to come from Mexico and proliferate in those regions. I happen to come from Texas. For if we do that, that would be one of the most disastrous public relations and foreign policy steps we could ever make. And my sensitivity to this hearing is that I am hearing Mexico, Mexico, Mexico continuously.

And so I am assuming that we are not trying to offend the gentleman who was misstepping in Colorado. I hope that we know that everyone missteps no matter who they are and I am a little bit sensitive to the tone of some of the witnesses in this room, not intentionally but I think it is important for the record to be made very clear.

And the reason, Mr. Chairman, let me do this. I would like to submit into the record a report from the Congressional Research Service on this question dated June 18, 2003, which speaks specifically—and I ask unanimous consent for the submission of this document.

Mr. HOSTETTLER. Without objection.

Ms. JACKSON LEE. It specifically indicates, for example, other cases where an individual does not have a passport and humanitarian cases, for example, and that the legislation that we are hearing about would totally knock them out of any kind of utilization of a document from their foreign government, aliens applying for asylum, aliens applying for temporary protective status, no passports, Cuban nationals arriving in the United States, no passports and aliens requesting humanitarian parole.

Let me ask two quick questions. First of all, Mr. Nelsen, can you tell me where is the constitutional position—where is it in the Constitution, the language of immigration in the Constitution that you are arguing? I don't understand it. Mr. Gutierrez, do you find—what is the difficulty if we do a broad brush with this concept of voiding these cards out of the Mexican consulates around the Nation because it seems as if we are saying that, and I am not sure whether others have creative ideas? What is the hardship of the broad brush if you could restate that?

Mr. Nelsen, could you give me a constitutional citation, because my knowledge is that we deal with immigration powers federally, but I don't know what the constitutional citation you use. What is your constitutional citation?

Mr. NELSEN. On immigration, the Constitution and the Supreme Court has found this over and over, as Mr. Chairman has said, this has been well-established for a long time, the Commerce Clause gives the Congress absolute power over all aspects of immigration policy by the Supremacy Clause. No State or local law can conflict with Federal law.

Ms. JACKSON LEE. I agree with you on that and the cards don't confer immigration status—they are identification cards. And I am just wondering if you could cite for me.

But let me go to Representative Gutierrez on the hardship. Cite the constitutional notation on the ID cards. This is not immigration. This is an ID card.

Mr. GUTIERREZ. I think you are absolutely correct that is what it is. The argument that is being made here by Members of this panel and other Members is that it is an immigration card. It is not an immigration card. Doesn't get you a visa. It doesn't get you a work permit. Doesn't get you a Social Security card. Doesn't get you any of those things. What it does allow for is a form of identification. The one thing it does allow you to do, because the FDIC has said so and because of our Homeland Security Department, it allows you to get a banking account.

And Congresswoman Jackson Lee, if we voided it tomorrow, all of these millions of undocumented workers—and let me just state for the record, most people in this country entering illegally into this country do not enter illegally, they enter legally and overstay their visas, number one. And most of them don't come through Mexico. But it seems as though we want to harp and harp and harp on one country, on one consular office, and I think that is unfortunate. But you know something, Congresswoman, it is nothing new. If this was the 1890's we would be referring to the Italians that the New York Times called unruly and uncivilized. And if this were the 1850's and we were in Boston, we would be talking about the menace of the Irish coming over here displacing the only real Americans; that is, the English that were here before that.

This is an old argument that we have heard before, and it is as old as the Mayflower, but I know this is a great Nation. Their contributions will be stated here in this country because that is what it is, and it is the largest growing minority, according to the Census Bureau.

What our challenge is if we want national security, you want to feel safe, I would feel safer tomorrow knowing that I had the fingerprints, the names, the photos of up to 10 million undocumented workers in this country. I would feel safer tomorrow because in the absence, Mr. Chairman, of the will and a purpose on the part and putting the resources and the purpose of our Government to deport them, we all know that this conversation is moot. We can come back here next year and there will be just as many of them, if not more, in this country because they don't come here for the Matricula. They come here as long as jobs are available to them that Americans will not perform.

Ms. JACKSON LEE. Thank you very much.

Mr. NELSEN. If I might respond to the question or——

Mr. HOSTETTLER. Oh, yes, actually ——

Ms. JACKSON LEE. I accepted his answer. You have an additional answer?

Mr. NELSEN. The question you asked me, I think you said that immigration—that these cards are about identity and not about immigration and therefore it is not a constitutional matter. Actually I think it is. The Federal law we cite says that no local government, no American can actually encourage an illegal American to remain illegally in the United States. A Matricula card which gives service to illegal aliens does encourage, we are arguing, someone to remain illegally in the United States, and therefore it is a violation of Federal law.

Ms. JACKSON LEE. And may I just conclude. The nexus that you make is totally with a lack of understanding as far as I am trying to understand you. I am asking for a constitutional nexus to this and you are talking about Americans, not the constitutional powers. Now there is a tenth amendment that certain issues are left to the States, and that is not the basis upon which I think you can make a constitutional nexus. But I will enjoy talking to you in the future, and I thank you for your response.

Mr. HOSTETTLER. The Chair now recognizes the gentleman from Arizona, Mr. Flake.

Mr. FLAKE. I thank the Chair. I thank the witnesses. I had a question about—let me say from the outset I think Matricula Consulars are a wonderful thing. I wish there were more of them. I wish that there are more out there because I like the identification. The question, though, here really is, as I understand it, is whether or not the U.S. Government or State and local governments ought to rely on that information. That is the real question here. Can we rely on that information? Does that have implications for national security?

So that is the real question that I am coming from here. And myself and Congressman Kolbe and Congressman Reyes, as you know, and others are working on a temporary worker bill that would allow individuals who are here undocumented to come out from under the shadows and work in a legal framework and be able to come and return home under a legal framework. In that case, a document would be issued that would be issued by the U.S. Government and could be relied upon. But the question about what banks can and cannot accept, is there not already a form there? And I am not arguing here and I think what the banks want to accept, whether it is a Matricula or something else, that is fine. Is there not a document already called an I–10 form that can be used?

Ms. Dinerstein, can you explain how that works?

Ms. DINERSTEIN. ITINs were created by the IRS in 1996 to encourage compliance with American tax law for people that were living overseas that owned U.S. securities and owed interest or something, and the IRS decided that the ITIN would also be an appropriate vehicle to use for illegal immigrants, and they only regarded it as a tax monitoring number and, therefore, when they sent their application form they requested people to send in things like copies of birth certificates, etcetera. But the IRS never made any serious effort to verify the authenticity of those documents because they are a tax gathering institution. They are not a document examining institution. And I think the IRS was probably totally appalled that this became a runaway best seller. And since 1996, 6 million ITINs have been issued. And less than 2 million of them have been in any way involved with filing U.S. taxes. So what is happening to the other 4 million ITINs? And the generally accepted answer is that they are being used as a replacement for a Social Security number. They are being used for identity purposes. The Treasury Department in its report to Congress on the USA PATRIOT Act went out of its way to say that the IRS was not appropriately verifying the authenticity of these documents and it could not be relied upon as an ID document.

Mr. FLAKE. Senator Andrews, I commend the State of Colorado for addressing the issue. Can you tell me what kind of scenario do you envision or can you envision where the U.S. Government or State and local government might rely on this form of identification and it lead to a breach in national security?

Mr. ANDREWS. Mr. Flake, when I said in my testimony that one concern about these nonsecure cards is that they help the bearer blend into American life, I think we have heard many vivid examples of that in the discussion of this hearing, bank accounts being the most prominent one. But without in any way denigrating individuals from any of the 20 countries issuing or proposing to issue those cards in the world of jet travel and the Internet, someone can pass through any country of origin and make their way into this country. And language and other cultural identities are increasingly blurred, and I can imagine nonsecure consular ID documents—leave Mexico out of it—from many different countries becoming a passport to—quasi-passport not to just financial participation but issuance of a driver's license. Bogus driver's licenses were used by several of the 9/11 aircraft hijackers. And it is a chain of legitimizing someone that broke the law to be here but gradually just blends into this vast sea, these 10 million individuals not here with proper legal status that Congressman Gutierrez has referred to.

The bigger the sea of people here illegally and not able to be tracked by our Government agencies, the harder it is to find the very few bad actors, and we know there are only a very few. But the bigger that pool into which they can disappear, the more I believe our national security is at risk.

Mr. HOSTETTLER. The Chair recognizes the gentleman from Texas, Mr. Smith.

Mr. SMITH. Thank you, Mr. Chairman. Several people have mentioned today that somehow issuing these consular identification cards makes it easier for people to remain in the country, somehow making for a safer country. And yet I think we ought to remember that 20 percent of all Federal prisoners today are illegally here in the country, 20 percent. If we want to do something about the crime rate in America, we need to do something about illegal immigration in America. When you look at the 20 percent of Federal prisoners who are illegal immigrants, if you look at their proportion of the population, that means someone who is in the country illegally is about 10 times more likely to be convicted of a serious crime than someone who is in the country legally, and we ought not forget that.

And as far as singling out Mexico, we don't need to be defensive about that because Mexico has basically singled herself out. About half of all illegal aliens come from Mexico. No other country is particularly close to that, and that just happens to be a fact. It is not singling out a country. That is just where the figures are and the facts are.

I was going to ask Senator Andrews about how these documents have a negative impact on homeland security as Congressman Flake just did. Did you have anything that you wanted to add before your time expired?

Mr. ANDREWS. I don't think so, Mr. Smith.

Mr. SMITH. Ms. Dinerstein, thank you for your contribution to today's discussion when you pointed out that no major bank headquarters in Mexico lists the Matricula Consular card among the several official identification documents they accept to start accounts. As I said earlier, that is just incredible that the United States banks might accept them but not the Mexican banks.

And, Mr. Nelsen, thank you for reminding us how strongly the American people think about some of these issues. Oftentimes those strong feelings are ignored by the media, but you pointed to two polls. One is a recent Roper poll that found nearly 9 out of 10 Americans want local police to enforce immigration laws. You also pointed out that 75 percent in another poll believe that those who opened bank accounts in the United States should be required to show legal residence. So oftentimes you have the media elite and others on one side and you have the vast majority of the American people on the other side, and I think this may be one of these issues.

And you also pointed out, and I referred to it earlier in my opening statement, that the Treasury regulations permit U.S. banking corporations—I want to ask you about this statement—to put profit above the public good and open bank accounts for illegal aliens. Do you think that some banks might put a few dollars profit ahead of homeland security?

Mr. NELSEN. Congressman Smith, I guess to give the benefit of the doubt, perhaps we don't realize the serious nature of the issue, but I think profit motive is clearly taking precedence here and they have admitted that.

Mr. SMITH. I think they are being shortsighted and might be tempted to put the profits ahead of what is good for the country in the long run.

Mr. GUTIERREZ. Mr. Smith, I don't want anybody to have the misconception here, but if you get a Matricula Consular you get a checking or a savings account. Someone said earlier that we are encouraging illegals, that this against the law, and we just heard about—not in my testimony, but Ms. Dinerstein's testimony—that there are approximately 4 million tax ID numbers that are issued by the IRS. And according to her testimony, there is no other reason she can figure out other than they are undocumented. So in other words, the Matricula Consular plus the IRS, the Internal Revenue Service, gets you a checking, a savings account, so we might want to look at the IRS officials.

Mr. SMITH. My time is almost up. The point is that a lot of the banks are using those cards, either alone or in combination with other documents, and you yourself used the word that these were used and you encouraged the use by undocumented immigrants to use them, and that is a fundamental difference in opinion that I think we have. I have to say I think there is a big difference between—you mentioned the Italians in the 1890's and the Irish in the 1850's, they all came in as legal immigrants as a part of the legal immigration process. We are talking about individuals here that you also acknowledged that are in the country illegally who are undocumented, documented. So I think there is a big difference between the two.

Thank you, Mr. Chairman.

Mr. HOSTETTLER. The gentleman's time has expired. The Chair recognizes the gentleman from Iowa, Mr. King.

Mr. KING. Thank you, Mr. Chairman. I would like to thank the panel for your testimony and I would pick up where Mr. Smith left off, I think, with regard to the sensitivity with regard to Mexico and I point out a few other things. The foreign policy of Mexico has been clearly to me the promotion of dual citizenship, the promotion of the ability to vote on both sides of the border, in fact the promotion of the elimination of the border between Mexico and United States entirely, and that is not something that they have been very shy about. They don't have the same policy on immigration with their contiguous neighbors as they do with the United States of America. Mexico enforces their southern borders and they encourage immigration into the United States, both legally and illegally.

The situation with them opposing our policy in Iraq doesn't sit very well with me. The violations of the NAFTA Treaty doesn't sit very well with me. Eighty-five percent of the meth that comes into my State, the State of Iowa, comes across the border from Mexico.

We heard at this very table a couple of weeks ago—excuse me, it was in the other room, but it was John Ashcroft, our Attorney General, who testified that 85 percent of those who are adjudicated deported simply disappear back into the masses and don't honor that deportation. People can be picked up 10 to 12 times by the INS or their successor administration and volunteer to go back to their home country, and in 85 percent of those adjudicated deported don't go back. We know that for sure there is not 85 percent of those who volunteer to return. Somewhere between 85 percent and 100 percent simply disappear back into the masses.

So I direct my question first to Mr. Nelsen. You made the statement that about 5 billion people on this planet live at a lower standard of living. I think what we are talking about here is we all have compassion for individuals and we would like to export our economy, our way of life and give everybody the same opportunities that we have here. But the question more is what does it take to sink the lifeboat? And if we have gotten an open borders policy with Mexico today, actually across the entire Western Hemisphere we have an open borders policy, anyone who wants to—that can make a credible allegation of U.S. citizenship and walk across these borders. We heard that testimony in this room just several weeks ago.

And so my point is this, if we announce to the world that we are going to erase our borders and allow people to travel back and forth as they please, that is really the question that is at stake here, what are the social implications, cultural implications and economic implications of such a policy because what we are talking about here with the Matricula Consular card is a piece of moving toward a policy of opening borders without restriction?

So first Mr. Nelsen and then Senator Andrews, I would like to hear from you on what you think this world would look like if we simply followed this thing fast forward, if we erased all borders and restrictions?

Mr. NELSEN. I mentioned in my statement that I went from being an open borders advocate in my 20's to realizing how foolish that is after living in China for a couple of years and just realizing the sheer magnitude of the numbers of desperately poor people in the world. It is hard for the—hard to get one's mind around a number the size of 5 billion, but it truly is an enormous and destructive number. This is one of the reasons that calls for amnesty are so irresponsible and destructive. Sometimes every now and then we hear about programs that include amnesties or we hear calls for blanket amnesties. I think Congressman Gutierrez just made one. Last year Representative Gephardt made one. Every time—while that plays well in certain constituencies, politically here in the United States, it is a huge devastating—sends out a huge cry to billions of desperately poor people around the world to go ahead and take the chance and try to get into our country illegally in hopes of being rewarded some day with an amnesty.

I think we all know that hundreds of people die every year on the borders who are lured across in that way. We think amnesties, Matricula Consular cards for Mexico and all the other countries that may start issuing theirs, it is a step toward this globalization, borderless, nationalist, unnationed world in which economic currents drive human life. It is hard to predict how it would look, but we know and we are confident that most Americans oppose that. And since it is their country, I think we should listen to them first rather than corporations.

Mr. ANDREWS. Mr. King, in my testimony I mention the concern that our law is written about secure and verifiable documents. And the simplest way to translate that is you can find out if someone is who he claims to be. And thinking about the D.C. sniper case that is back in the headlines, we were all mystified and frightened for a couple of weeks and suddenly there was a news break and these men had been traced to Alabama and then to Washington State and then the TV cameras circled in on this stump that had been used for target practice on the other side of the United States. That is because of traceability of people's criminal records and their movements in our society.

We all have privacy concerns but we have to be real about the danger in our midst. And if the Matricula card or other nonverifiable ID cards become common from these 20 countries—it is not Mexico bashing. Poland is involved—if these cards become common then it is like the breakdown of the Soviet economy. Fifteen years ago the joke was we pretend to work and they pretend to pay us. In this case I pretend to be someone that I am not by presenting you this handsome laminated card that has been described and law enforcement pretends to make a record of it, but what don't they do? They can't transmit it to the INS. The INS has said they don't want it. It is not on the NCIC criminal database.

Congressman Gutierrez mentioned fingerprints. I would love to have fingerprints shared. Mr. Cannon mentioned the sharing of information. If the information was shared so that you get to a seamlessly traceable record by which we can find people who are the wrongdoers, then we are getting somewhere. That is why we have tried to write our law in Colorado with some nuances, with some allowances for law enforcement.

My son the police officer sees these Matricula cards in the tough neighborhoods of northeast Denver every day, but we have to find a way to get it plugged into a seamlessly traceable system of records where privacy is respected, but at the same time where security can be safeguarded.

Mr. HOSTETTLER. The Chair recognizes the gentleman from Utah, Mr. Cannon.

Mr. CANNON. Thank you, Mr. Chairman. You are going in a very interesting direction, Mr. Andrews.

Mr. Nelsen, when you say at the end of your testimony you think time is coming very soon when we will have a national sort of standards for driver's licenses, you think that will happen by when?

Mr. NELSEN. By the end of this year. There is a system called Intelli-Check. I think three States already have it implemented on their driver's licenses or State IDs issued through their Departments of Transportation in which an embedded marker——

Mr. CANNON. I understand where you are going. Let me just say that that is not going to happen in Utah. That is not going to happen federally because those are subject—my Subcommittee, the Commercial and Administrative Law—and I really don't like the idea of invading America's privacy with those kinds of standards. On the other hand, when you are dealing with a Matricula Consular there are issues that really pertain there. And one of the things that my good friend Mr. Smith pointed out is that we have a lot of agreement on some of these issues and there are some huge chasms that divide us.

One of the things that unites us, Ms. Dinerstein, you said that there are a few bad actors and then Mr. Smith pointed out that is probably 10 times the number of people who are bad actors among illegal aliens as in the population as a whole. I view that as pretty consistent. I happen to agree with that. The problem with our system today is we have 8, probably as a minimum, maybe as many as 11 million illegal aliens. Among them, in the shadows where they are hiding, there are many criminals, a significantly disproportionate amount, not a huge number, but many bad actors as you call them. So the question is what do we do and how do we solve this problem, and there are many choices. We could have a national—an American national ID and if you don't have the ID you then get ground up in the system. I don't think that is particularly what we are going to do.

By the way, Mr. Andrews, I am going to be the guest of your Governor tonight. I am going out to your fair State. When you talk about a secure and verifiable card, I heard from your statement you would not mind a consular ID being used as that if it met some of the standards that Ms. Dinerstein talked about and that you consider essential.

Mr. ANDREWS. Not at all. I wouldn't mind it at all, Mr. Cannon, if we can weave it into the system, if we could have safeguards despite of who he claims to be.

Mr. CANNON. I want to move this in a direction. We have an issue that is going to come up next week, I think, on the Department of Justice Reauthorization Act, where this issue may be relevant. You agree that if we have standards, do you think it would be appropriate for America through our Department of State to negotiate with Mexico on what those standards should be?

Mr. ANDREWS. Yes, I certainly do. What I am troubled by, though, suppose you need a visa stamp on your passport to show you legally entered the United States. If we start giving those visa stamps to foreign governments inside our borders we just gave away the store.

Mr. CANNON. If I might take a minute because I only have a minute left, if you and Ms. Dinerstein would each take a couple of minutes to talk about—Ms. Dinerstein, you mentioned that all we are using is a birth certificate. It is hard to use that. But are there documents out there or trails that we can use to validate a person's identity so that you have one card for one person, and have either of you thought about that and what would those standards be? Clearly a birth certificate would be one, but are there others?

Ms. DINERSTEIN. There are ways—it would need to be authenticated in Mexico. They would need to corroborate the breeder documents and the only way to do that is to authenticate them in Mexico and that would make it more reliable.

Mr. CANNON. Let me add one layer here. If the Mexican government were willing to work with us. There are two things that the Mexican government can do, tell us who they are and how many people are here with these IDs or they can tell us what their process is and allow us to do an audit to assure that that process results in a verifiable single ID for a single individual. If we had a process like that in place the Department of State could put together, do you, the two of you think that would change your views on the consular ID?

Ms. DINERSTEIN. I am opposed to United States entities accepting a consular ID. I believe that it should be—we should be accepting in this——

Mr. CANNON. Reclaiming my time, when you spoke you said there is one profound defect. That is America can't understand what the basis for the issuance of the card was. If you could solve that profound defect, if you could do that, would that mean that the consular ID would have a place to resolve what we all agree is an enormous problem?

Ms. DINERSTEIN. In my mind, no. The profound defect was with regard to the reliability and verification and authenticity of that document. I still do not believe that we should be accepting in this country anything except U.S.-issued identification to foreign nationals proving that they have a legal right to be in this country.

Mr. CANNON. You didn't quite address the question, and if I might have Senator Andrews to respond to that question.

Mr. ANDREWS. I hear you describing so many modifications and restrictions to the Matricula card that it wouldn't look like the Matricula card at all, and so it is tough to answer the question except to say that when you and I get on the plane to go to Denver tonight, I don't want to see people bypassing the metal detector and the security check and just walking through a side door where they don't get checked. And right now to me the Matricula card or any consular card from Poland or Peru or anybody is a side door because somebody can walk up to the consular desk in Denver and not be asked if they broke the law to get into this country.

If there was a way to say no proof of legal residency then you don't get a consular card, the consular card would be like a passport or like a visa and I would have no problem with it. The reason that they are being not just issued for 130 years but marketed so aggressively in the last year or two is that it is a bypass around legal immigration, and that is what bothers me.

Mr. CANNON. With all due respect, Mr. Chairman, if I might have 10 seconds, the bypass happens of people coming across the border from all places and the question is how do we deal with 8 to 11 million people, which include a huge disproportionate number of bad actors, and that is the question and that is what we are going to have to deal with in a slightly different context in the State of Colorado because it is our jurisdiction.

Mr. ANDREWS. If I may just finish then. If any country's consular card, I don't care what country, if it was blue when you proved you were here legally and orange when you couldn't prove you were here legally, then you are taking your chances when you flash that orange card the next time you go anywhere, it would be better.

Mr. CANNON. Can I ask unanimous consent for another 30 seconds just to point out that——

Mr. HOSTETTLER. The gentleman's time has expired. We will have time for a second round.

Mr. CANNON. The rest of the Committee may have time for a second round.

Mr. GUTIERREZ. Mr. Chairman, I have a 4 o'clock meeting with Senator McCain that I finally got after 3 weeks to talk about immigration issues. Could I have 60 seconds and then I will be permitted to leave? The proponents of Matricula don't want to ask me any questions and the opponents don't.

Mr. HOSTETTLER. My second round, I will ask questions.

Mr. GUTIERREZ. I would like to see the Senator. If I just could I would like to summarize very quickly.

Mr. HOSTETTLER. Does the gentlelady from Tennessee——

Mrs. BLACKBURN. I will yield for a couple of minutes but it is—you know, we all have places to go and we are sitting here with Blackberries going off and we have a vote coming up at 4 o'clock. So very briefly I will yield.

Mr. HOSTETTLER. The Chair recognizes the gentlelady from Tennessee and she yields to you.

Mrs. BLACKBURN. I will yield to you.

Mr. GUTIERREZ. I appreciate it.

Listen, the Matricula should not be a get out of jail card and I don't think it is. And I think if a police officer finds someone doing something illegal they should be arrested and prosecuted. And I don't get what the Matricula does to stop that prosecution. They should be prosecuted to the fullest extent of the law. If we want secure borders and we have millions of undocumented workers and we should get rid of the bad apples, then we should have people come forward and have a way of registering them; that is, getting their fingerprints, finding out their work history, finding out if they have ever been involved with the law and if they have, so we can have hard working, tax paying—since 4 million have taxpayer IDs from the IRS—and law-abiding working people that are undocumented and bring them into the fold and we can get rid of the bad actors.

I want to thank the Committee, and I thank the gentlelady. I said I needed 60 seconds. And I know that we have many, many things to do. On a serious note no one has—and I know you will—I assure you when we get together, I am sure we will have that conversation and discussion. Thank you all for having me here this afternoon.

Mr. HOSTETTLER. The gentlelady is recognized.

Mrs. BLACKBURN. Thank you, Mr. Chairman. And thank you for our panel for your patience and for allowing us to be up and down and to visit with you today. I thank you, too, for submitting your statements in advance so we can prepare. I am going to kind of follow along where Mr. Cannon was and Mr. Andrews, or Senator Andrews, speak with you.

I am new in Congress to this year. I came out of the Tennessee Senate. And in Tennessee we have wrestled with an issue where illegal aliens could sign a document that they never had a Social Security number and receive a driver's license which I think, as Ms. Dinerstein quoted in her testimony, that it is a passport to American society. It is something that concerned me greatly, and I worked diligently in Tennessee to close that loophole. And I have read with interest what you all did in the Colorado Senate, and I wanted to know if there was one activity or one occurrence that triggered the action and the movement of this bill?

Mr. ANDREWS. Mrs. Blackburn, it was the cumulative concern that these cards are proliferating from many countries but in Colorado it happened to be our proximity to Mexico and the activity of the Mexican consulate to issue these things by the tens of thousands. There were actually waiting lines. People couldn't get them fast enough and there were no questions asked between the legal and the illegal resident.

I am aware of Tennessee's driver's license policy. I arranged for passage of a bill in Colorado a year ago that ended reciprocity where any other State's driver's license could be exchanged for a Colorado driver's license, no questions asked, because there were concerns about Tennessee and other States that gave these to illegal residents of the United States. And knowing the tragic role that driver's licenses played in 9/11, we didn't want Colorado anywhere near that.

Our bill closing the door on the nonsecure foreign issued ID card that passed this year didn't come from any one shocking incident.

It just came from the sense of mounting concern that we are turning a blind eye to the rule of law, that it didn't matter if you snuck into this country or came here obeying the rules.

Mrs. BLACKBURN. I found it very interesting, Ms. Dinerstein, that you had commented that Mexican banks do not accept the Matricula Consular. I missed the explanation as to why that is, if you do not mind repeating that for me.

Ms. DINERSTEIN. I wish I could. I don't know why Mexico doesn't. I do know that Mexico has far, far better identification than the Matricula. They were—they spent a lot of money in the early 1990's to make their voter registration card a very good ID card because there had been a lot of fraud in their elections. And those cards contain fingerprints as opposed to—Congressman Gutierrez seems to be under the impression that fingerprints are contained on the Matricula. They are not.

Mrs. BLACKBURN. Thank you very much. Let me ask you this. And you and Mr. Nelsen may be able to answer this for me. If an individual—would there be reason for suspicion that a person, an individual was illegally in the country, if they only had the Matricula Consular card as a form of ID? And I am saying this if a bank—if an employer were to see that, would that be a reason for suspicion?

Ms. DINERSTEIN. Yes. All employers are supposed to request a Social Security card. If I can just speak personally, if I am in a position where I am being asked to present ID to board a plane, because I have been pulled over for a traffic infraction or for whatever reason, I am going to give the best piece of ID I have to whoever is requesting it, and therefore, if the only piece of ID that is being presented is the Matricula, I think that a reasonable person could conclude that that individual does not have any U.S.-issued ID and is here illegally.

Mrs. BLACKBURN. I have some questions on technology but I know we are short on time, and I yield back.

Mr. HOSTETTLER. I thank the gentlelady. We will go for another round of questions if the panel can abide by that, and once again we will hold to the 5 minutes.

I would just like to once again bring us back to the focus of this hearing and, as was stated in the memorandum that was given to the panel members, the reason for the hearing is to discuss the issuance, acceptance and reliability of consular ID cards.

Is it the understanding, Mr. Nelsen, and your understanding, Ms. Dinerstein, that the issuance of the consular ID cards are issued by consulates of foreign nations in the United States? Is it your understanding that that is the case?

Mr. NELSEN. Yes, that is true.

Ms. DINERSTEIN. That is correct.

Mr. HOSTETTLER. And the acceptance of consular ID cards are essentially to be accepted by consulates in foreign nations in the United States?

Mr. NELSEN. Do you mean by other nations?

Mr. HOSTETTLER. The reason why—the people that accept—the people that accept the consular ID cards with regard to identification are whom—who cares about the identification traditionally should care about the identification that is on a consular ID card?

Mr. NELSEN. Only the issuing country historically.

Mr. HOSTETTLER. At the consulate essentially?

Mr. NELSEN. Yes.

Mr. HOSTETTLER. Not a bank, not a local housing entity, not anyone. The reason why consular ID cards traditionally exist is for acceptance of consulates, for the identification of a foreign national?

Ms. DINERSTEIN. That is exactly right. The host country has never been involved whatsoever with anything to do with a consular card until quite recently, a year-and-a-half to 2 years ago.

Mr. HOSTETTLER. And so we want to make sure that the reliability of that process is between the foreign national and the national Government in the form of a——

Ms. DINERSTEIN. I don't frankly care how reliable it is or it isn't if it is being issued by a foreign government and the foreign government is the only one that has anything to do with it. Why I care about the reliability of it is at this point the United States entities are being asked to accept it, and I care a lot now about the reliability.

Mr. HOSTETTLER. If we talk about a card or a mode of identification that steps out of what we know is traditionally the consular ID card, we are no longer talking about a consular ID card, correct, in the traditional sense? If we talk about biometrics, verifiability or whatever other characteristic of a form of identification, we are no longer talking about a traditional consular ID card, am I correct in that?

Mr. NELSEN. I think that is correct. It has become something like the Mexican green card. Basically, it is a green card issued by Mexico.

Mr. HOSTETTLER. Or Poland or Guatemala or whoever is doing that. I think that is an important point to make, about the reason for this hearing is, because we are talking about—we are talking about IDs that are being used for purposes outside of their traditional views. And that is the concern, because there are essentially two people in America today, two different types of people in America today, there are citizens and there are noncitizens. Because article 1, section 8, clause 4 of the Constitution says that, to reiterate, Congress shall have the power to establish a uniform rule of naturalization, that we are dealing with fundamentally, an issue of naturalization, a subset of that, which is immigration.

And so that is the Federal Government's role. And when people come here that are not citizens, it is the Federal Government's obligation and prerogative, solely, to deal with issues of naturalization, a subset of that which is immigration.

And so I just wanted to get us all on track, maybe back to the record as to why we are here today. And the concern that many of us have that a form of identification that was traditionally held as a means of identification between a foreign national and their foreign mission in the United States, is not that any more. And other countries—and because one country has set a precedent, that country happens to be Mexico, it could be someone else, and other countries are wishing to follow that precedent.

And that is why we are here. Senator Andrews.

Mr. ANDREWS. If I might just add, Mr. Chairman. The analogy occurs to me, I belong to the Rotary Club. The Rotary Club is in more countries of the world than even the United Nations. I have got a Rotary Club membership card. It is good when I go to any Rotary Club in this country or any other.

But, it is of no use or shouldn't be, for me to prove to any government in this country or any other country that I am not using an alias, and I am not breaking their laws. And, you have put your finger on it. The problem that has arisen with the consular cards in the last couple of years is that so many governmental and private entities in this country are now willing to say, you show me a card from a consulate, and I will assume you are not using an alias, and you are not breaking our laws.

And those two assumptions are what I have said on other questions a few minutes ago, it concerned us in Colorado so very much, that is why I said it is like the police pretend to believe that I am who I claim to be. But all they are doing is pretending, because I am giving them something that could be phony. And they are not bothering to find out if it is phony.

Mr. HOSTETTLER. Thank you very much. The Chair recognizes the gentlelady from Texas, Ms. Jackson Lee.

Ms. JACKSON LEE. Thank you very much, Mr. Chairman.

There is clearly a difference of opinion in this room. The good news is that we have had this hearing. And I would like to associate myself with, I think, the line of reasoning and the line of questioning that my good friend from Utah was expressing when he kept trying to probe the witnesses as to what changes would make them happy.

And because I could not seemingly hear from them any answers or solutions, again, I go back to the point whether or not this is just either bashing immigrants, generally speaking, and bashing those that come from Mexico.

I would like to put into the record, Mr. Chairman, an article that I am going to applaud from the Rocky Mountain News, Wedding Bells Are in the Cards. Now, I probably will get chastised for the proponents of the cards, because they are not understanding what I am saying. I am consistent.

These cards are not to be and are not used for immigration status. There is a separation of powers. The 10th amendment leaves to the State what it desires to do, and leaves to the Federal Government, its responsibilities. Immigration is a responsibility of the United States Federal Government. It is a power that one can detect, read, associate under the Constitution.

But, identification issues and a State's desire to accept identification is their prerogative. It is administrative in my interpretation. It is not a Constitutional Act. So we understand that a Ms. Garcia and a Mr. Ramos attempted to get married, and they went to the Denver Clerk and Recorders Office. They came away disappointed and discouraged, possibly after this law. I guess this is June 17, 2003, how apropos, I was celebrating my 30th wedding anniversary on that day, the very young woman that I am. And I was married——

Mr. HOSTETTLER. And the record so reflects that.

Ms. JACKSON LEE. I was married as a baby bride, not even a child bride. So my sympathies to this couple that could not get married. But, Mr. Ramos had a Matricula Consular card and an expired Mexican passport. He was rejected.

And Ms. Garcia, who had the proper identification, was okay. Well, I would argue, rightly so, to a certain extent, because there may be questions of immigration status. I am not sure questions were asked by the clerk, but if it had to do with status, and then that State made a determination that status had not been shown, Federal status had not been shown. If that was the question, if there was not provisions that said, we just need ID.

But the only reason I use that as an example is so that my good friends will know where I am going on this point, is that if it was that you have rules in Colorado that you can only marry people with documentation as to immigration status, then you rightly did not accept the card, and if you were basing that on Federal law.

And so it worked. And I don't know the State laws, what questions were being asked by the clerk. The card was only—if you only have requirements of ID, then have you a problem with this. But I applaud it if it had to do with status, because that is my argument, this is an identification card.

And so I don't know where this hearing will take us, but I would like to join in the words of the Congressman from Utah and ask, Mr. Chairman, that we try to provide guidelines, and we work to fix it. But if you broadly eliminate the utilization of this card, you are broadly, first of all I think, interfering with Federal law, when we should engage the State Department on the devastating damage, because on a humanitarian basis all of the asylum seekers will be without passports, and they will be walking around with nothing, to our disadvantage.

In the Homeland Security hearing I just came from, these were my pronounced words: We are not secure. Period. But, this process does not aid in security. Because what you are doing is, maybe what we should do, Ms. Dinerstein, is require fingerprints. I have not probed that with the consulars, because they interact with the State Department. But, I think they have done what they have tried to do, to make a card that cannot be counterfeited or smudged, and that is an improvement for us.

It is also an improvement that if they go and open a bank account, and there is identification, then if they are money launderers, that is an improvement for us. I will raise this question, last question, Mr. Chairman, and say this: Mr. Berman, who had another meeting on my side of the aisle and is very knowledgeable on these issues, begged us not to allow ideology to overtake common sense.

So we need to be able to reform or fix, but not to eliminate or undermine. Senator Andrews, you were attempting to respond, because—and I am sorry, Mr. Chairman, I would like unanimous consent to put this article in the record from the Rocky Mountain News dated June 17, 2003.

Mr. HOSTETTLER. Without objection.

Ms. JACKSON LEE. Senator Andrews.

Mr. ANDREWS. Congresswoman, I compliment you on your research, and I am flattered that you would enter an article from my hometown paper into the record, that is this week. And 30 days ago, Mr. Ramos and Ms. Garcia could have shown up to the Denver

County Clerk and obtained that marriage license on the strength of the Matricula.

What has changed in the last 30 days is that Colorado House Bill 1224 was signed into law in the meantime, and the Denver County Clerk is attempting to comply, and in this case, I believe, properly complied with this new State law.

Had the gentleman presented a valid Mexican passport, then I assume that the marriage license would have been issued. And the intent of the law is, to this small extent, operating because, I believe the Colorado General Assembly was listening to our constituents, and we were seeking to require valid ID that would reassure State agencies someone wasn't breaking the law, being in this country illegally, before they could obtain various State and local government services, even something like a marriage license.

So the new bill took effect here, and the new bill seems to be working as we hoped it would work.

Ms. JACKSON LEE. Mr. Chairman, I conclude by simply saying, that that is where we have the conflict. And I will have to read that bill. Because if they were rejecting it because he did not have proper ID, I consider that a legitimate role of the State. If they are trying to make an assessment of his immigration status, the card did not confer status. And I would raise the question of whether or not we are taking this card and penalizing it as an ID card, because we are saying that it is a card to equal status, and that is not what it is.

We should let it stand on what it is, Mr. Chairman, an ID card. And as it relates to immigration status, that is our responsibility, and we then need to fix whatever has to be fixed to make those cards viable.

I yield back, and I thank the Senator.

Mr. HOSTETTLER. Thank the gentlelady. The Chair now recognizes the gentleman from Iowa for 5 minutes, and that will put us 10 minutes to the end of the vote. Mr. King.

Mr. KING. Thank you, Mr. Chairman.

I was prepared in our second round to address my question to Representative Gutierrez. Reading through his testimony, he states that 13 States acknowledge the Matricula card as a means to acquire a driver's license. I would appreciate it if my office could receive that list of those States. I would be very interested in that.

I would point out that that number is very close to the same number of States that require citizenship before one can vote. And I don't have that list at my disposal, but even though there is a Federal requirement for citizenship in a local election, the States under the 10th amendment have that jurisdiction.

And only about 13 or 14 States have taken the trouble to legislate the obvious, that casting a ballot is an exercise in citizenship. It should require citizenship to cast a ballot at any election in this country, in my opinion. The States have not moved forward on that.

But I point that out as a kind of an interesting coincidence. But, I will say that when the Matricula card is used as a driver's license, and that driver's license is used as identification, and a person goes in any one of those other States, other than those 13 or 14 that require citizenship, and casts a ballot, then, in fact, they have opened the door to citizenship of the United States through the Matricula card—and it is controlled by the Mexican Consulate.

So that is what we are talking about here. And I posed the question earlier to the gentleman, and I will pose it now to the lady. And I am still interested in the broader subject matter here the steps that we take that cheapen citizenship and open our borders, move us in a direction of open borders.

And if we are going to recognize where we are going as a Nation, we have to find a way and have this open debate across this country, and fast forward ourselves into what are the results of an open borders policy, because we know what incrementalism is. It is a designed and calculated method to open borders, bring down barriers. And some people believe in a one-world government. I happen to believe that almost all of the blessings that humanity has contributed to, with the help of God, came from sovereignty of the Nation, and being able to have solid policies that are consistent, so that our currency is solid and our culture is consistent as well.

So, Ms. Dinerstein, can you then speculate what this world looks like if we fast forward down this path of open borders and one world. What does the United States look like in 50 years or a hundred years in your mind's eye?

Ms. DINERSTEIN. I think what it would be like is something very dissimilar to what is it today. And part of that is that the United States is the most technologically advanced country. The most entrepreneurial country. The country, you know, to our detriment now with respect to the Middle East, is viewed as so dominant in world affairs that we have now, it is coming back and biting us.

The people that are sort of compelled to come here are by their nature the poorest people. The people who have no opportunity in their own countries at all. Their own countries don't educate them. They don't provide them jobs. And, therefore, were there to be open borders, there would be a wave of people so grateful for the opportunity to come to this country that it would overpower us really.

They are hard working, but their skill level is such that they can't earn a decent living, and, therefore, they would become a public charge. You know, I just—it is a very interesting question. I sort of haven't gone there in my thinking because it is a little upsetting.

Mr. KING. I would state that I am surprised that of the three testifiers here on this panel that I have asked that question to, that you don't seem to have explored that out to the end, a generation or two down the road. I suspect that most of this Nation has not done that either.

So we are dealing with minutia policy, short-term vision here, instead of applying the long-term effect of what it is that we might be doing. And I think, though, that Mr. Nelsen did make some comments with that regard on our shortsightedness. I think that we might need to be much more farsighted in our policy that we establish, and know where it fits in the long scheme.

I thank you all very much for your testimony. And thank you, Mr. Chairman. I yield back.

Mr. HOSTETTLER. The gentleman yields back his time. I want to thank the witnesses for appearing today and for your testimony, as well as your responses to our questions.

We will leave the record open for 7 days for any additional information that the Members of the Subcommittee or witnesses may want to submit.

And I will also want to mention that we will be having a second hearing on consular identification cards next week on Thursday, June 26th, at 11 a.m. In this room. We will be holding a hearing on the Federal Government's response to the issuance and acceptance in the U.S. of consular identification cards.

At that hearing the Subcommittee will review the steps that Federal agencies have taken to review, regulate and oversee the issuance of consular ID cards in the U.S., as well as foreign government lobbying efforts to seek acceptance of the cards by States, localities and businesses in the United States.

Ms. JACKSON LEE. Mr. Chairman, I associate myself with your remarks on the appreciation to the witnesses. I would like to ask unanimous consent to submit into the record acceptance of Mexican Consular IDs is not only legal, it improves public safety and enhances the economy prepared by MALDEF.

Mr. HOSTETTLER. Without objection.

Ms. JACKSON LEE. Thank you.

Mr. HOSTETTLER. The business before the Subcommittee being complete, we are adjourned.

[Whereupon, at 4:20 p.m., the Subcommittee was adjourned.]

FEDERAL GOVERNMENT'S RESPONSE TO THE ISSUANCE AND ACCEPTANCE IN THE UNITED STATES

THURSDAY, JUNE 26, 2003

HOUSE OF REPRESENTATIVES,
SUBCOMMITTEE ON IMMIGRATION,
BORDER SECURITY, AND CLAIMS,
COMMITTEE ON THE JUDICIARY,
Washington, DC.

The Subcommittee met, pursuant to call, at 11:11 a.m. in Room 2237, Rayburn House Office Building, Hon. John N. Hostettler (Chair of the Subcommittee) presiding.

Mr. HOSTETTLER. The Subcommittee will come to order.

Today, the Subcommittee is holding its second hearing on consular identification cards, cards issued by foreign agents in the United States. In order to devote as much time as possible to this important topic, we have postponed Subcommittee action on four private bills until the week of July 14.

A few points became clear from the testimony at that hearing that was previously held last Thursday. The first point is that issuance of consular cards in the United States is not a new phenomenon. In fact, consular cards have been issued for approximately 130 years. Those cards have traditionally been issued by consular officials to nationals abroad to allow those nationals to seek their home country's assistance when they need help—for example, when they are injured or arrested.

Historically, therefore, the intended recipient of a consular card issued by a foreign government in the United States is the foreign government itself, not our Government and certainly not a locality in the United States. The second point is that while the issuance of consular cards is a fairly old process, attempts by foreign government agents to lobby States and localities to accept the cards are not. None of the witnesses at last week's hearing and no information that has come to the Subcommittee suggests that any foreign country issuing consular cards ever attempted to convince States or localities to accept those cards for domestic identification purposes before 2001.

Therefore, in the 130-year history of foreign government issuance of consular cards, foreign governments have only lobbied localities to accept those cards for the past 2 years. A third point about which there is little disagreement is that foreign governments are allowed to issue consular identification cards in the United States. Even those critics who believe that consular identification cards are insecure and unreliable believe that foreign countries have the right to issue them to their nationals. Critics do oppose, however, efforts by foreign government agents to lobby State and local officials in the United States to accept the cards. It is only in the context of such foreign government lobbying and domestic acceptance of consular cards that the security, reliability and verifiability is a concern for our country.

A fourth point is that consular cards do not convey any immigration status. None of the foreign governments that issue consular cards that the Subcommittee has examined appear to have any interest whatsoever in whether an applicant for the card is in our country lawfully; rather, it appears that those countries acknowledge the fact that most of the aliens applying for those cards in our country are here illegally and need the card because they have no form of lawful identification. In fact, some have argued that if an alien's only identification is a consular card, the alien is most likely illegally in the United States and should be arrested by the immigration authorities and removed.

A fifth point is that no domestic government entity in the United States at the present time regulates the issuance of consular cards or the lobbying efforts of foreign governments to convince States and localities to accept those cards. On a similar point, it is apparent that no domestic government entity in the United States has access to the databases of cards that have been issued by foreign government agents in the United States, even where those agents have lobbied States and localities to accept the cards.

It is against this backdrop that the Subcommittee calls this hearing today. It has been approximately a year and a half since foreign agents began a widespread effort in the United States to lobby States and localities to accept consular cards for domestic identification purposes. The Subcommittee is interested in determining what steps the Federal Government has taken in response to those efforts. The Subcommittee is also interested in determining what the Federal Government has done to investigate complaints that foreign governments have been lobbying States and localities to accept cards that are not secure and that are not reliable and that are susceptible to fraud.

Finally, the Subcommittee is interested in determining what the Federal Government's policy is with respect to domestic acceptance in the United States of consular cards. It is clear that the United States Government must play some role in this process, be it regulating domestic acceptance of consular cards or, at a minimum, providing guidance to States and localities that have been lobbied by foreign government agents to accept those cards.

For more than 6 months, the Subcommittee has been closely following the efforts of various Federal Government agencies—departments, excuse me, and agencies—to establish a uniform policy on and consider a response to the local acceptance of consular identification cards. We are still waiting for that policy to be issued. While that process has been ongoing, foreign government agents have continued to lobby localities to accept consular cards for local identification purposes. The Subcommittee has been told that some of those localities have come to the Federal Government looking for guidance but that no guidance was forthcoming because the Federal Government has failed to agree on a policy for accepting consular cards.

Because the Federal Government has been silent on this issue, localities have had to decide on their own whether to accept consular identification cards based on the information that was available to them, information provided by interested and concerned citizens and the statements of the lobbying foreign governments themselves. In the absence of Federal guidance, many localities have decided to accept those cards while the Federal Government has been assessing what its position on the acceptance of the cards should be.

In fact, on Monday, Indianapolis, IN, to accept the Mexican identification card known as the Matricula Consular. The fact that so many localities have made the decision to accept consular cards for domestic identification purposes without guidance from the Federal Government is a source of concern, particularly in light of testimony that this Subcommittee received at last week's hearing.

Marty Dinerstein, who appeared before the Subcommittee last week, explained why secure documents are essential to homeland security. She recounted the shock felt by the American people when they learned that 18 of the 19 September 11 hijackers, cold-blooded murderers of innocent men, women and children, possessed State-issued or counterfeit driver's licenses and ID cards.

Witnesses at that hearing told the Subcommittee, however, that consular identification cards, the acceptance of which has skyrocketed since September 11, 2001, are not secure. Witnesses also argued that consular identification documents are not reliable; that there is no assurance that the document accurately identifies the bearer of the card. In particular, the Subcommittee has been told that the breeder documents used to obtain consular cards are not authenticated. The lack of such authentication is an issue, because reports indicate that counterfeit birth certificates are readily available.

As Steve McCraw notes in his testimony, Mexican birth certificates, for example, are easy to forge and are a major item on the project list of the fraudulent document trade currently flourishing across the country and around the world. At that hearing last Thursday, Ms. Dinerstein also told the Subcommittee that there are no safeguards in place to prevent the multiple issuance of Matriculas to a single individual. There appears to be substantial merit to this claim. This Subcommittee has received credible reports that aliens have been arrested carrying multiple consular identification cards bearing their own pictures but with different names. Of particular note is a memo sent by the Border Patrol agent in charge in Riverside, California, to the sheriff of San Bernardino County, who was considering allowing his deputies to accept the Matricula. The Patrol agent in charge explained that his office had arrested many Mexican aliens who had, in their possession, multiple valid Matriculas in different names.

These arrestees, including one known alien smuggler with an extensive criminal history, found in a house with 25 smuggled aliens who had seven Matriculas in his possession, each bearing his picture and each with a different name. This claim is also borne out in the FBI's testimony.

Witnesses at the June 19 hearing also identified other issues raised by local acceptance of consular cards for issues that were unrelated to the reliability and security of the cards. Witnesses explained how local police acceptance of consular cards leaves a local police officer wholly reliant on a consular official, an agent of a foreign country, to verify the authenticity of the card or to gain access to any of the background information submitted with the card.

As Ms. Dinerstein stated, "this renders U.S. law enforcement agencies impotent to conduct a thorough background investigation," if such a card is presented to a police officer. Witnesses at that hearing also discussed the fact that the documents could hide possible criminal and terrorist activity. Senator Andrews from Colorado put it best when he compared local acceptance of consular cards to people at an airport bypassing the metal detector and the security check and just walking through the side door.

To understand the potential criminal and national security risks that consular identification cards pose, it is important to note the critical work that the State Department's consular officers do at our consulates abroad. They review the background of aliens who are seeking visas to come to the United States. They work to ensure that aliens are not admitted to the United States if they have committed crimes in their home countries. In certain cases, they request additional guidance from other U.S. agencies to ensure that an alien seeking admission will not pose a terrorism risk to the American people.

It is also important to note the important role that inspectors at our ports of entry play in protecting our national security. Those inspectors closely examine identification documents from aliens seeking admission at the ports of entry. They check databases of known criminals and security risks. They evaluate whether an alien may be inadmissible on any ground. They screen those who want to come to our country.

No background checks are run, however, when an alien applies for a consular identification card. No investigation is undertaken to assess the possible risk that an alien poses a risk to the American people. In the best-case scenario, an alien applying for a consular identification card fills out a form and presents identification documents to the consular officer. That is it. No criminal grounds for denial; no risk assessments. The foreign government's only interest is the welfare of the alien, not the wellbeing of the American people.

Witnesses at last week's hearing also explained how local acceptance of consular cards undermines our nation's immigration policies. Acceptance of consular cards by States and localities provides cover for aliens in the United States. It allows aliens to bypass the system that Congress had established to allow aliens to come lawfully to the United States and enjoy the freedoms and blessings that our country offers.

It gives a document to undocumented aliens. I question whether the States and localities that have agreed to accept consular cards for domestic identification purposes would have made that choice if they were aware of these issues. I doubt that States and localities would have taken the chance of accepting the cards if they believed that acceptance could expose their citizens to aliens who pose an unchecked criminal or national security risk. I also doubt that they would have deliberately made a decision that could have been at odds with our nation's immigration laws or that would have been unfair to the thousands of aliens who wait patiently abroad to enter our country legally.

Because the Federal Government has failed to formulate a policy on domestic acceptance of consular cards and because the Federal Government has failed to undertake an investigation into the liability and security of those cards, States and localities have been placed in a position in which they have had to take those chances and make those decisions however.

I would like to make one last point before we continue. Testimony for this hearing was due at 11 a.m. on Tuesday. This deadline was set to allow Members sufficient time to prepare for this hearing. Testimony was not received, however, until yesterday evening. This is unacceptable. This Subcommittee has not only the authority but also the duty to oversee the implementation of our immigration laws and policies. Late submission of testimony hinders the Members of this Subcommittee in preparing for oversight hearings and in fulfilling that duty. I expect all testimony from all witnesses to be submitted in a timely manner. I especially expect testimony from Federal Government witnesses to be submitted in accordance with the time frames set by this Committee.

I have on many occasions expressed my willingness to ensure that the three Federal departments represented today have sufficient resources to carry out their immigration responsibilities. This Subcommittee's relationship with each of your departments is a two-way street, however. I expect in return that each of your departments and this Administration will be responsive to this Subcommittee in a timely manner. And I realize the three witnesses before us today had very little to do with the timeliness of the submission of your testimony, but if you could take that message back for us, we would surely appreciate it.

I now turn to Representative Howard Berman, who is serving as Ranking Member today, for an opening statement that he would make.

Mr. BERMAN. Well, thank you, Mr. Chairman. A little while ago, the Ranking Member, Sheila Jackson Lee, asked me if I would sit in as long as I could this morning because of her obligations on the Homeland Security Committee, where she also serves. I would like initially permission for her statement to be included in the record.

Mr. HOSTETTLER. Without objection.

Mr. BERMAN. The Chairman has given a very extensive, thorough opening statement, and while there are points in that opening statement that I agree with, there are a number I question. But rather than—I did not take notes as he spoke and have not had a chance to read his testimony, understanding that he is not obligated to give me his testimony on Tuesday at noon. Rather than hit and miss, I would just make a couple of points. I would bring into question the assertion that the only interest of the consulates that provide these cards is in helping the alien. If the implication of that is that the consulates are knowingly giving cards to people who are not the people that they claim they are, and the consulate is not doing anything to verify whether or not that person is the person that he or she asserts he is; I do not believe that. I do not believe that is true of the consulate in Los Angeles in my area. I am sure it is not, and I do not think we should attribute motives to institutions of our neighbor Mexico or any other government without a more fundamental foundation being laid for making that kind of conclusion about motivations.

Secondly, there are non-State institutions in this country that have concluded that these identifiers are accurate enough to give them the assurance to do things like cash checks and handle money for an individual that if they did not would otherwise force that person to go to loan sharks and usurious check cashing institutions to make any financial transactions.

By and large, the banking institutions in this country are not frivolous about the kind of identification that they will use to assure that the individual is who he or she says he is. I am sure mistakes happen, but I would not be so quick to challenge the security of these cards, and it is unclear to me exactly why these cards are any less secure than the passports that we commonly, in the Federal Government commonly accepts as secure identifiers to justify all kinds of privileges.

To the extent that one has questions, and I listened with interest to the Chairman's citation regarding some specific incidents, and I think they are worth following up on, but to the extent one has doubts about the security of those documents, one could also have doubts about the security of passports.

And the final point is September 11. The vast majority of the terrorists who engaged in that conduct were here on visas issued by United States Government agencies. They were not here based on illegal entry and then obtaining identifiers from their government's consulates in this country. And so, I think we should be careful to—we had serious problems in dealing with watch lists and integration of different agency functions which must be corrected. But to sort of deflect that issue and take the emotionality of that issue and apply it to the issue of these consulate-issued identifiers I think creates an impression which is not very fair.

And with that, I yield back the balance of my time.

Mr. HOSTETTLER. I thank the gentleman.

The Chair now recognizes the gentleman from Texas, Mr. Smith, for an opening statement.

Mr. SMITH. Thank you, Mr. Chairman, and Mr. Chairman, thank you once again for having a hearing on a very timely subject and also, thank you for your very strong opening statements.

Just a couple of comments: one is in regards to one of our witnesses, Mr. Verdery, who was simply sworn into his present position yesterday at the Department of Homeland Security and is testifying today. He is off to a fast start and for that reason probably ought to be entitled to at least one pass on one question. [Laughter.]

Mr. HOSTETTLER. Not necessarily. [Laughter.]

Mr. SMITH. The other, Mr. Chairman, is that unfortunately, I have two other Committees that are meeting and are marking up legislation, so I will not be necessarily able to stay for all of the testimony, but I hope to shuttle back and forth. Finally, Mr. Chairman, I thought it might be of interest to the Members of the Subcommittee as well as perhaps to our witnesses, the results of several public opinion polls that have been conducted in just the last several months and that I have put together and I thought might be relevant today.

This is a Roper Poll just a couple of months ago. The question was how serious of a national problem do you think illegal immigration into the United States is? Eighty-six percent of the American people thought that illegal immigration was a serious problem. On another question, again, the same Roper Poll, 85 percent of the American people agree with this statement: Congress should pass a law requiring State and local governments and law enforcement agencies to apprehend and turn over to the INS illegal immigrants with whom they come into contact. And a third question, I will not go into a lot of them; a lot of the questions dealt with both illegal and legal immigration, but a third question dealing with illegal immigration was this: that 83 percent of the American people agree that the Federal Government should strictly enforce present laws calling for heavy fines for employers who knowingly hire illegal immigrants.

Now that question, I think, can be related to the use of the Matricula cards by banks, because they are basically employers giving recognition to individuals who are in the country illegally.

Mr. Chairman, these percentages, 86 percent, 83 percent, are astronomical in almost any context when you ask the American people how they feel about issues. And I think the point here is simply to point out that there are a number of interest groups, many editorial writers and not a few politicians and perhaps a few individuals associated with the Administration who are simply on the wrong side of the vast majority of the American people. And I think we ought to keep that in mind as we go forward with hearings and legislation.

Mr. BERMAN. Will the gentleman yield?

Mr. SMITH. I will be happy to yield to my friend from California.

Mr. BERMAN. I question the methodology of the poll, because I would have a hard time believing that there are 14 percent of the American people who are not against illegal immigration.

Mr. SMITH. Does that mean you would have said you thought illegal immigration was a serious problem? You would have voted the way the American people would have?

Mr. BERMAN. If voting the way you vote is the way most of the American people would have voted on some of these issues, perhaps not. [Laughter.]

But I would certainly answer affirmative to the question that I think illegal immigration is a serious problem and has to be dealt with.

Mr. SMITH. To reclaim my time, I read the questions. I thought they were accurate and objective questions. And it is reassuring to me if the gentleman from California seemed to agree with most of the American people on these poll results. But I appreciate his comments and yield back, Mr. Chairman.

Mr. HOSTETTLER. The Chair now recognizes the gentlelady from California, Ms. Sánchez, for an opening statement.

Ms. SÁNCHEZ. Thank you, Chairman Hostettler and Acting Ranking Member Berman.

I am not going to make a long statement this morning, since I was able to speak at last week's hearing on this topic. I just want to emphasize a few points that I made then.

Consular identification cards have been used for over 100 years. And recently, however, people have begun raising concerns about the use of these cards. And frankly, it is not exactly clear to me why. For example, I have heard it argued that people use them so that they can skirt immigration laws. But the reality is that these cards do not establish any kind of immigration or other benefits. They merely are used to allow foreign visitors to this country to establish their identity.

Others have argued that the consular ID cards are not secure documents, but my understanding, based on information that I have, is that they are more secure than many types of ID, including U.S. passports. I would agree that it may be possible for someone to make a false consular ID card, but my question to those who are concerned about it is what document in existence today is impossible to forge? It seems to me that there is a great deal of fuss being made about cards that, in essence, are just helping police and other officials do their jobs.

I look forward to hearing from the witnesses, and I hope that at the end of the day, we will be able to agree that the use of consular ID cards actually works to enhance the security of this nation, not to break it down.

Thank you, and I yield back the balance of my time.

Mr. HOSTETTLER. I thank the gentlelady.

The Chair now recognizes the gentleman from Arizona, Mr. Flake, for an opening statement.

Mr. FLAKE. I thank the Chairman. I spoke also at the last hearing.

I just want to say that consular IDs, as have been mentioned, have been around for 100 years. They are in use. I think it is a great thing. I am glad they are out there. I am glad that identification exists to this extent. I do have issues, though, with whether or not the Federal Government should accept them for identification, and the fact that they are not secure is a concern to me. I have legislation of my own on driver's licenses. Many of the terrorists, as has been mentioned, came here with a temporary visa and were able to get long-term driver's licenses. In my own State of Arizona, they issue driver's licenses for up to 44 years. If you are 16; you are here; you can get it until you are 60.

A lot of States are going that direction, where you have a driver's license that is good for a number of years. If you are here on a temporary visa, you can go in and get a driver's license that lasts a lot longer than your temporary visa. My legislation would say that your driver's license can last no longer than your temporary visa, the expiration date.

This is in a similar vein to the legislation that Representative Gallegly has. It simply says that the Federal Government should not use this for secure identification. And that is my position. I look forward to this testimony this morning.

Mr. HOSTETTLER. I thank the gentleman from Arizona.

The Chair now recognizes the gentleman from California, Mr. Gallegly, for an opening statement.

Mr. GALLEGLY. Thank you very much, Mr. Chairman.

Mr. Chairman, I believe it is important to respond to a number of the arguments that have been made by supporters of the foreign consulate cards being used for legitimate ID. Supporters of these cards claim that the consular cards have been used for over 130 years, as Representative Sánchez just mentioned. And that is true.

However, while issuing them has been a routine activity for many countries, there has always been an assumption that the cards were issued to people who were legally in the host country. In addition, no country I am aware of has ever accepted foreign-issued consular cards for identification purposes or domestic services.

In March of 2002, the Government of Mexico began issuing the cards wholesale to illegal immigrants in the United States. According to published statements by the Mexican officials, they have issued more than 1.2 million cards in the past year alone. The Government of Guatemala, likewise, has started to issue consular cards to illegal immigrants, and other countries have announced their intent to do so, including Brazil, Poland, Nicaragua, El Salvador and Haiti.

In the case of Nicaragua, the government officials there have stated that they are modeling their program after Mexico's. All of this, Mr. Chairman, is unprecedented. It is also true, as stated by consular card supporters, that all six of these countries are well within their rights to issue the cards, and many showed good faith by working with the State Department to develop the program.

The problem is that our Government's own failure to act responsibly in the interests of the safety of our citizens. The only people who need these cards are illegal immigrants, somctimes criminals or maybe terrorists. The State Department, foreign governments and the supporters of these cards do not deny that illegal immigrants are the principal beneficiary of these programs. Yet, the State Department representatives acknowledged in Congressional briefings that they had an active dialogue with Mexico in designing its program, and a U.S. Embassy cable from Managua explicitly asked the State Department in Washington for guidance regarding the implementation of Nicaragua's consular card program.

Supporters of the consular cards also state that those who need these cards are not terrorists but hard-working and undocumented immigrants who work in the lowest-paying jobs in our agriculture and hotel industries. That card only allows them to bank and send money back to their relatives. While it is correct that the overwhelming, almost total number of those seeking cards, are not terrorists, it is equally true that the terrorist states are certainly watching this program to see how it may be exploited.

Within the next few years, six countries could be 60. Are we willing to accept consular cards from the Saudis, from the Syrians, from Colombia, who are also seeking low-paying jobs. The truth is that Poland, Mexico, Nicaragua, and other countries that are trying to expand their consular programs in the United States are doing so in an effort to force a de facto amnesty for their nationals illegally in the country and allow them to receive services to which they are not entitled, among which is the ability to use cards to board commercial airliners, Mr. Chairman, a dramatic step back toward the type of security we had prior to 9/11.

In a recent cable from the U.S. Embassy in Managua to the State Department, a U.S. official noted that the Nicaraguan Government wanted its nationals to have the cards to open bank accounts, obtain utility service and possibly get driver's licenses. As we all know, 9/11 terrorists used driver's licenses as their key to operate freely in the United States, and under the Nicaraguan law, a person needs no documentation to prove identity; only two witnesses to vouch for them with no one vouching for the vouchers.

Mr. Chairman, the current consular programs are direct assaults on this country's sovereignty. Issuing consular identification cards to illegal immigrants undermines the immigration enforcement policies of the United States, and it weakens the security and puts Americans at great peril. Supporters have stated that there is no political will to deport illegals in this country and that these people should be integrated into our community, perhaps through the distribution of consular cards. To that, I say the desire of Americans to never repeat 9/11 is will enough to eliminate this program.

I have authored and introduced an Identification Integrity Act of 2003 with the exceptions of passports, which are issued under strict guidelines provided by the Government, it would prevent the Federal Government's recognition of foreign-issued IDs. This legislation has now almost 100 cosponsors, and the price, Mr. Chairman, is far too high not to end this practice.

I would just like to conclude by saying that one of my very good friends on the other side of the aisle, a Democrat from California, said to me that he was very puzzled at why people would spend money to buy a consular card that does nothing more than proves they are an illegal immigrant.

I yield back.

Mr. HOSTETTLER. I thank the gentleman.

Now, at this time, I would like to introduce our panel of witnesses: Steve McCraw is the assistant director of the Office of Intelligence for the Federal Bureau of Investigation. Throughout his 20-year career with the FBI, Mr. McCraw has served in numerous supervisory positions, including director of the Foreign Terrorist Task Force. Prior to his appointment to the FBI, Mr. McCraw was a State trooper for the Texas Department of Public Safety and taught political science at the university level. Mr. McCraw holds a master's and an undergraduate degree from West Texas State University.

Roberta S. Jacobson is the acting deputy assistant Secretary of State for the Bureau of Western Hemisphere Affairs. Ms. Jacobson joined the Department of State as a Presidential Management Intern in 1986. She has also served at the State Department as deputy chief of mission at the U.S. Embassy in Lima, Peru; director of the Office of Policy Planning and Coordination in the Bureau of Western Hemisphere Affairs and Coordinator for Cuban Affairs within the Bureau of Western Hemisphere Affairs. She was also at the National Security Council. Ms. Jacobson holds a master's of arts in law and diplomacy from the Fletcher School of Law and Diplomacy and a bachelor's degree from Brown University.

C. Stewart Verdery, Jr. is the Assistant Secretary for Border and Transportation Security Policy and Planning at the Department of Homeland Security. He was confirmed to this position last Friday. Prior to coming to DHS, Mr. Verdery was the senior legislative counsel for the Government Affairs and Public Policy Office at Vivendi, Universal Entertainment, Universal Music Group, and Vivendi Universal. Before he joined Universal, he was general counsel to the United States Senate Assistant Republican Leader Don Nickles of Oklahoma. Mr. Verdery also served as counsel to two Senate Committees and to Senator John Warner. He received his undergraduate degree from Williams College and his law degree from the University of Virginia.

Elizabeth Davison is the director of the Department of Housing and Community Affairs for Montgomery County, Maryland. She is an urban economist who has spent her 30-year career in both the private and public sector. Prior to joining the county, she was vice-president of Hammer, Siler, George Associates and Real Estate Research Corporation. Ms. Davison received her undergraduate degree from George Washington University; her graduate degree from Washington University in St. Louis and has attended the Kennedy School of Government at Harvard University.

Once again, I want to thank all of the witnesses for your appearance today. Without objection, your full testimony will be entered into the record, and if you can limit your comments to 5 minutes, we would most surely appreciate it.

Mr. McCraw, you have the floor.

STATEMENT OF STEVEN McCRAW, ASSISTANT DIRECTOR, OFFICE OF INTELLIGENCE, FEDERAL BUREAU OF INVESTIGATION

Mr. McCRAW. Thank you, sir.

Chairman, if I may, with me today is Robert Matamoros, who is the unit chief for the money laundering unit. If you have questions relating to money laundering in that regard, he is behind me, sir.

Mr. HOSTETTLER. Thank you.

Mr. McCRAW. And thank you for the opportunity to be here. Good morning to you, sir, and to the rest of the Committee. The one thing I would like to do is since my full testimony is going to be placed in the record is just dispense with it at this time and just discuss the issue a little bit with your permission, Chairman.

Mr. HOSTETTLER. Yes.

Mr. McCRAW. As you are aware—certainly, everyone is aware—terrorism is the most important thing that the FBI does and the Department does right now. The President directed and charged the FBI and the Department to make it a number one priority. It is. And with the support of Congress, that is what we are doing.

The issue of a fictitious or a fraudulent consular ID, years ago, pre-9/11, we would simply view it in the context of a criminal matter. It would not be something that the FBI would be overly concerned about, other than the fact that they could be exploited by criminals, as they often do with fictitious IDs.

In the post-9/11 era, I mean, the FBI is charged with assessing threats and vulnerabilities. And clearly, this is a threat and a vulnerability. And as long as terrorists—and it was a very good point.

The 19 hijackers, in fact, used their own names. And even though they obtained, you know, State ID cards, they did use, in fact, their own identifications, even if they overstayed their visas. However, you know, it is absolutely prudent that we in the FBI and the Department and also other Government agencies look at in terms of their adaptability.

Our number one threat is clearly Al Qaeda. They are consistent; they are patient; and clearly, they are adaptable. And frankly, any ability to get fictitious identification, they are going to exploit. Specifically, and coming from my latest assignment at the San Antonio Division of the FBI, which had 650 miles of the border, our concern there and concern nationwide in the FBI has been the number of countries that have a strong Al Qaeda presence that are exploiting the tri-border area and utilizing long-established and very well-disciplined alien smuggling organizations in Mexico to transit individuals, foreign nationals, through Mexico and into the United States. It was a concern when I was there; it is still a concern with us.

Of course, a part of the process is fictitious IDs. And anywhere, an average price, perhaps $10,000, even greater that Mexican alien smuggling organizations use and charge to transit these individuals, these foreign nationals, into the United States. So naturally, the threat that we see is in terms of them having legitimate identification in the United States; utilizing either forged consular ID cards or utilizing fraudulent ones because of birth certificates that were obtained without the proper or at least the type of authentication that we would like to see is a concern to us. There is no question about it.

One quick example to further exploit or expand upon some of the written testimony is, as alluded to, the foreign national from the Middle Eastern country. It was an Iranian arrested by the Texas Department of Public Safety officer on February 23 of 2003. He was arrested along with four individuals. The only thing that was noted—in fact, the trooper called and was supported by legacy INS, Border Patrol agents showed up there; is that the Iranian had a Matricula Consular identification on his body. And through their investigation, they determined that he obtained it through his girlfriend, who got a fraudulent birth certificate through her father in Mexico and who was able to convert that into a State ID in California in the consular office in San Bernardino.

Now, I mentioned four other instances in there, and I am not saying there are not other documents in the same category. In fact, we are concerned about all documents that are vulnerable, not just this particular one. But right now, we do have concerns about it because of what we have seen in recent months and over the last 2 years.

Thank you.

[The prepared statement of Mr. McCraw follows:]

PREPARED STATEMENT OF STEVE MCCRAW

Chairman Hostettler, Ranking Member Jackson Lee, and Members of the Subcommittee, the Federal Bureau of Investigation is pleased to have the opportunity to appear before you today to discuss the important issue of consular ID cards. The Department of Justice and the FBI have been charged by the President, with the support of Congress, to protect the American people from the continuing threats of terrorism and the crimes associated therewith. It is in the context of our post-9/11 world that we present our views and concerns to the Subcommittee today.

Over the past two years, we have all seen a dramatically increased effort to promote and utilize consular ID cards as forms of identification for foreign nationals who are present in the United States. The Government of Mexico has been particularly aggressive in marketing the use of its consular ID card, the Matricula Consular. As a result of the extensive efforts to promote the use of the Matricula Consular, a number of other foreign countries are now considering the issuance of their own consular ID cards. The crucial element in the acceptance of any consular ID card is the ability to verify the actual true identity of the bearer of the card. In today's post-9/11 world, this element is all the more important because, in order to protect the American people, we must be able to determine whether an individual is who he purports to be. This is essential in our mission to identify potential terrorists, locate their means of financial support, and prevent acts of terrorism from occurring.

Since Mexico's Matricula Consular is currently the predominant consular ID card in existence, I will focus my comments today on this particular card. It is believed that consular ID cards are primarily being utilized by illegal aliens in the United States. Foreign nationals who are present in the U.S. legally have the ability to use various alternative forms of identification—most notably a passport—for the purposes of opening bank accounts, gaining access to federal facilities, boarding airplanes, and obtaining a state driver's license. In addition, foreign nationals who are present in the United States, either legally or illegally, have the ability to obtain a passport from their own country's embassy or consular office.

The U.S. Government has done an extensive amount of research on the Matricula Consular, to assess its viability as a reliable means of identification. The Department of Justice and the FBI have concluded that the Matricula Consular is not a reliable form of identification, due to the non-existence of any means of verifying the true identity of the card holder. The following are the primary problems with the Matricula Consular that allow criminals to fraudulently obtain the cards:

> First, the Government of Mexico has no centralized database to coordinate the issuance of consular ID cards. This allows multiple cards to be issued under the same name, the same address, or with the same photograph.
>
> Second, the Government of Mexico has no interconnected databases to provide intra-consular communication to be able to verify who has or has not applied for or received a consular ID card.
>
> Third, the Government of Mexico issues the card to anyone who can produce a Mexican birth certificate and one other form of identity, including documents of very low reliability. Mexican birth certificates are easy to forge and they are a major item on the product list of the fraudulent document trade currently flourishing across the country and around the world. A September 2002 bust of a document production operation in Washington state illustrated the size of this trade. A huge cache of fake Mexican birth certificates was discovered. It is our belief that the primary reason a market for these birth certificates exists is the demand for fraudulently-obtained Matricula Consular cards.
>
> Fourth, in some locations, when an individual seeking a Matricula Consular is unable to produce any documents whatsoever, he will still be issued a Matricula Consular by the Mexican consular official, if he fills out a questionnaire and satisfies the official that he is who he purports to be.

In addition to being vulnerable to fraud, the Matricula Consular is also vulnerable to forgery. There have been several generations of the card; and even the newest version can be easily replicated, despite its security features. It is our estimate that more than 90 percent of Matricula Consular cards now in circulation are earlier versions of the card, which are little more than simple laminated cards without any security features.

As a result of these problems, there are two major criminal threats posed by the cards, and one potential terrorist threat.

The first criminal threat stems from the fact that the Matricula Consular can be a perfect breeder document for establishing a false identity. It is our understanding that as many as 13 states currently accept the Matricula Consular for the purpose of obtaining a drivers' license. Once in possession of a driver's license, a criminal is well on his way to using the false identity to facilitate a variety of crimes, from money laundering to check fraud. And of course, the false identity serves to conceal a criminal who is already being sought by law enforcement. Individuals have been arrested with multiple Matricula Consular cards in their possession, each with the same photograph, but with a different name. Matching these false Matriculas are false driver's licenses, also found in the criminals' possession. Such false identities are particularly useful to facilitate the crime of money laundering, as the criminal is able to establish one or more bank accounts under completely fictitious names. Accounts based upon such fraudulent premises greatly hamper money-laundering investigations once the criminal activity is discovered. As the Subcommittee is well aware, the FBI is particularly concerned about fraudulent financial transactions in the post 9/11 environment, given the fact that foreign terrorists often rely on money transferred from within the United States.

The second criminal threat is that of alien smuggling, a crime that has resulted in many deaths within the past year. Federal officials have arrested alien smugglers who have had as many as seven different Matricula Consular cards in their possession. The cards not only conceal the identity of the smuggler, they also serve as a magnet for the victims who are enticed to entrust their lives to the smugglers, believing that the Matricula Consular that awaits them will entitle them to all sorts of benefits within the United States.

These criminal threats are significant, but it is the terrorist threat presented by the Matricula Consular that is most worrisome. Federal officials have discovered individuals from many different countries in possession of the Matricula Consular card. Most of these individuals are citizens of other Central or South American countries. However, at least one individual of Middle Eastern descent has also been arrested in possession of the Matricula Consular card. The ability of foreign nationals to use the Matricula Consular to create a well-documented, but fictitious, identity in the United States provides an opportunity for terrorists to move freely within the United States without triggering name-based watch lists that are disseminated to local police officers. It also allows them to board planes without revealing their true identity. All of these threats are in addition to the transfer of terrorist funds, mentioned earlier.

In addition, it is important to note that the White House Homeland Security Council is currently chairing an interagency working group that is developing recommendations on Federal policy for Federal acceptance of these cards as well as guidance to state and local governmental agencies on acceptance. The interagency group is examining policy for acceptance of all consular identification cards. They are also specifically examining counterfeit and fraud concerns with the Mexican consular identification card that would impact its acceptance for identification purposes. The Department of Justice is an active participant in that group.

The events of 9/11 forever changed our world. As unpleasant as it may be, we must face the realities of our current world as they relate to protecting the people of the United States. This requires continual vigilance—particularly when it comes to being able to detect and deter those who might abuse the system to directly cause harm, or those who might aid and abet the financing of terrorist operations. Thank you.

STATEMENT OF ROBERTA S. JACOBSON, ACTING DEPUTY ASSISTANT SECRETARY OF STATE FOR THE BUREAU OF WESTERN HEMISPHERE AFFAIRS

Ms. JACOBSON. Thank you, Mr. Chairman.

Chairman Hostettler, Mr. Berman, Members of the Subcommittee, I am pleased to have this opportunity to appear before you today to discuss foreign consular identification cards. My name is Roberta Jacobson. I am currently acting deputy assistant secretary for the Bureau of Western Hemisphere Affairs, and in that capacity, I am charged with overseeing our bilateral relations with Mexico and Canada.

Before addressing the issue of the Federal Government's and in particular the Department of State's response to consular identification cards, I want to emphasize that it is our top priority to ensure the safety and security of the United States and its citizens. The events of September 11 and the possibility of future terrorist attacks resonate throughout the Department and have significantly affected how we do business.

Since the start of our deliberations on this issue, safety and security have been material to the development of a policy on the issuance of foreign consular identification cards. Safety and security are also central themes in the bilateral relationship with Mexico. Every day, I witness the strong spirit of cooperation that exists between the United States and Mexico to improve the security not only of the United States but all of North America.

Indeed, just last month, in Washington, Mexican Foreign Secretary Derbez affirmed that security and counterterrorism represented the number one priority for Mexico in its bilateral relationship with the United States.

Mr. Chairman, the Administration has not taken an official position on the issuance or acceptance of foreign consular ID cards. State and other Executive Branch agencies are working to establish a comprehensive Federal Government policy on consular identifications, a policy that will affect documents now being issued or that may be issued in the future by any nation to its nationals in the U.S.

The need for a Government-wide policy became evident as Mexico and other countries have become more active in issuing or exploring the possibility of issuing such documentation and as questions about acceptance of foreign consular identification cards were raised. Beginning last year, the Department of State chaired an interagency group tasked with developing that policy. Earlier this year, the Homeland Security Council assumed the leadership of the interagency process, and we continue to support this endeavor.

All of us involved in drafting the policy are aware of the intense interest and desire for a final product that will address the many aspects of the issue. Any policy on the issuance and more importantly the acceptance of foreign consular identifications must address questions of security, reciprocity and protection for Americans abroad, our international treaty obligations, law enforcement and State and local legislation. Topics that were discussed while the Department chaired the interagency process included the effect of foreign consular identification cards on homeland security; the rights and privileges granted to the United States as well as other countries under the Vienna Convention on Consular Relations, U.S. obligations regarding consular protections, foreign policy goals, questions of federalism and the regulation of financial services.

The complexity and diversity of the issue, which extends well beyond the purview of the Department of State, argues for a thorough development of any policy and underscores the need for a coordinated approach. In addition to concerns about national security, the State Department has two additional interests in the development of any policy on consular identification cards. The first is the impact of a policy on the Department's ability to carry out its responsibilities in consular affairs both domestically and abroad. On the domestic front, the Department views consular identification cards as a possible tool for facilitating consular notification by accountable law enforcement officials.

The Vienna Convention on Consular Relations requires that a foreign national who is arrested or otherwise detained in the United States be advised of his or her right to request the appropriate consular officials be notified of the detention without delay. The issue of consular notification is a serious one for the Department, and we are working assiduously to assure U.S. compliance.

Because foreign consular identification cards are a means to identify an individual as a foreign national, the bearer's possession may alert responsible law enforcement authorities to the need to provide notification. The Department also believes that the U.S. Government must carefully avoid taking action against consular identification cards that would foreclose our options to document or assist Americans overseas. The Department itself issues documentations other than passports for U.S. citizens abroad and at times issues similar identity cards or travel documents.

Should a foreign country decide to limit acceptance of such documentation or other traditional documentation such as State-issued IDs or driver's licenses, the actions of American citizens abroad could be seriously restricted. The Department's goal is a single, uniform policy that is applicable to all countries that issue consular identifications. While the Mexican card has recently been highlighted, it is not a new program, as you have stated. The Vienna Convention on Consular Relations, to which we are a party, allows for sending states to perform consular functions to help assist and protect their nationals.

What has clearly changed is the scope of the Mexican program and the Government of Mexico's vigorous efforts to secure acceptance of the card by local governments and financial institutions at a time of heightened security concerns.

Given these changes, we have contacted the Government of Mexico to learn more about the technical nature of the card, and we have found the Embassy and the Ministry of Foreign Affairs to be responsive to our requests for information about the issuance process, security features and card production.

Thank you, Mr. Chairman, for the opportunity to present this testimony, and I would be pleased to respond to any questions you have.

[The prepared statement of Ms. Jacobson follows:]

PREPARED STATEMENT OF ROBERTA S. JACOBSON

Chairman Hostettler, Ms. Jackson Lee, and members of the Subcommittee, I am pleased to have this opportunity to appear before you today to discuss Foreign Consular Identification Cards.

My name is Roberta S. Jacobson, and I am currently the Acting Deputy Assistant Secretary of State for the Bureau of Western Hemisphere Affairs, and in that capacity, I am charged with overseeing the United States' bilateral relations with Mexico and Canada.

Before addressing the issue of the federal government's and, in particular, the Department of State's response to consular identification cards, I want to emphasize that our top priority is ensuring the security and safety of the United States and it's citizens. The events of September 11 and the possibility of future terrorist acts resonate through the Department and have significantly affected how we do business. Since the start of our deliberations, safety and security have been material to the development of a policy on the issue of foreign consular identification cards. Safety and security are also central themes in the bilateral relationship with Mexico. Everyday I witness the strong spirit of cooperation that exists between the United States and Mexico to improve the security of not only the United States, but all of North America. Indeed, just last month in a speech in Washington, Mexican Foreign Secretary Derbez affirmed that he understood and accepted that security and counter terrorism represented the number one priority for Mexico in its bilateral relationship with the U.S.

Mr. Chairman, the Administration has not taken an official position on the issuance or acceptance of foreign consular identification cards. State and other executive branch agencies are working to establish a comprehensive USG policy on foreign consular identifications, a policy that will affect documents that are being issued now or may be issued in the future by any nation to its nationals in the United States. The need for a government wide policy came evident as Mexico and other countries have become more active in issuing—or exploring the possibility of issuing—such documentation and as questions about acceptance of foreign consular identification cards were raised. Beginning last year, the Department of State chaired an interagency group tasked with developing that policy. Earlier this year, the Homeland Security Council assumed the leadership of the interagency process. The Department continues to fully support this endeavor. All of those involved in drafting this policy are aware of the intense interest and desire for a final product that will address the many aspects of this issue.

Any policy on the issuance and, perhaps more importantly, acceptance of foreign consular identifications must address questions of security, reciprocity and protection for Americans abroad, USG international treaty obligations, law enforcement, and state and local legislation. Topics that were discussed while the Department of State chaired the interagency process included: the effect of foreign consular identification cards on homeland security; the rights and privileges granted the United States as well as other countries under the Vienna Convention on Consular Relations (VCCR); USG obligations regarding consular protections; foreign policy goals and objectives; questions of federalism; and the regulation of financial services. The complexity and diversity of the issue—which extends well beyond the normal purview of the Department of State—argues for prudence and thoroughness in the development of any policy and underscores the need for a coordinated, interagency approach.

In addition to concerns about national security, the State Department has two additional interests in the development of any policy that addresses foreign consular identification cards. The first is the impact of a policy on the Department's ability to carry out its responsibilities in the area of consular affairs, both domestically and abroad. On the domestic front, the Department views foreign consular identification cards as a possible tool for facilitating consular notification by accountable law enforcement officials. The Vienna Convention on Consular Relations (VCCR) requires that a foreign national who is arrested or otherwise detained in the United States be advised of his or her right to request that the appropriate consular officials be notified of the detention without delay. The issue of consular notification is a serious one for the Department, which is working assiduously to ensure U.S. compliance. Because a foreign consular identification card is a means to identify an individual as a foreign national, a bearer's possession of this card can alert responsible law enforcement authorities to the need to provide consular notification.

The Department also believes that the U.S. Government must also carefully avoid taking action against consular identification cards that foreclose our options to document or assist American citizens abroad. The Department itself issues documentation other than a passport for U.S. citizens abroad and at times occasionally issues similar identity cards or travel documents. Should a foreign country decide to limit acceptance of such documentation or other traditional documentation such as state issued identifications or driver's licenses, the actions of American citizens abroad could be seriously restricted.

The Department's goal is a single, uniform policy that is applicable to all countries that issue consular identifications. While the Mexican card has recently been highlighted, the Mexican "matricula consular" is not a new program. Mexico has issued cards to its citizens in the United States for more than 100 years. The Vienna Convention on Consular Relations, to which we are party, allows for sending States to perform "consular functions" to help, assist, and protect their nationals. What has changed is the scope of the Mexican program and the Government of Mexico's vigorous efforts to secure acceptance of the card by local governments and financial institutions at a time of heightened security concerns.

Given these changes, we have contacted the Government of Mexico to learn more about the technical nature of the card. We have found the Mexican Embassy and the Ministry of Foreign Affairs to be very responsive to our requests for information about the issuance process, security features, and card production.

I would like to thank the Committee for the opportunity to present this testimony today, and I would be pleased to respond to any questions that the Committee may have at this time.

Mr. HOSTETTLER. Thank you, Ms. Jacobson.

Mr. Verdery?

STATEMENT OF C. STEWART VERDERY, ASSISTANT SECRETARY FOR POLICY AND PLANNING, BORDER AND TRANSPORTATION SECURITY DIRECTORATE, DEPARTMENT OF HOMELAND SECURITY

Mr. VERDERY. Chairman Hostettler, Ranking Member Acting Berman and Members of the Subcommittee, I am pleased to have this opportunity to appear before you today to discuss foreign consular identification cards. My name is Stewart Verdery. I am the assistant secretary for policy and planning in the Border and Transportation Security Directorate, known as BTS, within the Department of Homeland Security.

I have had the pleasure of working with many of you while a staffer in Congress and in private practice, and I am looking forward to continuing those relationships in my brand new capacity.

The Department of Homeland Security and the policy office within BTS in particular has been involved in the interagency process led by the Homeland Security Council to develop a comprehensive United States Government policy on foreign consular identification cards. Historically, various forms of these cards have been utilized by many countries for a variety of purposes. Foreign consular ID cards do not establish or indicate lawful U.S. immigration status and should not be viewed as valid for that purpose. Nor do they establish a foreign national's right to be or to remain in the United States.

Immigration status of an alien in the United States can only be determined by reference to documents issued by the United States Government or, in the case of some nonimmigrants, to a U.S. Government annotation in the alien's passport. In addition, the Federal Protective Service within the Bureau of Immigration and Customs Enforcement, which is also part of BTS, does not accept the Matricula Consular or other foreign consular identification cards as identification for entry into secure Federal buildings.

In recognition of our national security requirements and interests and given the expanding use of these ID cards, it is clear that we need to develop a Federal policy on the acceptance and use of these cards for other purposes as well as guidance to State and local government agencies and appropriate private entities such as banking institutions that require identification. That work is being done through the interagency process which I and other witnesses have referred to, and I am confident that such a policy will be developed expeditiously.

The interagency group is also specifically examining counterfeit and fraud concerns with the Mexican consular identification cards, the Matricula Consular. These cards have been issued by Mexican consulates to Mexicans living abroad and have been in existence in various forms since the 19th Century. A foreign government may issue documents to its nationals. However, given the increase in the volume of requests for these cards in the past year or so and in light of the heightened security concerns in the post-9/11 environment, we are concerned at DHS about the use and acceptance of these cards.

We believe that individuals have been able to obtain multiple cards under multiple names, an occurrence which poses a significant security issue and impacts the reliability as valid forms of identification. Another concern is the extent to which consular identification cards are used as breeder documents; that is, to more easily gain access to other documentation such as driver's licenses. We are concerned that foreign consular identification cards fraudulently obtained could aid criminal activity such as money laundering by facilitating the creation of false identities.

We at DHS and within the United States Government need to examine and are examining not only the security features of these cards but also the security of the issuance process and the documented requirements for obtaining them. The Bureau of Customs and Border Protection, known as BCBP, also one of the bureaus within BTS, has disseminated an intelligence alert that contains background information about the consular identification cards, including an example of a Matricula Consular.

BCBP requires reporting on the interdiction of individuals who have been caught carrying multiple cards. Further, they are working closely with other BTS agencies to coordinate any information or intelligence arising from such cases. Our goal is to develop a uniform and sound policy which will define legitimate uses for foreign identification cards while ensuring that the security of our nation is not compromised.

In developing a policy, we should ensure that foreign consular identification cards are not being used as a means for avoiding the immigration laws of the United States.

Again, I would like to thank the Committee for the opportunity to present testimony on behalf of the Department of Homeland Security. I would be pleased to respond to any questions you might have.

Thank you.

[The prepared statement of Mr. Verdery follows:]

PREPARED STATEMENT OF C. STEWART VERDERY, JR.

Chairman Hostettler, Ranking Member Jackson Lee, and Members of the Subcommittee, I am pleased to have this opportunity to appear before you today to discuss Foreign Consular Identification Cards.

My name is Stewart Verdery, and I am the Assistant Secretary for Policy and Planning in the Border and Transportation Security (BTS) Directorate of the Department of Homeland Security.

The Department of Homeland Security, and the policy office in BTS in particular, has been involved in an interagency process led by the Homeland Security Council to develop a comprehensive U.S. Government policy on foreign consular identification cards.

Historically, various forms of consular identification cards have been in use by many countries for a variety of purposes. Foreign consular ID cards do not establish or indicate lawful U.S. immigration status and should not be viewed as valid for that purpose, nor do they establish a foreign national's right to be or remain in the United States. Immigration status of an alien in the United States can be determined only by reference to documents issued by the U.S. Government or, in the case of some non-immigrants, to a U.S. Government annotation in the alien's passport. In addition, the Federal Protective Service within the Bureau of Immigration and Customs Enforcement does not accept the matricula consular as identification for entry into secure Federal buildings.

However, in recognition of our national security requirements and interests, and given the expanding use of consular identification cards, it is clear that we need to develop Federal policy on the acceptance and use of these cards for other purposes, as well as guidance to state and local government agencies and appropriate private entities such as banking institutions. That work is being done through the interagency process to which I referred. I am confident that such policy will be developed expeditiously.

The interagency group is also specifically examining counterfeit and fraud concerns with the Mexican consular identification cards. The matricula consular, issued by Mexican consulates to Mexicans living abroad, has been in existence in various forms since the 19th century. A foreign government may issue documents to its nationals. However, given the increase in the volume of requests for these cards in the past year, and in light of heightened security concerns in the post 9/11 environment, we are concerned about the acceptance and use of these cards. We believe that individuals have been able to obtain multiple cards under multiple names, an occurrence which poses a significant security issue and impacts their reliability as valid forms of identification.

Another concern is the extent to which consular identification cards are used as "breeder documents," that is, to more easily gain access to other documentation, such as drivers' licenses. We are concerned that foreign consular identification cards fraudulently obtained could aid criminal activity—such as money laundering—by facilitating the creation of false identities. We need to examine not only the security features of these cards but also the security of the issuance process and the documentary requirements for obtaining them.

The Bureau of Customs and Border Protection (BCBP) has disseminated an intelligence alert that contains background information about the consular identification cards, including an example of a matricula consular. BCBP requires reporting on the interdiction of individuals who have been caught carrying multiple cards. Further, they will work closely with other BTS agencies to coordinate any information and intelligence arising from such cases.

Our goal is to develop a uniform and sound policy which will define the legitimate uses for foreign consular identification cards while ensuring that the security of our nation is not compromised. In developing a policy, we should ensure that foreign consular identification cards are not being used as means for avoiding the immigration laws of the United States.

I would like to thank the Committee for the opportunity to present this testimony and I would be pleased to respond to any questions that the Committee may have.

Mr. HOSTETTLER. Thank you, Mr. Verdery.

Ms. Davison?

STATEMENT OF ELIZABETH DAVISON, DIRECTOR, DEPARTMENT OF HOUSING AND COMMUNITY AFFAIRS, MONTGOMERY COUNTY, MARYLAND

Ms. DAVISON. Thank you very much, Chairman Hostettler; Acting Ranking Member Berman and other Members of the Committee. For the record, my name is Elizabeth Davison, and I am the director of the Department of Housing and Community Affairs for Montgomery County, Maryland, adjacent to the District of Columbia.

And I am here really presenting the views of our County Executive, Douglas Duncan, on the use of the Matricula Consular or the ID cards that are issued by the Government of Mexico for over 100 years and most recently also by the Government of Guatemala to citizens of their countries who are living in the U.S.

Montgomery County has a very large base of Hispanic residents. According to the Census of 2000, there were over 100,000 Hispanic residents. That is about 12 percent of our county, which is a county of roughly 900,000 population; clearly, it is a very large community.

Many of these residents are legal; many of them have passports. But an increasing number do not. And clearly, with that number, it is very difficult for the county to deal with tens of thousands of people with no documentation; no identity. Our County Executive, Douglas Duncan, recently announced that Montgomery County will accept the Matricula Consular as identification for all county services. And I do want to stress that this initiative was not based on these foreign governments lobbying the County Executive. This came up because I heard news reports about these cards; talked with our County Executive after doing some research with some other local governments about how they used them and what they were.

I also went to the Mexican Consulate here in Washington, DC with one of my Hispanic staff members; saw the operation; asked them questions about how did this work; how did they determine people's identity. And so, we did see firsthand how this operation was conducted.

At that point, we then contacted some of the other Hispanic governments, South American, Central American, to find out what they were doing. Because this seemed like a way that we could work with this population and have a little bit more, I guess, assurance of who the people were. While the county local government does not have a role in immigration, we do have a role in public safety, public health, education, and other basic local services. That is really the major reason why we have determined to accept these cards.

Why are there benefits to having these cards from a local government's point of view? Let me go through several reasons. First of all, with the banks that have been accepting these cards, it then becomes a first step to establishing credit. And credit is an extremely important thing in this society. We found without credit or without a bank account that this population becomes a target for crime, including muggings, and many of the apartment complexes which house these immigrants find that they have a very high break-in rate, because thieves know that there is cash perhaps hidden in a drawer or perhaps in a mattress, the same way that they know that these residents are likely to be carrying cash because they cannot put it in a bank account.

Also, without a credit rating, it is becoming increasingly difficult in this metropolitan area and I am sure in others to be able to rent an apartment, because they do a credit check on you. If you cannot get access to one of the apartment complexes run by a major management company, you are much more likely to go to an unlicensed, unregulated apartment complex, sometimes with unscrupulous landlords; other times with landlords who just think they are doing you a favor.

We have had experiences; perhaps you saw in the local press last year a family that was burnt alive because they were in an illegal, unlicensed basement apartment with no means of egress. My department inspects apartments, but we cannot look in every single house in Montgomery County to see if there is an illegal basement apartment, and increasingly, both the combination of the high price of housing; the scrutiny of credit checks and other background checks, and if you do not have credit, you cannot pass a credit check.

Fourth reason that the county needs to know who a person is is to establish whether they are a resident of Montgomery County. We pride ourselves on a very high level of local government services, but we clearly cannot provide those services to anybody who shows up who may—I have gotten calls from people in Arlington County when they heard we were giving away free fire detectors because of these fires, wanting us to send them to their address in Arlington County. Obviously, we got wise to that one, but if someone presented themselves at our office one of these ID cards with a local address, we would at least have some verification of them being a citizen. We cannot not plow a street when it snows if we think that there are people who are citizens of foreign countries living there. Our services are provided to all residents, whether they are legal, illegal; whether they are citizens or not citizens.

Fifthly, when you have people who do not have access to bank accounts, they often end up using check cashing services, often which charge very high fees and also create a very run-down and unsavory appearance in our business districts. We have been working very hard, spending a lot of money to improve areas like Silver Spring, which I think is fabulous now; other areas like Wheaton, Long Branch, other parts of our community. The more there are these check cashing services, payday loan joints, the worse our business districts look and the more run-down they become.

We have also found that there are many unscrupulous and predatory businesspeople who target this population. We recently found out about a travel agent called Tiva Travel who had taken large amounts of cash from many people for trips home during the Christmas holidays but failed to actually make the reservations and buy the tickets. Many of the people who did not have bank accounts gave the cash, multiple thousands of dollars. In addition to being out that cash, they did not get their trip home.

If they had a credit card, they could have put this on a credit card and would have been protected. So we are finding that this practice of not being able to have access to a bank account is creating predatory business practices. And lastly, obviously, with homeland security, it is important for people to know who we are dealing with. During the sniper shootings in Montgomery County and throughout this region, there were some witnesses who were afraid to come forward because they were afraid they would be deported. There are other situations of witnessing crimes where, without some identification, we do not know who they are; they are afraid of coming forward.

In closing, I would just like to say our County Executive was concerned that without any kind of Federal policy in this area that it was being left to Montgomery County or other local counties to make up a foreign policy, in effect. And so, we have decided to accept these cards, because we cannot have tens of thousands of people with no kinds of identification, and we are actively promoting other governments of Central and South America to use these cards.

Thank you very much. I would be happy to answer any questions.

[The prepared statement of Ms. Davison follows:]

PREPARED STATEMENT OF ELIZABETH B. DAVISON

Good Morning. For the record, my name is Elizabeth B. Davison, Director of the Department of Housing and Community Affairs for Montgomery County Maryland. I am here to present the views of our County Executive on the use of the Matricula Consular, or ID cards that are issued by the Government of Mexico for over 100 years, and most recently by the government of Guatemala to citizens of their countries who are living in the U.S.

Montgomery County Maryland has a large base of Hispanic residents, over 100,000 according to the US Census 2000. This is about 12 percent of the close to 900,000 population of the county. With such a large base of Hispanics from many countries, it is becoming increasingly important that they have identification. Certainly many do have passports or are American citizens with Social Security cards and other identification, but an increasing number do not.

Our County Executive, Douglas Duncan recently announced that Montgomery County will accept the Matricula Consular as identification for all County services. It is of course important that these cards be authentic. The County is in this position because these people are residents, and a local government must deal with them as they have an effect on our community. We do not have a role in immigration, but we do have a role in public safety, public health, education and other basic local services.

Because of this need to document who people are, we have been working over the last year with several Latin American and Central American Consulates to issue these cards, since many of our residents are not from Mexico or Guatemala.

There are many reasons why having a document such as the Matricula Consular is important.

1. Several banks have been accepting this card as an ID in order to open a bank account, which is the first step to establishing credit.
2. Without a bank account, this population becomes a target for crime, including muggings and break ins to apartment complexes because they are known to carry large amounts of cash;
3. Without a credit rating, it is increasingly difficult to rent an apartment, making it more likely they are living in unlicensed and unregulated living arrangements which may be unsafe. People have died in fires in this kind of living situation, which is a great tragedy for them and their relatives and associates.
4. The County needs to know if a person is a resident of the County in order to provide them County services. This identification carries a local address. Montgomery County services are very good, but clearly we need to be sure that the person who is requesting those services is indeed a resident of the County.
5. The non banked population often ends up using check cashing operations, and other very costly and often not legitimate services. These in turn create a run down appearance in our business districts, leading to further decline in these areas.
6. Other predatory business people target this population and can thrive on the proceeds. Recently my staff uncovered a travel agent who was taking people's money for plane tickets to their home countries over the holidays, and in many cases accepted cash, but did not provide authentic tickets. If these people had paid with a credit card, they would not have lost the many thousands of dollars that they did.
7. As homeland security becomes more important, we need for people to have identification that is valid, which we understand the Matricula Consular to be, since the governments of the issuing countries check very carefully to establish the identity of the person before issuing the card.

Thank you very much for the opportunity to share our views with your committee on this issue which is very important to our community in Montgomery County, Maryland.

Mr. HOSTETTLER. Thank you, Ms. Davison.

The panel will now turn to a period of 5-minute questions per Member. Ms. Davison, my first question is to you. When Montgomery County employees, in the course of their jobs, confront a consular ID card, confront an individual who puts forward a consular ID card for identification, and your employees contact the consulate, and they ask for the status of the alien, how often do they determine that the alien is in the country illegally?

Ms. DAVISON. Well, we do not do that. I mean, we do not ask if people are legal or illegal. Sometimes, we will need to have some identification just to know who the name of that person is and that they are a resident of the county. That is as far as we go with checking their identification.

Mr. HOSTETTLER. And you are familiar with the traditional purpose of the consular ID card, as testified by Ms. Jacobson, in that a Government official in the United States generally contacts a consulate to—and that is the purpose of a consular ID card. But you do not do that in Montgomery County?

Ms. DAVISON. No, we are just trying to determine if they are residents of the county. And if they have no ID, we do not know. If they have this card which does have a local address, we can determine that they are residents of the county. Our services are not based on whether someone is here illegally or legally or whether they are a citizen of the U.S. or they are not.

Mr. HOSTETTLER. And that is a point in your testimony that you make when you say it is not your role to deal with immigration law, which is intriguing to me, because right after that, you mention—let me quote it correctly here—"that we have been working over the last year with several Latin American and Central American consulates." And in your oral testimony, you say that was actually initiated by your office.

Ms. DAVISON. That is right.

Mr. HOSTETTLER. I am intrigued, as Montgomery County does not feel that it is their obligation to deal with Federal immigration law, how do you make the distinction with regard to dialogue with foreign governments on issues whose jurisdiction is international agreements, such as the Vienna Convention on Consular Relations? How do you draw the distinction between not dealing with Federal immigration law but initiating conversations, dialogues with foreign governments?

Ms. DAVISON. Well, as I said, we are kind of left in a situation where we have a large number of people that we need to know who they are. Our conversations with these consuls have been to try and find out if they are thinking of issuing them; just what the status of it was and telling them that we would accept the card if they did that. Clearly, it does not go any further than that kind of discussion.

Mr. HOSTETTLER. Thank you.

Mr. McCraw, in your testimony, you state that individuals have been arrested with multiple Matricula cards which bear the individual's picture but a different name.

Mr. MCCRAW. Yes, sir.

Mr. HOSTETTLER. In what ways could the possession of multiple consular ID cards assist a criminal to engage in money laundering?

Mr. MCCRAW. Well, one of the ways is to get multiple bank accounts, and in terms of void and in terms of suspicious activity reporting; and a number of reasons in terms of when you are a criminal, hiding your identity is important, especially if you are dealing with the money laundering side of it but also in terms of, in today's society, and as Ms. Davison pointed out, you know, you need identities to get certain types of services, whether it is apartment services or banking services. And it is very important to us, looking from a national security standpoint or working a criminal case to make sure that that individual that we go back and we track and we trace is, in fact, that same individual. And it certainly increases the ease of actually linking individuals to terrorism and also to other criminal acts.

And so, it is critically important that we do it one way or the other. Certainly, when you have something that is being used that is systemically flawed, and there are a number of things that are a problem with it. And believe me, we do not—the FBI and the Department, we do not—certainly, I would like to say that the Government of Mexico has been tremendous in terms of working with us in terrorism along the border.

This has nothing to do with that. It just has to do with this particular card. And there are four vulnerabilities that we see with this particular card that are in my testimony. And the first thing is that there is no database, centralized database. The databases are not interconnected. And the fundamental flaw is the authentication is, in fact, birth certificates. And we have problems with that even in the United States. And when we are able to seize, you know, large loads of these documents, and we know that these documents are out there, and we have got examples in terms of how they can get it, then, it makes it much more difficult to make sure that that individual is who he or she says they are.

Moreover, it is a breeder ground for additional documents. If individual governments allow it to be, you know, what we view as a problematic document to be valid, then, of course, they can produce and get driver's licenses and State IDs from there, which means, you know, you can continue on. And if you have seven different ones, then, you can get seven different driver's licenses, and you can have seven different bank accounts. And you can continue to hide behind this.

I did not mean to continue on, but those are the problems, as we see it. Again, we are assessing the vulnerability of that particular card as it relates to a threat.

Mr. HOSTETTLER. Thank you, Mr. McCraw.

The Chair now recognizes the gentleman from California, Mr. Berman, for 5 minutes.

Mr. BERMAN. Thank you, Mr. Chairman. I thank all the witnesses for their useful testimony on this issue.

Mr. McCraw, let me read you something from—it is a report by the Migration Policy Institute.

Mr. MCCRAW. Yes.

Mr. BERMAN. Focused specifically on local law enforcement, it essentially concludes that they are among the most enthusiastic backers of the consular IDs and cites reasons why. Police departments welcome the cards for the following reasons: when the police stop someone without identification on a minor charge, they are forced to hold them overnight when a citation would otherwise suffice. Resources are also wasted; people without identification are also more likely to flee when stopped by the police. The Matriculas make it easier to identify dead or unconscious people. By facilitating the use of banks, the cards help immigrants avoid carrying or stockpiling large amounts of cash, which makes them targets for robbery and home invasions; in some cases, the police themselves have asked local banks to accept the Matricula. Having identification encourages people to report crimes and to come forward as witnesses. It allows police to keep better records.

Now, I would be interested in your comments on that. And the more general comment: I think it is a mistake for people—I think one can conclude that these cards are a good thing, even accepting what has been assumed by many that large numbers of undocumented people are getting these cards or that that is the primary motivation for at least some people to get the card; that there are two different issues here: how to deal with stopping illegal immigration and, in a country which has anywhere from 6 million to 10 million—who knows exactly?—undocumented immigrants, what is the role of this card?

Why is law enforcement better off with people having no identification card than this identification card, even with the limits that there may be on the extent to which that identification card reflects the true name and address? And then, I have one follow-up question.

Mr. MCCRAW. Well, I think you make some very good points, and I think Ms. Davison made some very good points. And from a former State trooper having the same dilemma, although a couple of decades ago, it was always problematic when you come in contact with no ID, and you have no basis to do anything. So clearly, something was always better than nothing, and I understand that.

Mr. BERMAN. I appreciate that admission. It does not mean this is foolproof. It does not mean this cannot be phony, but by and large, something is better than nothing.

Now, your first reason for concern, I am curious about in terms of—well, the databases. Compare with me. Let's take Mexico. The question of getting a passport, which is by and large accepted as a pretty darn good identifier, versus one of these cards. What is the nature of the database that is used in Mexico to issue a passport that makes it so much more likely to be valid? In other words, we are not talking about phony passports here; we are talking about real passports issued to people; makes the passport so much better than this card in terms of the databases used?

Mr. MCCRAW. You bring up a good point, you know, passport, you know, from our standpoint is a better document. It is scrutinized more. The State Department has controls for standards. I know they are working toward a number of different things.

Mr. BERMAN. How does the State Department control Mexican passports?

Mr. MCCRAW. Well, there are some agreements, and certainly, INS—excuse me; I have not changed with the initials—but legacy INS will work on it; maybe next two or 3 years, they will get it right.

They know; those inspectors are trained in what to look for in terms of forged documents as they come through in terms of passports. At least from the forgery standpoint, and I think there are some universal standards——

Mr. BERMAN. Well, forgery——

Mr. MCCRAW. Yes.

Mr. BERMAN. But I am talking here about a valid passport issued by the Mexican Government.

Mr. MCCRAW. Yes.

Mr. BERMAN. It is not a forgery.

Mr. MCCRAW. No, sir.

Mr. BERMAN. The question is, is it being issued to that person?

Mr. McCRAW. Yes, and I cannot answer your direct question. I do know that we have not seen the trend of criminals utilizing fraudulent or forged passports, Mexican passports, in the U.S., not compared to the trends I discussed in my written testimony. You know, we are just describing a vulnerability right now, and I understand.

Mr. BERMAN. But on the basic question, is it fair to say that you, at this point, could not tell me why the database used by the Mexican Government for the issuance of passports——

Mr. McCRAW. No, sir.

Mr. BERMAN.—is totally different than the database used by the consulates to issue the consular ID cards?

Mr. McCRAW. Sir, I could not even tell you if they had a database——

Mr. BERMAN. All right.

Mr. McCRAW.—from the State Department for the passports.

Mr. BERMAN. Thank you.

Mr. HOSTETTLER. I thank the gentleman.

The Chair now recognizes the gentleman from California, Mr. Gallegly.

Mr. GALLEGLY. Thank you, Mr. Chairman. And this has been a very informative hearing so far.

Mr. McCraw?

Mr. McCRAW. Yes, sir.

Mr. GALLEGLY. I read your testimony before I got here this morning, and you have talked about the vulnerability of the Matricula Consular to forgery and so on and so forth. You also in your testimony refer to several generations of this card, saying that there have been some integrated security in recent cards, although 90 percent of the cards that are out there are the older generation which are very vulnerable to counterfeit, forgery and so forth.

You also mention in your statement that it is your understanding that as many as 13 States currently accept Matricula Consular for the purposes of obtaining a driver's license as a breeder document.

Mr. McCRAW. Yes, sir.

Mr. GALLEGLY. Could you just follow up with that a little bit and give us a little bit better understanding of why we are concerned about this as a breeder document?

Mr. McCRAW. Well, because once you have it, you know, once you have established—in the United States, it is one of the documents recognized for you to fly; a bank account; a number of different functions once you have a State either ID or a State driver's license. So any document that will allow you to get that, of course, is important, the source documentation. So if we take it back to the Matricula Consular, and if there is a flawed process, and we perceive there are vulnerabilities in it, then, the driver's license—it does not matter what the State does in terms of the precautions they place on that driver's license. They can have all of the safeguards in the world, and they can scrutinize all they want. But if they are depending upon the breeder document, and that breeder document is flawed, then, of course, that driver's license or that State ID is going to be flawed as well.

Mr. GALLEGLY. And 90 percent of these are really blatantly flawed because of the vulnerability with absolutely minimal validity to start with for the——

Mr. MCCRAW. They are very susceptible——

Mr. GALLEGLY. To forgery.

Mr. MCCRAW. Yes, sir, that is correct.

Mr. GALLEGLY. Ms. Jacobson, who needs Matricula Consular in the United States other than an illegal immigrant?

Ms. JACOBSON. I do not know that I could speak to exactly who else might use them but——

Mr. GALLEGLY. But you say that is the principal beneficiary?

Ms. JACOBSON. I really do not know that. We have not studied that. But Mexican citizens living in the United States are asked to register at consulates for purposes of being notified by their Government. Matriculas Consular, unlike passports, would have a local address so that the consulate could contact them. So there are other purposes for which they are issued, primarily the fact that they have the residence on them.

Mr. GALLEGLY. Ms. Jacobson, you have said that you have been involved in discussing with the Mexican Government, and they have been very cooperative and sensitive to our concerns about forgery and validity of these documents, and they want to work with us on that. Is that correct? They want to work with us to make sure that the document is secure?

Ms. JACOBSON. As secure as possible, right.

Mr. GALLEGLY. Do you think the Mexican Government, after Mr. McCraw's testimony that 90 percent of these documents are the earlier generation that they would be prepared to invalidate that 90 percent?

Ms. JACOBSON. I am not entirely sure about the 90 percent figure; I have heard——

Mr. GALLEGLY. Well, do you think they would be prepared——

Ms. JACOBSON. I understand.

Mr. GALLEGLY.—with their spirit of good faith to invalidate all of those documents that do not possess the security issues that the latest generation have?

Ms. JACOBSON. What the Mexican Government has told us is that they are very interested in replacing those old cards, in part because they believe that the old card——

Mr. GALLEGLY. Well, they are interested in doing it, but what are they going to do about it?

Ms. JACOBSON. They are beginning to work on a plan to replace all of the old cards. Since March 2002, they have issued only the new cards.

Mr. GALLEGLY. But do they have a program that, effective September 12 or whatever, those are invalid?

Ms. JACOBSON. It is my understanding that that is what they are working on now. They have not announced one yet.

Mr. GALLEGLY. We have a very limited amount of time, and I appreciate your succinct answers.

Ms. Davison, who needs Matricula Consular other than illegal immigrants?

Ms. DAVISON. I do not know.

Mr. GALLEGLY. Is public housing and public benefits in Montgomery County, do you have an overabundance of public housing and really limited demand, or do you have a demand equal to the amount of services you are able to provide?

Ms. DAVISON. In terms of public housing, we have a little bit more trouble filling that up than some others, partly because it is not as well maintained as some of the private sector housing, because the Federal Government has cut back on that money. But we do have a need for affordable housing.

Mr. GALLEGLY. For the record, you have stated that you have absolutely no discretion or care to be concerned whether a person gets public benefits in Montgomery County whether they are illegally in the United States or not; is that correct?

Ms. DAVISON. Our services are available to anyone who is a resident of the county.

Mr. GALLEGLY. Is it also true that Montgomery County last year got $1,102,029 in SCAP funds from the Federal Government?

Ms. DAVISON. I do not know. That is not my area of authority.

Mr. GALLEGLY. The Federal Government has provided certain funds to Montgomery County; is that correct?

Ms. DAVISON. Certainly, yes.

Mr. GALLEGLY. Mr. Chairman, I see my time has expired. I yield back.

Mr. HOSTETTLER. I thank the gentleman.

The Chair now recognizes the gentlelady from California, Ms. Sánchez, for 5 minutes.

Ms. SÁNCHEZ. Thank you, Mr. Chairman, and thank you to all of the witnesses for providing your testimony here today.

Mr. McCraw, can you provide specific data on the number of cases successfully brought against individuals for using fraudulent consular ID cards? And how would this number compare with fraudulent use in the United States, say, of driver's licenses for underage drinkers or fraudulent U.S. passports used abroad?

Mr. MCCRAW. I do not have any statistics on that.

Ms. SÁNCHEZ. Would you consider Matricula Consulares acceptable as long as you were satisfied that they were as fraud-proof as possible?

Mr. MCCRAW. Absolutely; if they were fraud-proof—we are looking at it from a vulnerability standpoint. If they were fraud-proof, and they could be authenticated, absolutely, and we did not have this trend; I mean, we only care from the standpoint of national security, not how it is used or not used.

Ms. SÁNCHEZ. Have you had an opportunity to review the multi-levels of security features on the Mexican consular ID card?

Mr. MCCRAW. The new one, I have seen documents, and I have been advised that they have improved dramatically over the first generation. And although there is a study that exists that says they can be still forged, they have dramatically improved since the first iteration. I think we are on the third generation now.

Ms. SÁNCHEZ. To your knowledge, is there any document in the U.S. or other foreign country that could not be forged?

Mr. MCCRAW. There are all varying degrees of forgery. It is a constant—you know, nothing is perfect, and I am sure, as I have testified earlier, that where there are vulnerabilities, they will be exploited.

Ms. SÁNCHEZ. Thank you.

Ms. Jacobson, could the failure to accept the safe and fraud-proof Mexican consular ID violate the Vienna Convention on Consular Relations? And if we were to violate the Vienna Convention that was signed by the U.S. back in 1963 and that guarantees that consulates can provide services to their nationals living abroad, what remedies would Mexico have for a violation of that?

Ms. JACOBSON. I am going to answer the second question first, if I might, because I do not know what remedies the Government of Mexico would have, and I would be happy to look into that. But on the first point, the fact is that, as you know, we have not prohibited use of the Matricula Consular nor have we accepted them. What the Vienna Convention says is that consulates have a right to issue—to carry out functions that help, assist or protect its nationals in the receiving state. And one of those functions may be to identify their nationals, as we do overseas when we issue identification papers or ask people to register with U.S. consulates.

But the Vienna Convention does not say that governments in the receiving state must accept those cards nor that they, you know, should prohibit them. It is silent on that subject. It is the right of the foreign government to issue them, but it makes no mention of responsibility of a party to the treaty to accept them.

Ms. SÁNCHEZ. Mister—sorry; I am probably going to mispronounce your name—Verdery, is that correct?

Mr. VERDERY. Perfect.

Ms. SÁNCHEZ. If, as has been stated by some of the Members of the Subcommittee, in fact, that the majority of people who use consular ID cards or the only reason for using them would be that you are in the country illegally, I guess I am trying to understand why would somebody create a fraudulent consular ID card which does not confer any type of immigration status? Would it not make more sense for folks to create false green cards or passports instead? What would be the advantage of creating a falsified consular ID card versus other types of identification that could confer immigration status?

Mr. VERDERY. Well, this is somewhat of a guess, but I think the answer would be that these are easier to forge. I know that the Bureau of Immigration and Customs Enforcement forensics lab has done an examination of comparing the Matricula Consular security features to the Mexican passport features and has found that the passport has much more security, even under the new card that is being issued. So my answer would be that I think it would be easier to forge those than the other types of documents you discussed.

Ms. SÁNCHEZ. So, again, if Matricula Consulares were as fraud-proof as possible, would you then say that it would be acceptable to accept them in the United States?

Mr. VERDERY. I could not give you that policy on behalf of the Administration today, but obviously, it would be a clear factor in our review of them if they were more fraud-proof. That would be a good thing. But I could not give you that determination today.

Ms. SÁNCHEZ. Thank you, Mr. Chairman. I yield back the balance of my time.

Mr. HOSTETTLER. I thank the gentlelady. The Chair now recognizes the gentlelady from Tennessee, Mrs. Blackburn.

Mrs. BLACKBURN. Thank you, Mr. Chairman, and thank you all very much.

Mr. McCraw, I enjoyed reading your testimony prior to coming here, and I thank you for submitting that to us. I come from Tennessee. I am a freshman legislator. I have been in the State Senate. I led the fight to close the loophole illegal aliens were using to get valid Tennessee driver's licenses and therefore access State services. And I agree with many of the points that you have made.

Ms. Jacobson, I would like to begin my questioning with you if I may, please, ma'am. I find it very troubling that the Administration has taken no official position on the issuance or acceptance of the foreign consular identification cards, and I think in the world in which we live, that is troubling, and I wanted to see if you had any idea when you felt that the Administration would develop a position on this.

Ms. JACOBSON. Well, I think that on that issue, Congresswoman Blackburn, I can speak for the three agencies here and all of the others involved in the interagency process that we really do desire to complete the process as quickly as possible. We realize there is a great need for a clear policy, and so, it will be done as expeditiously as possible, but I am afraid I cannot give you a date.

Mrs. BLACKBURN. So there are no ongoing discussions of when a policy will—there is no target for when a policy will be achieved?

Ms. JACOBSON. I think we would not want to set a target that might actually, you know, delay implementation or a policy. We just want to do it as quickly as possible. I do not know that there is a target date.

Mrs. BLACKBURN. Let me ask you this: when is the Office of Foreign Missions going to demand that these consulates link their databases and address the concerns that Mr. McCraw brought out in his testimony?

Ms. JACOBSON. I think that the Office of Foreign Missions at the State Department has not determined that we have the ability to demand of the Mexican Government a particular way in which they set up issuance of the cards. However, in our discussion with the Mexican Government, we have made very clear that among the concerns that all of the agencies of the Federal Government have is the ability to get multiple cards. And we have been told by the Mexican Government that they are greatly concerned with that issue. They are currently implementing linkage of databases and that the consulates should be fully connected to check those records by the end of this year.

Mrs. BLACKBURN. How responsive is the Mexican Government to your expressed concerns of the problems that we have with this card?

Ms. JACOBSON. Well, so far, I would say our evaluation has been that they have been quite responsive, increasing the levels of security on the card, as Mr. McCraw has mentioned; beginning a plan to replace the cards that are not that highest quality; continuing to improve the features, not stopping just with the six or seven that are in the current card but looking ahead to more. So they have been trying.

Mrs. BLACKBURN. All right; thank you, ma'am.

Mr. Verdery, who needs a Matricula Consular card other than an illegal alien in the United States?

Mr. VERDERY. Well, if I might answer your question in the reverse, if you are here legally in this country, you would either have a passport with a visa; you would have a Border Crossing Card if you were a frequent traveler that is basically the equivalent of a visa, or you would have a Permanent Residency Card.

Mrs. BLACKBURN. Can you answer for me the question—we found out in a hearing last week that banks in Mexico do not accept the Matricula Consular card as positive identification. Can you answer for me why that is? Our witnesses last week were unable to answer that question for me. I would like an answer to that one.

Mr. VERDERY. Well, unfortunately, I have to join that crowd. I am not aware of the specifics of why the Mexican banks do not accept the card, if that is actually the fact. But we would be happy to look into that and get back to you.

Mrs. BLACKBURN. Okay; thank you.

Ms. Davison, thank you for being with us. I am sure you are familiar with the Foreign Missions Act, and the Senate report on that act states that the Office of Foreign Missions has responsibility for ensuring the national security interest of the United States, taking into consideration when foreign governments seek to operate missions in the United States. In light of the fact that the 19 September 11 hijackers were aliens in the United States, do you believe that controlling immigration is a national security interest of our country?

Ms. DAVISON. Well, unfortunately, I am not familiar with the act that you cited. I do think that it is important for the Government to control immigration, yes. It is also up to local governments to deal with the people who are here.

Mrs. BLACKBURN. Now, let me you ask you this: were you aware that banks in Mexico do not accept the Matricula Consular cards as identification?

Ms. DAVISON. I do not know whether that is true or not. I am not aware of that.

Mrs. BLACKBURN. Thank you very much.

Mr. HOSTETTLER. I thank the gentlelady.

The Chair now will entertain a second round of questions, and I will begin my questioning at this time. And before I go to the questions, I would just like to point out a few things.

The context of this hearing is knowing that consulates have issued consular ID cards for over 100 years in this country. That is not contested. That is, we are not trying to stop that. In fact, we cannot stop that according to the Vienna Convention mentioned earlier. What we are concerned about is the fact that they are being utilized in a manner that is irregular and does not comport with the traditional usage of the consular ID card, especially the fact that there is this effort afoot for ID cards to be used by local governments.

And I would like to highlight a fact that has been alluded to or been discussed or the idea of the passport, the Mexican passport being on the same level with regard to being tamper-proof and verifiable and credible as a Mexican Matricula, for example. In fact, in a report dated April 23 of this year, the Bureau of Immigration and Customs Enforcement Forensic Document Laboratory assessed how the security features of the most recent version of the Mexican Matricula rate in comparison to those of the Mexican passport. The Forensic Document Laboratory concluded that the present version of the Mexican passport, "contains many more components and features that make it a much more secure document," end quote, finding that the, quote, "overall complexity of the passport makes it a more difficult document to counterfeit or alter."

The Bureau of Immigration and Customs Enforcement, an agency of the United States Federal Government, has already determined that in the case of the consular ID card issued by the Mexican Government, namely the Mexican Matricula, is far less verifiable and is a much easier document to counterfeit or alter. So I just wanted to make those points for the record.

I would also, Ms. Jacobson, like to ask you a question in regard to Article 55.1 of the Vienna Convention on Consular Relations, which states, and I quote: "Without prejudice to their privileges and immunities, it is the duty of all persons enjoying consular privileges and immunities to respect the laws and regulations of the receiving state. They also have a duty not to interfere in the internal affairs of that state," end quote.

Ms. Jacobson, do you believe that in lobbying U.S. States and localities to accept their consular cards for identification purposes, an action that would appear to only benefit essentially illegal aliens in the United States, that foreign countries are encouraging those countries to violate U.S. immigration policy, and to follow onto that, are they not also violating the terms of the Vienna Convention on Consular Relations with regard to the interference of internal affairs of the United States?

Ms. JACOBSON. Mr. Chairman, thank you. I am going to answer as much as I can of that question not being a lawyer from our legal advisor's office. I do have someone here from the legal advisor's office who may have a bit more to add to fully complete our answer.

One of the things I would note is that the Vienna Convention also, in Article 38, talks about the ability of consular officials in receiving nations, that is, those in the United States, to interact with local officials and the national government to take actions to, as we have discussed before, help, assist or protect their citizens in that country. And so, we have, up until this point, viewed the lobbying effort by the Mexican Government as consistent with their efforts to promote the Matricula, which would help them help, assist or protect their citizens in this country.

Now, that is promoting of Mexican citizens in this country getting a Matricula Consular, not necessarily speaking to the acceptance of that card by State, local or Federal authorities in this country. That is the provision of the card, not the acceptance of it, as I stated earlier. I do not know, Carol, whether there is anything further you would like to say.

Okay; sorry. In addition, I think one of the main purposes that we have always been comfortable with foreign governments lobbying our State and local authorities is that we actively seek to do the same overseas. We want the ability to be able to contact and lobby national and local officials in foreign governments to pursue our interests and protect our citizens, and as you know, diplomatic international law is based highly on reciprocity, and that is not a benefit that we would like to see infringed overseas.

Mr. HOSTETTLER. So it is the testimony of the Department of State that the Department of State lobbies local entities abroad to allow a consular ID card for the purposes of a driver's license, housing, and other State benefits?

Ms. JACOBSON. We lobby local officials on all sorts of issues. I do not believe we lobby them on their driver's licenses or housing privileges, but we certainly would contact local authorities in terms of accepting our documentation for services overseas.

Mr. HOSTETTLER. For services, for all types of services?

Ms. JACOBSON. No, for services we believe our citizens might be entitled to, services that we might provide to our citizens, that that document be accepted or departure from the country, for example, if people are being evacuated that they be allowed to do so based on a document we would give them; functions of that sort. I do not believe that we would necessarily be lobbying for things like driver's licenses or housing.

Mr. HOSTETTLER. I yield myself an additional minute, because I want to make this clear, because we are looking at an issue of traditional usage of a consular ID card versus a new usage of a consular ID card, and as well as—let me ask you this: does the United States Government determine if the U.S. citizen abroad is legally in the country when they ask for a consular ID card?

Ms. JACOBSON. I do not believe so. I can ask my experts, but I believe we offer support and assistance to any U.S. citizen overseas. That is our job.

Mr. HOSTETTLER. And you issue them a consular ID card.

Ms. JACOBSON. We may in certain circumstances, yes, absolutely.

Mr. HOSTETTLER. So you do not issue consular ID cards in every circumstance?

Ms. JACOBSON. No; I mean, it would depend on the circumstance as to whether that document was really needed and they did not have another one that could be used. But certainly, if they did not and were in need of a document that would allow them to travel, re-enter the United States, et cetera, we would, and we have.

Mr. HOSTETTLER. Right; I thank the gentlelady.

The Chair now recognizes the gentleman from California, Mr. Berman, for 5 minutes.

Mr. BERMAN. Well, thank you, Mr. Chairman.

Ms. Jacobson, are you telling me that our U.S. embassies abroad do not consider themselves responsible for enforcing those countries' immigration laws?

Ms. JACOBSON. We certainly consider ourselves to be in compliance with the foreign country's immigration laws, and we certainly——

Mr. BERMAN. No, the embassies do not take on the responsibility of enforcing the foreign country's immigration laws?

Ms. JACOBSON. We do not, sir.

Mr. BERMAN. I am shocked! [Laughter.]

Do you find it that we may be going down a slippery slope to the extent that we focus our attentions in trying to prohibit or constrain a foreign government's ability to lobby either Federal or local officials on particular policies that it might end up on the fundamental principle of reciprocity restraining us from our ability to use our diplomatic personnel to lobby for what is determined to be in the interests of the United States? Do you see a slippery slope there?

Ms. JACOBSON. I do not know, Congressman, if I would call it a slippery slope, but I think that is the one thing that the State Department brings to the table in these kinds of discussions. That is precisely a perspective that we have to offer, which is that every time we take actions affecting the activities of foreign governments in the United States, we must be cognizant of the implications that those actions could have on our activities overseas to protect our citizens. That does not mean we will not take such actions. We just need to be aware.

Mr. BERMAN. I remember the State Department asking me to lobby local officials in India to site an Enron power plant near Bombay. I mean, you know, the Administration——

Ms. JACOBSON. We do lobby overseas.

Mr. BERMAN. The Administration actively—and every Administration actively has—economic, political, intelligence, military interests in what goes on in countries.

Ms. JACOBSON. And consular.

Mr. BERMAN. And lobbies and asks other representatives of the U.S. Government to engage on those issues with those foreign governments, be they national or local. Is that not true?

Ms. JACOBSON. I do not know that we always ask others to do that. We certainly do it ourselves.

Mr. BERMAN. Well, when you can hook others to do it, you try. I have no further questions.

Mr. HOSTETTLER. I thank the gentleman.

At this time, the Chair recognizes that Mr. McCraw has been very patient but has another appointment that he needs——

Mr. BERMAN. Mr. Chairman, could I just ask you to give me 30 more seconds? I totally forgot the one question I wanted to ask Mr. McCraw.

Mr. HOSTETTLER. The gentleman is recognized.

Mr. MCCRAW. Yes, sir?

Mr. BERMAN. As I hear what is said here, the issue is not—if you could really get to the security of these cards, if you could really get to the security of these cards and strengthen that, that the real concerns that the FBI has and others might have, to the extent you enhance that security and the inability to forge that document, the problems with that document diminish and evaporate; is that a fair conclusion?

Mr. MCCRAW. That is; in fact, Mr. Berman, you nailed it. If we can eliminate the fraudulent part on the front end and the forgery on the other end, and that is why in the testimony we referred to the passport. There is a higher standard, according to the Department of—what is it now?—Immigration and Customs Enforcement; their laboratory analysis, you know, concluded that it is a much more——

Mr. BERMAN. Their conclusion was about not whether it was easier to get a passport; it was that it was harder to forge——

Mr. MCCRAW. Correct.

Mr. BERMAN.—a passport.

Mr. MCCRAW. Correct.

Mr. BERMAN. And as you make that card more secure—no one has laid a foundation for me that it is harder for the actual person to get a passport than it is to get one of these cards.

Mr. MCCRAW. That is correct; it is just that we do not see a trend that that is being the level that we are with the Matricula Consular. The one thing that I did say to you, Mr. Berman, and I apologize. I left the impression that the FBI may not be concerned, and I was about, you know, no document is better than some document. And the problem with that is I think that is true. I think that there are many good arguments, as Ms. Davison pointed out and others have pointed out, you know, that there is some value to it; even yourself in terms of a law enforcement officer.

But the slippery slope I am concerned with is that it breeds—once you have it, once you have that fictitious ID to start with and are able to build additional IDs, up to 7, 10, 15, it is very problematic from a security standpoint.

Mr. BERMAN. Fictitious ID?

Mr. MCCRAW. Yes, sir.

Mr. BERMAN. So if it is an authentic ID, producing breeder documents is not a law enforcement concern.

Mr. MCCRAW. Exactly.

Mr. BERMAN. Okay.

Mr. HOSTETTLER. I thank the gentleman.

The Chair now recognizes the gentleman from California, Mr. Gallegly, for 5 minutes.

Mr. GALLEGLY. Thank you, Mr. Chairman.

Before Mr. Berman leaves, could I just ask him—he made a statement about the situation in Bombay. For the record, did that lobbying start with the previous Administration?

Mr. BERMAN. As a matter of fact, it did.

Mr. GALLEGLY. I thank the gentleman.

Mr. BERMAN. Goes to show. [Laughter.]

Mr. HOSTETTLER. If the gentleman will yield.

Mr. BERMAN. But in all fairness, I do not believe the State Department in the previous Administration was familiar with the auditing and accounting practices of that particular company at the time they asked me to do that. [Laughter.]

Mr. GALLEGLY. I appreciate it.

Mr. HOSTETTLER. If the gentleman will yield, Mr. McCraw, thank you for——

Mr. MCCRAW. Thank you very much, Mr. Chairman, Members of the Committee.

Mr. HOSTETTLER.—being here.

Mr. MCCRAW. I appreciate it.

Mr. HOSTETTLER. You are excused.

Mr. GALLEGLY. Thank you very much, and I want to thank Mr. McCraw, and I would urge my colleagues who have not read his complete testimony to please do so. I think it is very telling. It is very articulate, and I think it is a very important part of the substance of this hearing.

Ms. Davison, after hearing the FBI's testimony—I do not know whether you had the opportunity to read the testimony of Mr.

McCraw, but after hearing his testimony, do you believe that Montgomery County should continuing accepting Matricula Consular?

Ms. DAVISON. Yes; I did have the opportunity to read his testimony this morning.

Mr. GALLEGLY. Do you believe they should still continue to accept Matricula Consular?

Ms. DAVISON. Yes, I do.

Mr. GALLEGLY. Okay; do you believe that the county, your county, has a duty not to contravene or subvert immigration laws?

Ms. DAVISON. Certainly.

Mr. GALLEGLY. Would your assessment of those that are using Matricula Consular as the only identification that they have—obviously, if that is the only thing they can present you with, and your argument for the use of it is they have nothing else; is that correct?

Ms. DAVISON. Often, that is the case, yes.

Mr. GALLEGLY. Would you believe that there is a high probability that those that have that as the only form of identification are illegally in the country?

Ms. DAVISON. Probably a number of them are; that is correct

Mr. GALLEGLY. Okay; having said that, do you also—on record, I believe, and correct me if I am wrong—that any person who has a Matricula Consular receives all of the same benefits that any American citizen would receive; is that correct, as far as housing, other social benefits?

Ms. DAVISON. No; there are some Federally-subsidized programs that the county offers where there are specific regulations. I mean, there could be additional qualifications for participation.

Mr. GALLEGLY. What about housing?

Ms. DAVISON. Well, in housing, most of what we do is actually county-funded. We do have some public housing, and I do not operate that. We have a separate housing authority.

Mr. GALLEGLY. Okay.

Ms. DAVISON. So I am not sure about the qualifications for that.

Mr. GALLEGLY. But there is a chance that with only Matricula Consular, they could receive public housing, because if that——

Ms. DAVISON. I do not know. I doubt that, but I do not know. I would have to check with the Housing Opportunities Commission.

Mr. GALLEGLY. The issue of accepting Matricula Consular for the purposes of opening bank accounts, Ms. Jacobson, I think you were the only one who did not get the question. Were you aware that the Mexican Government themselves will not accept the Matricula Consular for the purposes of identification to open bank accounts in their own country, yet they are heavy lobbying the U.S. for the U.S. to do that when they will not do that themselves?

Ms. JACOBSON. It is my understanding, Congressman, that it is not accepted widely in Mexico because it is not designed to be used by Mexicans, so it is simply not a common card for Mexicans to use. They are not familiar with it. They have other forms of domestic ID. It is also my understanding that an increasing number of Mexican banks in the northern part of the country do accept the card, as they begin to actually see it.

Mr. GALLEGLY. But I would like to try to get back to that issue that we talked about on the first round relative to the cooperation of the Mexican Government. Do we have any specific, concrete, iron-clad understanding or agreement with the Mexican Government to invalidate the 90 percent plus or minus of the Matricula Consular documents that the FBI identified as really impossible to verify as legitimate documents?

Ms. JACOBSON. All I can tell you, Congressman, is that the Foreign Minister has told the Secretary of State that they are planning to do that.

Mr. GALLEGLY. They do not have a date? To date, it is kind of happy talk?

Ms. JACOBSON. They do not have a date. They have not given us a date.

Mr. GALLEGLY. Okay; thank you very much, Mr. Chairman.

Mr. HOSTETTLER. I thank the gentleman.

The Chair now recognizes the gentlelady from Tennessee, Mrs. Blackburn, for 5 minutes.

Mrs. BLACKBURN. Thank you, Mr. Chairman. I appreciate that.

Mr. Verdery, you have mentioned in your testimony the concern over our national security requirements and interests, and then, you go on and mention the need to develop some policies and also some guidance to our State and local governments on the acceptance of the Matricula Consular and other forms of identification from foreign governments.

If you would please list for me or give me an idea of what you envision as being the guidance. What are the type programs that you would see implemented? What are the type instructions or rules that you would see given to our State and local governments for recognizing fraudulent or forged documents for developing a way to understand what true identification is?

Mr. VERDERY. Well, your question goes to the heart of the matter that is being looked at in the public policy review process that is undergoing, in the interagency process at the Homeland Security Council, and so, the specifics as to what the guidance might look like at the end of the day to State and local governments is still under development. I assume it will end up including things such as, you know, what type of security checks should be reviewed; concerns we have about creating identities, multiple identities; concerns about our general enforcement of immigration laws.

As you know, the Department has not only the antiterrorism mission that has been assigned to it by Congress, but the BTS also has the responsibility, through the Bureau of Immigration and Customs Enforcement and the Bureau of Customs and Border Protection, to enforce our immigration laws. And so, we have obviously concerns—any concerns that the cards would raise in terms of enforcement of immigration laws is also something that should be on the table in terms of our guidance. But that guidance is under development, and I could not give you any more specifics on it than that.

Mrs. BLACKBURN. If it were up to you or in your opinion, would you put the Matricula Consular card on a list of recommended documents that State and local governments accept for positive identification?

Mr. VERDERY. That is not up to me is the short answer, and so, you know, that is really a decision that would be made through the

Homeland Security process, and for our Department, Secretary Ridge would make that recommendation to that process.

Mrs. BLACKBURN. Do you think that accepting the Matricula Consular card makes it more difficult for our State and local law enforcement agencies to know the true identity of a person?

Mr. VERDERY. Well, it is clear that there are two sides of the coin on this. I forget which Member asked Mr. McCraw—Mr. McCraw read a report in about some police agencies believing that it was helpful and that it provided identification for people who might not otherwise have identification; it might allow people to come forward during criminal investigations and the like. So you would have to balance those pro-law enforcement benefits, so to speak, with the problems of multiple identities being created to allow organized criminal activity, money laundering, terrorist activity.

So those are kind of the law enforcement pros and cons that are being weighed in this homeland security process undergoing at the Administration as we speak.

Mrs. BLACKBURN. Thank you very much.

Thank you, Mr. Chairman.

Mr. HOSTETTLER. I thank the gentlelady.

I have a question or two remaining for the witnesses. I appreciate your forbearance.

But Mr. Verdery, in our post-September 11 world, it is crucial that every step be taken to protect the American people from further possible attacks, especially in relation to airline travel. Is it true that anyone in possession of a Mexican consular ID card can board an airliner today with no questions asked and it be received as a Government-issued ID?

Mr. VERDERY. It is my understanding that those cards are being accepted by TSA when a person arrives in an airport to board a plane just as any other official Government ID would be accepted, again, to prove that the person is who they say they are. Of course, it should be remembered that this is in terms of a screening process, that anybody who raises particular concerns would then go to secondary screening. But yes, the ID would be accepted as any other Government ID.

Now, I should add, though, that that policy that has been in place is part of the review that is going on at the Homeland Security Council, and so, that is on the table as well.

Mr. HOSTETTLER. It is part of the interagency discussion that is going on?

Mr. VERDERY. Yes, sir.

Mr. HOSTETTLER. All right; I thank you very much.

I thank the panel of witnesses very much for your time and your testimony and your service to us. I would remind the record that the record will stay open for seven legislative days for any Member who wishes to make an addition.

The business before the Subcommittee being completed, we are adjourned.

[Whereupon, at 12:59 p.m., the Subcommittee adjourned.]

APPENDIX

MATERIAL SUBMITTED FOR THE HEARING RECORD

PREPARED STATEMENT OF THE HONORABLE SHEILA JACKSON LEE, A REPRESENTATIVE IN CONGRESS FROM THE STATE OF TEXAS

It is unfortunate that the Matricula Consular card has become an immigration issue. The Matricula is not issued as an immigration document, and it has no immigration purpose. The Government of Mexico has been issuing Matriculas at their consulates around the world for more than 130 years. The consulates do this to create an official record of its citizens in other countries. The Matricula is legal proof of registration with a consulate. This registration facilitates access to protection and consular services because the certificate is evidence of Mexican nationality. Last year alone, more than a million of these cards were issued to Mexican citizens living in the United States. It does not provide immigrant status of any kind, and it cannot be used for travel, employment, or driving in the United States or in Mexico. The Matricula only attests that a Mexican consulate has verified the individual's identity.

The Matricula, however, does have some non consular uses. For instance, because it is an identification card, it provides Mexican nationals in the United States with access to banking services. Without an acceptable identification card, many Mexican nationals in this country cannot open checking or savings accounts or use any other banking services.

In 2002, Latino immigrants sent more than $30 billion to their families in Latin America. The cost of making such transfers is much higher if the person making it has to use a money transmitting business such as Western Union or MoneyGram instead of a regulated financial institution such as a bank or a credit union. Moreover, the banks and credit unions want the Latino banking business. United States banks plan to spend at least $8.5 billion through 2005 to attract Hispanic customers.

The availability of banking services is a safety issue too. Latinos are more likely to be victims of violent crime than any other racial or ethnic group. Much of this crime relates to the perception of criminals that because Latinos do not have bank accounts, they carry large amounts of cash. As a result of this problem, police departments across the country support the use of the Matricula to enable Latinos to use mainstream financial institutions as a means of reducing crime and violence.

In an attempt to assist efforts to destroy the financial networks that support Al-Qaeda and other terrorist organizations, the Committee on Financial Services enacted legislation to reform money laundering laws. The enacted provisions were incorporated into the USA PATRIOT Act.

Customer identification provisions in this Act have a direct impact on the use of the Matricula as a legitimate form of identification to allow consumers to open bank accounts. Specifically, Section 326 of Title III adds a new subsection that requires the Secretary to prescribe regulations setting forth minimum standards for financial institutions that relate to the identification and verification of any person who applies to open an account. These regulations permit banks to accept identification cards issued by foreign governments from customers opening new accounts, including the Matricula. The regulations went into effect on June 9, 2003, but anti-immigrant groups and some state and federal officials have expressed opposition to the regulations. Consequently, there will be further consideration of the regulations, including an additional comment period.

Congressman Elton Gallegly has introduced a bill that would make it more difficult for Mexican citizens in the United States to use a Matricula card. His bill, the Identification Integrity Act, H.R. 687, would prohibit the federal government from accepting identification documents issued by a foreign government, except for a passport that is accepted for such purpose. I have many concerns about this bill.

It seems to me that the unintended consequences of such a law far outweigh any good that Mr. Gallegly thinks the bill would achieve.

For instance, certain classes of aliens applying for humanitarian relief are not required to be in possession of a valid passport and typically will not have one in any event. This includes many aliens who are applying for asylum; aliens applying for Temporary Protected Status; Cuban nationals who arrive in the United States; and aliens requesting humanitarian parole. If the government cannot accept identification documents issued by a foreign government, how will people seeking such humanitarian relief establish their identities if they do not have passports?

Similarly, what will happen in the cases of aliens who have been exempted by law, treaty, or regulation from being required to carry a passport? At the very least, this presents difficult questions of international law.

Many people are included in this category, such as, Canadian nationals, except after a visit outside the Western Hemisphere; Mexican nationals in possession of a border crossing card with a biometric identifier who are applying for admission as temporary visitors from contiguous territory; alien employees entering pursuant to the International Boundary and Water Commission Treaty between the United States and Mexico; citizens of the Republic of the Marshall Islands, the Federated States of Micronesia, and the Republic of Palau, in accordance with the Compacts of Free Association between these entities and the United States; certain aliens in transit through the United States; and aliens entering from the U.S. insular areas of Guam, Puerto Rico, or the U.S. Virgin Island.

If laws are to be enacted to prevent Mexican nationals from using the Matricula in our country, they need to be much narrower than a provision that simply would prohibit the federal government from accepting identification documents issued by a foreign government.

Thank you.

PREPARED STATEMENT OF THE HONORABLE ELTON GALLEGLY, A REPRESENTATIVE IN CONGRESS FROM THE STATE OF CALIFORNIA

Mr. Chairman, Mexican consulates began mass distribution of matricula consulars—identification cards issued by the Mexican government to illegal immigrants in the United States—just more than a year ago. They gained favor among illegal immigrants when banks began to accept the cards as legitimate identification to open bank accounts. Then local governments began to accept them as legitimate identification as well. Attempts are now being made the accept these cards at the federal level.

Let me clear about one point, the only people who need these cards are illegal immigrants, criminals, and terrorists.

If we accept identification issued by Mexico as legitimate in the United States, where does it stop? And what protections do we have against terrorists taking advantage of the program when we've turned over to foreign governments our sovereign right to identify people within our borders?

Mexico, Poland, Nicaragua, and other countries trying to expand their consular ID programs in the United States are doing so in an effort to force a de facto amnesty for their nationals illegally in this country and to allow them to receive services to which they are not entitled.

And, while it's correct that the vast majority of those seeking the cards are not terrorists, it is equally true that terrorists are certainly watching this program to see how they may exploit it. Are we willing to accept consular cards from illegal Saudi Arabians, Egyptians or Colombians?

Equally disturbing is that our government is actively supporting these programs. State Department representatives admitted in a congressional briefing that the department helped Mexico design its program. And a U.S. embassy cable from Managua explicitly asks the State Department in Washington for guidance regarding the implementation of Nicaragua's consular card program.

Giving up our sovereign rights during a time of war is foolhardy and irresponsible.

To combat this threat to our security, I have authored and introduced the *Identification Integrity Act of 2003*. With the exception of passports—which are issued under strict guidelines provided by the U.S.—it would forbid the federal government's recognition of foreign-issued IDs.

The price is just too high not to end this practice now.

Prepared Statement of the Honorable Steve King, a Representative in Congress From the State of Iowa

Chairman Hostettler, Thank you for holding this hearing today. I have serious concerns about the acceptance of consular identification cards issued by foreign governments, including the "Matricula Consular" card issued by the government of Mexico. Other governments are also considering offering similar cards.

My first question that occurs to me, is why would a Mexican national in the US need or want such a card? Legal aliens in the United States already possess all of the necessary documents issued by our government. In additional, Mexican nationals can obtain a passport from their government, a highly-secure and internationally accepted form of identification. It appears to me that only illegal aliens would need to carry such cards for identification purposes—issuance and acceptance of these cards encourages people to flout our immigration laws. I am also concerned that acceptance of this card, which is not as secure as a passport, will severely hamper the ability of the government to track money laundering, or accurately identify people who use the cards to open accounts.

Acceptance of the Matricula Consular card is a serious issue of national security. These cards are known by federal law enforcement officers to be insecure. Illegal aliens are often apprehended with multiple cards under multiple names. It is my understanding that according to some estimates, more than a million cards have already been issued in the U.S. with little or no regard for source documents, identity confirmation with Mexican public records, or even reliable record keeping as to the names printed on the cards.

Given our concern about national security, it is clear that the "Matricula Consular"—or any other identification card susceptible to fraud issued by a foreign government—should not be recognized or accepted as a secure identification document by any federal agency or in any program or activity falling under federal regulatory jurisdiction.

I look forward to hearing from the witnesses here today, on this important issue of vital national security.

LETTER FROM THE FEDERATION FOR AMERICAN IMMIGRATION REFORM (FAIR)

FAIR

FEDERATION FOR AMERICAN IMMIGRATION REFORM
1666 CONNECTICUT AVENUE, NW, SUITE 400 • WASHINGTON, DC 20009
PHONE: (202) 328-7004 • (877) 627-FAIR • FAX: (202) 387-3447 • WWW.FAIRUS.ORG

June 17, 2003

The Hon. John Hostettler
Chairman, Immigration, Border Security, and Claims Subcommittee
1214 Longworth House Office Building
Washington, DC 20510

Reference: Hearing on "The Issuance, Acceptance, and Reliability of Consular Identification Cards", June 19, 2003

Dear Representative Hostettler,

In connection with the referenced hearing, I would appreciate your taking into consideration the following views of the Federation for American Immigration Reform (FAIR) and your including those views in the record of the hearing.

Today's massive problem with illegal immigration, estimated to number between 8-11 million persons, has severe consequences for national security as well as for the nation's economy, social services, and law enforcement. Against this backdrop, FAIR firmly believes that any recognition of a foreign-government issued document other than a passport for internal purposes in the United States exacerbates those problems.

The Mexican government's *matricula consular* is unexceptionable as a document for identifying Mexican citizens for purposes of the Mexican government. However, when Mexicans are residing in the United States, there is no reason that they should be exempt from the requirement that they identify themselves with a Mexican passport. The international standards for the issuance of passports offer protections against identity fraud that are not available for the Mexican consular identity cards.

To the best that we have been able to establish, the Mexican government makes no effort to verify the identity of the persons to whom it issues these cards with any federal or state database of information to verify names or dates of birth. We have even seen press accounts to the effect that the Mexican government is issuing these cards to persons who have no official Mexican identity document and is accepting a form of affidavit as a substitute. Needless to say, this means that little if any credence should be given to the *matricula consuslar* as a true identity document by our government or for any official purpose regulated by the government.

In substantiation of the valuelessness of the Mexican identity cards, we have received information from immigration officials who have personally found instances of multiple issuance of these cards to the same individual in several different names. This would be precluded if there were any form of identity verification exercised by the Mexican authorities.

While the likelihood of the Mexican government issuing a *matricula consular* to a terrorist in the United States may be slim, because of the lax documentary standards required for those cards, it would seem less likely that a terrorist would have obtained a Mexican passport. Thus it would be common sense to hold to the requirement that a Mexican present a passport or a green card attesting to legal presence in the United States for official purposes in this country.

FAIR also believes that action must be taken to discourage the flow of illegal aliens into our country and to encourage those who are here now to return to their home country. Any actions that serve to accommodate and facilitate the activities of illegal aliens as if they were legally resident in the country work at cross-purposes to that objective. The sea of illegal aliens in our country within which intending terrorists may hide and plan their operations is an issue of serious concern. We owe it to the American public to take all reasonable actions that will lessen and reverse that problem.

We support H.R. 687 and H.R. 502, which are both designed to bar acceptance by the federal government of identification cards issued by foreign governments, but that, by itself, does not fully address the problem. As long as other institutions, such as banks, which are federally regulated, are free to give standing to the Mexican identity cards, the screening process designed to deny banking facilities to terrorists and terrorist-supporters and to hinder a normal life style for illegal residents in our country will be undermined.

Finally, the success to date of the campaign by the Mexican government to gain recognition in our country for their consular identity cards has encouraged other governments to follow suit. If the federal government does not now call a halt to the proliferation of uses for these documents, a time is likely to come when we find such identity documents in the hands of terrorists, either before or after they have committed another atrocity against the American public.

Sincerely,

Dan Stein
Executive Director

CONGRESSIONAL RESEARCH SERVICE REPORT SUBMITTED BY REP. JACKSON LEE

Congressional Research Service

Memorandum June 18, 2003

TO: House Immigration, Border Security and Claims Subcommittee
Attention: Nolan Rappaport

FROM: Andorra Bruno
Analyst in American National Government
Domestic Social Policy Division

SUBJECT: Certain Classes of Aliens Not Subject to a Passport Requirement When Seeking Nonimmigrant Admission to the United States or Humanitarian Relief

---

In response to your request regarding documentary requirements for aliens, this memorandum identifies certain classes of aliens that are not subject to a passport requirement when applying for nonimmigrant admission to the United States or for certain forms of humanitarian relief. The classes enumerated here are intended as examples and do not represent an exhaustive list of all nonimmigrants or humanitarian cases not subject to a passport requirement. The information is drawn principally from the Immigration and Nationality Act of 1952, as amended,[1] and regulations issued by the former Immigration and Naturalization Service (INS).[2]

Nonimmigrants

Under INA §212(a)(7)(B)(i)(I), aliens seeking temporary admission to the United States as nonimmigrants must be in possession of a passport that is valid for at least 6 months beyond the initial period of admission or contemplated initial period of stay. There are a number of exceptions to this requirement, however, established by law, treaty, or regulation. A passport is not required for the following classes of nonimmigrants to gain admission:[3]

- Canadian nationals, except after a visit outside the Western Hemisphere;

---

[1] Act of June 27, 1952, ch. 477; 8 U.S.C. 1101 *et seq.*

[2] The Homeland Security Act of 2002 (P.L. 107-296, November 25, 2002) abolished INS, which had been part of the Department of Justice (DOJ), and transferred most of its functions to the Department of Homeland Security (DHS) as of March 1, 2003.

[3] For additional information about these exceptions, see 8 CFR 212.1; 22 CFR 41.1; and 22 CFR 41.2.

- Aliens resident in Canada or Bermuda having a common nationality with Canadian nationals or with British subjects in Bermuda,[4] except after a visit outside the Western Hemisphere;

- Mexican nationals in possession of a border crossing card with a biometric identifier who are applying for admission as temporary visitors for business or pleasure from contiguous territory;

- Alien employees entering pursuant to the International Boundary and Water Commission Treaty between the United States and Mexico;

- Citizens of the Republic of the Marshall Islands, the Federated States of Micronesia, and the Republic of Palau, in accordance with the Compacts of Free Association between these entities and the United States;

- Certain aliens in transit through the United States;

- Certain alien members of the U.S. Armed Forces coming to the United States under official orders or permit of such Armed Forces;

- American Indians born in Canada having at least 50% American Indian blood;

- Aliens entering from the U.S. insular areas of Guam, Puerto Rico, or the U.S. Virgin Islands;

- Certain Armed Services personnel of a North Atlantic Treaty Organization (NATO) member; and

- Certain Armed Services personnel attached to a NATO headquarters in the United States.

---

[4] This reference is considered to include citizens of all Commonwealth countries and Ireland.

The INA also authorizes the Attorney General and the Secretary of State acting jointly to waive the documentary requirements of INA §212(a)(7)(B)(i), including the passport requirement, on the basis of unforeseen emergency in individual cases.[5]

Even in cases in which passports are required for nonimmigrant admission, they may not need to remain valid (unexpired) throughout the period of stay. According to *Immigration Law and Procedure*:

> The six-month margin of validity required of passports has been effectively eliminated in most cases. Many countries have entered into agreements with the United States by which their passports are recognized as valid for return to the country concerned for six months beyond the expiration date shown in the passport. As the six months needed for INA §212(a)(7)(B)(i) are automatically built into such passports, their bearers can be admitted to the United States until the validity date shown on their face.[6]

Humanitarian Cases

Certain classes of aliens applying for humanitarian relief are not required to be in possession of a valid passport. These classes include the following:

- Aliens applying for asylum;
- Aliens applying for Temporary Protected Status (TPS);[7]
- Cuban nationals who arrive in the United States; and
- Aliens requesting humanitarian parole.

I hope this information is helpful. If you have any questions or require further assistance, please contact me at 7-7865.

---

[5] INA §212(d)(4)(A). The Homeland Security Act transferred most immigration-related functions from DOJ to DHS. It is uncertain as of this writing whether this waiver authority remains, in whole or in part, with DOJ and the Attorney General.

[6] Charles Gordon, Stanley Mailman, and Stephen Yale-Loehr, *Immigration Law and Procedure*, vol. 2, March 2003, §12.04[2].

[7] Although a passport is not required to apply for TPS, it is the preferred document under immigration regulations for TPS applicants to evidence their identity and nationality (8 CFR 244.9(a)(1)).

ARTICLE FROM ROCKY MOUNTAIN NEWS SUBMITTED BY REP. JACKSON LEE

Wedding bells aren't in the cards
Betrothed dealt headaches in getting marriage licenses

By Robert Sanchez, Rocky Mountain News
June 17, 2003

Fidela Garcia and Francisco Ramos arrived Monday at the Denver Clerk and Recorder's Office looking to get married.

They came away disappointed and discouraged with a system they said took away their most basic right.

"I'm just really upset," said Garcia, 48, whose fiance was forbidden from getting a marriage license because he presented the Mexican Consulate's matricula-consular card and an expired Mexican passport as his identification.

"I'm not sure what to do," said Garcia, who had proper identification.

Clerks across Colorado are struggling with the Secure and Verifiable Identity Document Act passed by state lawmakers this year. It forbids government workers from accepting some forms of identification in issuing licenses and documents.

Much of the confusion surrounds foreign-issued documentation, including passports, birth certificates and matricula-consular cards. Some clerks accept them as valid ID, while some don't.

Before the law passed, foreign passports and birth certificates were accepted in all counties. Now the law states: "Secure and verifiable document means a document issued by a state or federal jurisdiction or recognized by the United States government and that is verifiable by federal or state law enforcement, intelligence or homeland security agencies."

Some clerks said the wording is too broad and will ask state officials - including Attorney General Ken Salazar - for a list of acceptable IDs.

Salazar had not received the request for clarification late Monday.

Since Gov. Bill Owens signed the law, Denver's Clerk and Recorder's Office rejected at least 50 marriage licenses for people from Chile, Ethiopia, Mexico, Russia and Switzerland.

That includes Garcia and Ramos, who met two years ago when they worked at Wal-Mart.

"I feel pretty bad about all of this," Ramos, 47, said through his fiancee.

Fifteen minutes earlier, Minerva Rodriguez was told her fiance's matricula-consular card wouldn't work, either.

"We only wanted to get married, nothing else," said Rodriguez, 30, a 20-year Denver resident who has two children, ages 8 and 4. "It's awful."

Sherry Jackson, Denver's clerk and recorder, said she would post a list of acceptable IDs on the city's Web site before the month's end.

The matricula-consular card - which critics argue lends legitimacy to illegal immigrants and can easily be counterfeited by potential terrorists - will remain on the unacceptable list.

News staff writer Javier Erik Olvera contributed to this report.

CABLE FROM STATE DEPARTMENT

```
Cable Text:
UTE8039
ACTION VO-01

INFO  LOG-00   NP-00    CA-01    CIAE-00  INL-00   DODE-00  WHA-00
      DS-00    OIGO-00  FBIE-00  UTED-00  VC-00    TEDE-00  INR-00
      IO-00    VCE-00   AC-01    NSAE-00  ACE-00   TEST-00  DSCC-00
      PRM-00   DRL-01   NFAT-00  SAS-00     /004W
                  ------------------60C2A7  062336Z /38
R 062222Z MAY 03
FM AMEMBASSY MANAGUA                    American Embassy
TO SECSTATE WASHDC 5570                 Secretary of State
INFO WHA CENTRAL AMERICAN COLLECTIVE
AMEMBASSY MEXICO
HQ INS WASHINGTON DC

UNCLAS  MANAGUA 001324

E.O. 12958: N/A
TAGS: CVIS, KFRD, PGOV, PREL, SMIG
SUBJECT: GON SEEKS TO EMULATE MEXICO WITH CONSULAR ID CARDS
```

Summary and Action Request

1. The GON plans to implement a consular ID card program similar to the one begun by the Mexican Government for Mexican citizens in the U.S. The ID card, which would be issued by the GON to Nicaraguans living in the U.S., would be used to open bank accounts and obtain utility services from local governments. The program would be initially implemented as a pilot in Miami and eventually expanded to other cities with large Nicaraguan populations. The GON is negotiating with the company that produces the ID cards for the Mexican Government and the Nicaraguan ID card will have security features similar to its Mexican counterpart. The ID card would be made available to any Nicaraguan citizen, regardless of legal status in the U.S. Although the GON has definite ideas regarding the major outlines of the program, it has not worked out the details. Furthermore, the card could be issued to an applicant lacking any identity documents, provided he has two witnesses who can attest to the applicant's identity. Post requests guidance for discussions with the GON. See action request at para 7. End Summary.

Responding to Citizens' Requests

2. After reading in the local press that the GON was proposing a consular ID program similar to the one recently implemented by the Mexican Government for Mexican nationals in the United States, Emboffs met with Consular Affairs Director Miriam Fonseca April 28, 2003, to inquire about the plan. Fonseca told Emboffs that the consular ID program was a direct response to numerous requests from Nicaraguans in

the U.S., who allude to Mexico's success with such ID cards and seek similar benefits. The program is currently designed as a pilot to be implemented first in Miami, where the GON believes there are 150,000 Nicaraguan citizens, and eventually expanded to other cities with large Nicaraguan populations, such as Los Angeles. The Foreign Ministry had initially planned for the program to be operational in June but is now projecting inauguration late this year.

3. Fonseca believes that the cards will be accepted to open bank accounts, obtain utility services from the city, and possibly get driver's licenses. The GON plans to install a card-making machine in the consular office and to provide ID cards on the spot. No approval will be required from Managua. The cost to the GON is projected to be USD 6 per card, for which individuals will be charged USD 25 each. In early April, the Vice-Foreign Minister presented the proposal for approval to the Supreme Electoral Council (CSE), a GON agency in charge of providing voting ID cards to Nicaraguans domestically. To date, the CSE has not responded.

Features Comparable to Mexican ID Cards
----

4. The GON is currently in negotiations with the same company that produces consular ID cards for the Mexican Government. The cards would presumably carry the same security features as the Mexican ID cards, but Fonseca was unfamiliar with the specifics. Although the security features of the card may be substantial and the card may be difficult to falsify, it is the criteria for issuance of the card that is problematic. Under Nicaraguan law, a person can usually establish his identity without documents when accompanied by two adult witnesses who can attest to the person's identity. For example, a person can use "witnesses" to be able to vote without a voter ID card and to obtain a copy of a birth certificate. According to Fonseca, this same "witness" process will be applied to the issuance of consular ID cards.

Legal Status Not a GON Concern
----

5. In issuing a consular ID card, the GON will not inquire as to the individual's legal status in the U.S. According to Fonseca, that is not a GON concern. The consular office will issue a card provided that the individual can establish his Nicaraguan citizenship with "appropriate documents." However, Fonseca conceded that legal Nicaraguan residents already have identification documents and only illegal residents are likely to benefit from the program.

Comment
----

6. It is fairly evident that although the GON may have determined the major outlines of the program, it has yet to focus on the details. For example, exactly what documents will be required to be presented to obtain the ID card have yet to be determined. In addition, requirements regarding

UNCLASSIFIED

age and residency in the U.S. have not been considered. Control of the database, and whether there will be Managua oversight, is unresolved. More importantly, the GON's practice of establishing identity with two witnesses is unlikely to impress bank, city, county, or State officials. To date, the GON has consulted with none of the entities to whom individuals are likely to present the cards. End Comment.

Action Request
----

7. Because the consular ID program is in its early stages and the Consular Affairs Director and Foreign Minister seem open to Embassy input, the U.S. Government has an excellent opportunity to influence the implementation of the program. Post requests Department guidance on what to tell the GON on this issue.
MOORE

NNNN

End Cable Text

ARTICLE FROM ROCKY MOUNTAIN NEWS SUBMITTED BY SENATOR ANDREWS

Rocky Mountain News

URL: http://www.rockymountainnews.com/drmn/local/article/0,1299,DRMN_15_1677393,00.html

Owens questions Mexican consulate

Colorado's chief exec wants official to clarify status of spokesman

By John J. Sanko And Hector Gutierrez, Rocky Mountain News
January 16, 2003

Gov. Bill Owens has asked the Mexican consulate in Denver to clarify the status of its spokesman after lawmakers said he is lobbying them without the proper credentials.

Gubernatorial spokesman Dan Hopkins said Owens sent a Dec. 27 letter to the Consulate General of Mexico asking for an explanation of Mario Hernandez's official status.

In the letter, addressed to Consul General Leticia Calzada, the governor writes:

"Recently, questions have been raised as to whether Mr. Hernandez should be registered as a foreign agent due to certain activities, such as lobbying state legislators and representing the consulate in matters involving press relations.

"The questions have been raised because it is not clear whether Mr. Hernandez is an employee of the Mexican Consulate, and if so, it is not clear that his activities are within the scope of his consulate position as determined by the Department of State."

Calzada has been out of the country and said she did not see the letter until this week. But after reviewing the letter, Calzada said Wednesday that she had no comment. Hernandez also declined to comment.

Hopkins said the governor believed that Hernandez, who identifies himself as a consular spokesman, had been active in a number of areas, including drivers license and in-state tuition legislation involving immigrants in Colorado.

"A number of people have expressed concern over Mr. Hernandez becoming increasingly active politically," Hopkins said.

"So the governor sent a letter inquiring about Mr. Hernandez's status."

Hernandez is considered one of Calzada's most trusted aides, who often travels with her to visit schoolchildren, business executives, state officials and migrant communities.

Fluent in English, Hernandez stands by Calzada to assist her when she needs help with translations.

He has helped arrange news conferences for the consulate's office and Mexican dignitaries who visit Colorado. Hernandez has been quoted frequently in a number of stories, including a dispute involving Jesus Apodaca, an 18-year-old Aurora honors student in the country illegally and not eligible for in-state tuition at Colorado colleges.

Calzada and Hernandez also have made presentations to law enforcement agencies and local governments about the matricula consular, the identification card that is issued to their compatriots by their office.

In his letter, Owens said the Foreign Agents Registration Act requires every agent of a foreign principal to register with the U.S. Justice Department.

However, it does exempt consular staff and employees from registration requirements while they are engaged "exclusively in the performance of activities which are recognized by the Department of State as being within the scope of the functions" of such employees.

Owens asked for Calzada's opinion as to whether Hernandez should register under FARA. If not, the governor asked whether he was in compliance with all other applicable federal law, including registration under the Lobbying Disclosure Act or notification of the Department of State.

Hopkins, Owens' spokesman, declined to identify lawmakers who have complained.

One lawmaker who is not complaining is Sen. Ron Tupa, D-Boulder, who said he has talked with Hernandez about legislation.

Tupa had nothing but praise for his work but said no lobbying was involved.

Tupa introduced a bill last year that would have allowed illegal immigrants to get drivers licenses in Colorado.

Tupa, who is expected to introduce similar legislation this year, said an estimated 50,000 immigrants in Colorado now drive without licenses or mandatory no-fault auto insurance.

His bill, which was killed in a Senate committee, would have allowed unauthorized immigrants to apply for and receive drivers licenses.

Tupa said he had discussed the issue with Hernandez and also with the consul general.

"I've talked to both her and her spokesperson," Tupa said.

"They definitely were not lobbying me. It was for information only."

Lisa Doran, a spokeswoman for Colorado Secretary of State Donetta Davidson, said Hernandez is not a registered lobbyist with the state.

Davidson said state law requires such registration for a person who is lobbying, whether a citizen or not.

U.S.C.A. § 1324, are irresponsible, false and frivolous. And since there is no underlying crime, there is no RICO-prohibited financial gain involved.

3. **Threats of civil liability are arbitrary, capricious, and without any legal merit.**

4. **State and local government officials are not charged with enforcing immigration laws, which under our constitutional system is an exclusive mandate of the federal government. Therefore, state and local governments, as well private entities and individuals, may not be held negligent or otherwise liable for any theoretical failure to enforce federal immigration laws.**

5. **In fact, state and local governments, as well as banks and other private entities or individuals, are prohibited from discriminating based on immigration status.**

6. **The international legal rules followed by the U.S. State Department prohibit non-recognition of the Mexican consular ID.**

7. **Eight hundred police departments, various local governments and at least 80 banks have accepted the matricula, because it increases public safety, national security and our economic competitiveness by enabling the reliable identification of millions of Mexicans living and working in the U.S.**

8. **The only viable alternative to acceptance of the matricula is to legalize the millions of Mexicans who are performing vital work and sustaining the U.S. economy.**

Analysis:

1. **Acceptance of the Mexican consular ID is not illegal-in fact is it currently permitted by the U.S. Treasury under the Patriot Act.**

In Colorado, where the anti-immigrant and anti-matricula campaign has been most vocal, the State Bank Commissioner, Richard Fulkerson, was copied on a "Legal Notice" addressed to all Colorado banking institutions, by anti-immigrant groups contending "that the matricula consular card is illegal and exposes the acceptor to legal liability." The State of Colorado decided to follow the lead of the federal government and refrain from prohibiting acceptance of matriculas. Commissioner Fulkerson reasoned that:

> "At this time, I am not aware that any of the federal banking agencies have officially taken a position as to the acceptability of the [Mexican consular ID] card. However, I would note that a footnote to a July 16, 2002, Department of Treasury press release concerning proposed rules implementing Section 326 of

U.S.C.A. § 1324, are irresponsible, false and frivolous. And since there is no underlying crime, there is no RICO-prohibited financial gain involved.

3. **Threats of civil liability are arbitrary, capricious, and without any legal merit.**

4. **State and local government officials are not charged with enforcing immigration laws, which under our constitutional system is an exclusive mandate of the federal government. Therefore, state and local governments, as well private entities and individuals, may not be held negligent or otherwise liable for any theoretical failure to enforce federal immigration laws.**

5. **In fact, state and local governments, as well as banks and other private entities or individuals, are prohibited from discriminating based on immigration status.**

6. **The international legal rules followed by the U.S. State Department prohibit non-recognition of the Mexican consular ID.**

7. **Eight hundred police departments, various local governments and at least 80 banks have accepted the matricula, because it increases public safety, national security and our economic competitiveness by enabling the reliable identification of millions of Mexicans living and working in the U.S.**

8. **The only viable alternative to acceptance of the matricula is to legalize the millions of Mexicans who are performing vital work and sustaining the U.S. economy.**

Analysis:

1. Acceptance of the Mexican consular ID is not illegal-in fact is it currently permitted by the U.S. Treasury under the Patriot Act.

In Colorado, where the anti-immigrant and anti-matricula campaign has been most vocal, the State Bank Commissioner, Richard Fulkerson, was copied on a "Legal Notice" addressed to all Colorado banking institutions, by anti-immigrant groups contending "that the matricula consular card is illegal and exposes the acceptor to legal liability." The State of Colorado decided to follow the lead of the federal government and refrain from prohibiting acceptance of matriculas. Commissioner Fulkerson reasoned that:

> "At this time, I am not aware that any of the federal banking agencies have officially taken a position as to the acceptability of the [Mexican consular ID] card. However, I would note that a footnote to a July 16, 2002, Department of Treasury press release concerning proposed rules implementing Section 326 of

the Patriot Act, specifically advises that '…the proposed regulations do not discourage bank acceptance of the 'matricula consular card that is being issued by the Mexican government to immigrants.' It is anticipated that the proposed [Patriot Act] rules requiring financial institutions to establish a formal customer identification program will be issued in the very near future.

"Unless contradicted by the issuance of the above referenced rules in final form, it is the position of the Division of Banking that Colorado state-chartered financial institutions may accept the matricula consular card as one form of identification, although it would generally be expected that one or more additional identifying documents also be obtained. Federal banking regulators have informally advised me that the federal agencies have adopted a similar position until such time as that final regulations are issued."

As the Colorado Bank Commissioner mentioned, Section 326 of the Patriot Act will "require financial institutions to establish minimum procedures for identifying and verifying the identity of customers seeking to open financial accounts." These requirements will be applicable once the Department of Treasury, along with all other federal financial regulators, complete their relevant rule-making procedures in order to implement Section 326 of the Patriot Act. In July 2002, proposed rules were issued jointly by Treasury with seven other federal financial regulators. In the case of non-citizens, the rules would require that:

"A financial institution is given the discretion to decide what type of information it will request of a non-U.S. citizen in place of a taxpayer identification number. A financial institution may accept any one or more of the following: a U.S. taxpayer identification number; a passport number and country of issuance; an alien identification card number; or the number and country of issuance of any other government-issued document evidencing nationality or residence and bearing a photograph or similar safeguard."

The U.S. Treasury's "Section 326 Summary" then included a footnote stating expressly that: "Thus, the proposed regulations do not discourage bank acceptance of the 'matricula consular' identity card that is being issued by the Mexican government to immigrants."

In sum, Treasury approved of the Mexican consular IDs in the context of the provisions of the Patriot Act designed to identify all account holders and report suspected terrorists. However, in the meantime, the anti-immigrant lobby convinced the General Services Administration ("GSA") that it should suspend acceptance of the matricula for purposes of entering the San Francisco Federal Building. The GSA asked the State Department to review the matter, and then an Inter-Agency Commission of the Departments of State, Treasury, Justice ("DOJ") including the Federal Bureau of Investigation ("FBI"), Health and Human Services, Education, and the new Department of Homeland Security ("DHS")(collectively, "Inter-Agency Commission") began reviewing the validity of accepting the Mexican consular ID. We understand that the final ruling will be issued by the State Department, and that is why we are writing to the State Department directly.

The Inter-Agency Commission should approve continued acceptance of the Mexican consular ID and similar foreign consular IDs. The rulings to date of Treasury, well-established law, the logic of the need to identify all persons within our borders, and the fact that the matricula is a better, more fraud-proof form of ID than any U.S. government-issued identification document, all clearly indicate that at this moment in history, our government should accept the Mexican consular ID as a valid and reliable form of identification. Moreover, Treasury has made clear that acceptance of the matricula by banks is perfectly legal in the meantime.

2. Allegations that accepting the Mexican consular ID would be considered as "aiding and abetting illegal immigration," in violation of 8 U.S.C.A. § 1324, are irresponsible, false and frivolous. And since there is no underlying crime, there is no RICO-prohibited financial gain involved.

As FILE correctly points out, Section 274 of the Immigration and Nationality Act (8 U.S.C.A. §1324, Bringing in and harboring certain aliens) provides criminal penalties for any person who "encourages or induces an alien to come to, enter, or reside in the United States, knowing or in reckless disregard of the fact that such coming to, entry, or residence is or will be in violation of law." Accepting the Mexican consular ID is not in violation of this statute. As a preliminary matter, banks and government officials that are accepting Mexican consular IDs are doing so from persons who already reside in the U.S. Therefore, the acceptance of the ID is not encouraging or inducing anyone to "come into, enter, or reside" in the U.S. The individual who carries the Mexican consular ID, whatever his or her immigration status is, has already come to, entered, and resided in this country well before he or she approaches a bank or local government official.

While highly unlikely, even in the case of an individual who has come to and entered the U.S. but not yet begun residing here, acceptance of a Mexican consular ID could not be legally considered as "aiding and abetting" the underlying crime of encouraging or inducing illegal immigration. This is because the statute requires that the accused was acting while knowing or in reckless disregard that an immigrant's residence in the U.S. is or will be in violation of the law.

The statute requires a level of intent or mental state to commit the crime of encouraging illegal immigration that does not apply to the circumstances of acceptance of a Mexican consular ID. The plain language of the statute makes clear that "knowing or reckless disregard" that the person's residence in the U.S. is in violation of immigration laws is required to prove criminal culpability. Bank officials are not knowingly or recklessly encouraging illegal immigration by accepting matriculas, because they are not even aware of the immigration status of the individuals with whom they are conducting business. Instead, they are only verifying identification for the purposes of opening bank accounts and conducting financial transactions.

The Mexican government issues consular IDs to any of its nationals living abroad who can provide sufficient documentation to meet Mexico's strict standards for issuance of matriculas. Any person born in Mexico and residing in the U.S. who has not naturalized is a Mexican citizen, even if he or she is residing in the U.S. legally and permanently. As such, holding a Mexican consular ID cannot be equated with being illegally present in the U.S. The Mexican consulates emphasize that the matricula does not provide, document or otherwise address immigration status. The fact that a person of Mexican origin is carrying a Mexican consular ID does not prove that the person is undocumented.

Neither banks nor police departments could be held liable for "aiding and abetting illegal immigration," because knowledge that a person has a Mexican consular ID does not mean knowledge of the person's immigration status. Furthermore, local police are not charged with enforcing federal immigration laws.

Police stop people either due to suspicion or for a random check. If local police stop a person for suspicion, they are responsible for verifying whether that person has committed the violation for which they were suspected. Further investigation would be unconstitutional. If, on the other hand, local police stopped a person for a check without articulable suspicion (in a checkpoint or similar stop), the United States Constitution requires that the stop is random, meaning that everyone is stopped on an egalitarian basis. Investigating outside the scope of such stops is unconstitutional. Furthermore, hundreds of police departments are accepting matriculas precisely because this increases public safety. In sum, state and local police accept the Mexican consular ID not for the purpose of checking immigration status, but because it increases public safety. For all these reasons, local police could not be held liable for failure to check the person's immigration status.

The same rationale applies in the case of government officials who ask for identification. The purpose of asking for identification documents are to know who the person is, e.g., that they are who their ID says they are, that they have the right to enter the building or public property in question, and that they are not a threat to public safety or security. People enter government buildings for a variety of purposes, such as paying traffic tickets, going to court, or trying to participate in democracy. Since checking immigration status is not part of such purposes, then government officials cannot be held liable for failure to check an ID holder's immigration status, unless such check is part of the express purpose of their mission. In that case, federal government officials should be asking for proof of immigration status, which the Mexican consular ID does not provide.

It is difficult to see why FILE would allege that banks would have the requisite criminal intent to be held liable for encouraging illegal immigration under the express terms of the Immigration and Nationality Act ("INA") they cite in their Model Complaint. The underlying crime of encouraging or inducing illegal immigration, as is prohibited under INA, is hardly committed by opening a bank account. There is no causation. The bank account does not encourage illegality-it is up to the federal government, and not private entities, nor the states and localities, to enforce immigration laws.

Moreover, study after study has shown that millions of undocumented immigrants are living and working here in the United States, with or without bank accounts. Their presence is not caused by banks, by local police, school boards or other local government officials, or federal government officials, except those who are directly working on federal immigration policy. Millions more legal immigrants, refugees, visiting businesspersons and tourists make financial transactions in the U.S. every day, providing immeasurable benefit to the U.S. If banks are responsible for facilitating these financial transactions that benefit the U.S. economy, then we should support their acceptance of foreign identification documents.

In sum, banks, police departments and government officials (except those expressly charged with enforcing federal immigration laws) are not criminally liable if they accept matriculas. Since there is no underlying illegal procurement of citizenship or naturalization, there can be no conspiracy to commit a crime or unlawful gains from such crime, and therefore the federal RICO statute is inapplicable.

Finally, FILE should be aware that there is no private right of action to enforce immigration laws. For all these reasons, the FILE allegations of criminal liability and threats to prosecute those who accept matriculas are irresponsible.

3. <u>Threats of civil liability are arbitrary, capricious, and without any legal merit.</u>

FILE claims that acceptance of the Mexican consular ID "opens the institution [that accepts the ID] to civil liability and personal injury lawsuits." However, in order for a bank to be held negligent for any damages caused to U.S. citizens by illegal immigration, the bank would have to have legally caused such damages. In order for a bank to have legally caused such damages, the damages would have to be foreseeable. Currently, the federal government sanctions acceptance of matriculas by banks, and therefore damages are not legally foreseeable.

Even if the federal government were silent on the matter, a bank official accepting a form of identification that proves who the person is, is not responsible for ascertaining the immigration status of that person. A person presenting a Mexican consular ID might or might not be here illegally. Therefore, bank officials could not have forseen any damages caused by a holder of a Mexican consular ID having a bank account here in the U.S, and could not be held liable for such hypothetical damages.

4. <u>State and local government officials are not charged with enforcing immigration laws, which under our constitutional system is an exclusive mandate of the federal government. Therefore, state and local governments, as well private entities and individuals, may not be held negligent or otherwise liable for any theoretical failure to enforce federal immigration laws.</u>

FILE is correct in one part of the "Legal Considerations" it published for citizens to send to banks. FILE correctly surmises that: "The courts have long recognized that by Article I, Section 8 of the U.S. Constitution (the Commerce Clause), Congress has 'plenary power' over all aspects of immigration law." This is correct, but the analysis and conclusion that FILE gathered from the original legal norm, set forth by the Supreme Court in 1893, fails to take into account a long series of cases decided in the interim. FILE asserts that because the power to regulate immigration belongs to the federal government: "Therefore, no public institution except the Federal Government may make *any policy that speaks in any way* to the presence in the community of foreign nationals." As will be shown below, this analysis is entirely incorrect.

Since 1893, the Supreme Court has repeatedly reaffirmed and further interpreted the general norm that enforcement of immigration laws is the exclusive mandate of the federal government. The Court has made clear that state and local officials are prohibited from legislating on immigration, unless their policies mirror the policies set forth by the federal government. Any state and local law regarding immigrants that differs from federal immigration law may be struck down as outside the mandate of state and local authority.

No matter which scenario is applied to matriculas, their acceptance by state and local governments is perfectly legal. FILE did not take into account that not everything that has to do with immigrants as people falls under the purview of the plenary power of the federal government to regulate immigration. For example, immigrants go to school, operate businesses, and are subject to state criminal and civil laws the same as any other person. The Supreme Court has ruled again and again that these types of matters do not fall under the federal plenary power to regulate immigration. Acceptance of matriculas has nothing to do with the plenary power or foreign policy, but is merely a means to accurately identify a person who wants to open a bank account, identify themselves for safety reasons, or pay a traffic ticket. In this case, relevant state and local policy would not unduly interfere with the plenary power of the federal government.

Assuming that acceptance of Mexican consular IDs falls under the federal plenary power to regulate immigration, as long as the federal government permits the acceptance of Mexican consular IDs, state and local governments may not enact contradictory policies. However, states and local governments may enact policies that mirror and further the federal policy, as long as federal constitutional protections are in place. Similarly, if the federal government were silent on the matter, states and localities may not enact anti-matricula laws for the purpose of involving themselves in immigration. This analysis was affirmed on January 29, 2003, by a recent final ruling of the Department of Justice and the Immigration and Naturalization Services ("INS").

In sum, (1) either acceptance of matriculas is simply regulation of immigrants that is not part of the plenary power because it has nothing to do with foreign policy, or (2) state and local regulation of immigrants falls under the plenary power, and therefore is subject to the authority of the federal government. In either case, acceptance of the Mexican consular IDs could not be an undue interference in the plenary power or foreign policy.

5. In fact, state and local governments, as well as banks and other private entities or individuals, are prohibited from discriminating based on immigration status.

Because state and local governments may not enforce immigration laws, except under limited circumstances with delegation of authority by and supervision of the federal government, their actions are subject to stricter standards of review than the federal government. As discussed, when the federal government enforces immigration laws, its actions fall under the plenary power to regulate immigration and act in matters of foreign policy. Therefore, U.S. courts reason that the federal government should have discretion as to how to conduct such activities. When state and local governments are taking actions under delegated federal authority, similar rules of law could apply.

However, when state and local governments are not regulating immigration, but instead regulating immigrants, they do not enjoy such wide discretion and their actions are subject to much stricter scrutiny. Similarly, private entities such as banks, which are not authorized to enforce immigration laws, do not enjoy discretionary authority and may not discriminate against or otherwise infringe upon the fundamental constitutional rights of immigrants, even those who are undocumented.

For example, the U.S. Supreme Court held in 1982 that children of undocumented immigrants are entitled to receive public education. It would be illogical to conclude the public schools are encouraging illegal immigration by providing education to deserving students, without discrimination based on immigration status. Similarly, if banks were to deny services to all Mexicans who presented matriculas, they could be charged with discrimination.

6. The international legal rules followed by the U.S. State Department prohibit non-recognition of the Mexican consular ID.

Mexico is a sovereign nation with the right to issue Mexican identification cards to its foreign nationals. The new Undersecretary of Border and Transportation Security, Asa Hutchinson, made this clear in recent public statements. Furthermore, the practice of consular registration has been recognized by international law. Mexican Consuls have been issuing consular ID documents since 1871. The purposes of consular registration are to enable consular officers to protect their nationals and provide access to consular services, and to help relatives and authorities of the sending State to locate their nationals overseas. As part of this mandate, the Mexican consulates explain to matricula applicants that the card does not provide any immigration status or legal access to benefits whatsoever. Its main purpose is to provide accurate identification of its holder.

Consular registration of Mexican nationals assists Mexican consulates in complying with the functions recognized by the Vienna Convention on Consular Relations. The Mexican consular ID assists in identifying the Mexican nationality of a person returning to Mexico from the U.S., and provides an official *Mexican* record of that person's residence for the time in which he or she was in the U.S. Consular registration also facilitates the access to protection and consular services, as the registration is considered evidence of Mexican nationality. For all these reasons, Mexican consulates issue matriculas to Mexicans living in any part of the world.

U.S. consular posts also provide consular registration services for U.S. nationals living in other countries, in order to better provide consular services to U.S. citizens living abroad. When Mexican nationals in the U.S. have problems, they turn to their consulates for help, the same as U.S. citizens turn to U.S. consulates for help when living overseas.

The Vienna Convention on Consular Relations permits many relevant consular functions, such as protecting and safeguarding nationals living abroad, providing them with services and legal advice, developing helpful bilateral relations, and certifying and issuing legal documentation. These functions are the legal framework for the services that both U.S. and Mexican citizens are entitled to from their respective consulates. Issuance of the Mexican consular ID and similar foreign consular IDs falls well within the legal boundaries of the consular functions permitted under the Vienna Convention. Moreover, as will be discussed below, compliance with this Vienna Convention is important to the United States.

Parity and Reciprocity

The Inter-Agency Commission studying the validity of accepting foreign IDs must take into account that the United States is party to and its citizens enjoy parity and reciprocity under a series of international treaties that permit U.S. citizens to travel and do business abroad. Enjoyment of the benefits of such treaties means that we must provide for parity and reciprocity of such benefits to other countries. The principle of parity and reciprocity is set forth in the non-discrimination provisions of the Vienna Convention on Consular Relations. This means that in addition to the requirement that the U.S. not discriminate among foreign Consuls, the Vienna Convention provides that better or worse treatment will not be considered discriminatory, as long as the same favorable or restrictive treatment is also applied to U.S. citizens in the "sending State."

Whatever treatment we give Mexican Consuls, the same treatment will be applied to U.S. Consuls in Mexico with regard to their ability to protect the myriad interests of U.S. citizens living, doing business in, or simply traveling to Mexico. U.S. Consuls issue birth certificates, death certificates, divorces, and provide many other documents, document authentications, and services for the nearly 500,000 U.S. citizens living in Mexico and the 15-17 million U.S. citizens visiting Mexico annually. The legal principle of parity and reciprocity means that whatever consular functions we engage in on behalf of U.S. citizens in Mexico, Mexico has the right to do on behalf of Mexican citizens in the U.S. On the other hand, whatever functions we deny to the Mexican Consuls in the U.S., Mexico has the right to deny to U.S. consulates in Mexico.

For all these reasons, non-acceptance of Mexican IDs could lead to non-acceptance in

Mexico of U.S. identification documents, including passports. There is no known international treaty that requires acceptance of U.S. passports, and if we fail to acknowledge the rights of foreign Consuls to issue IDs to their nationals, the rule of reciprocity and parity means that other nations could also restrict the rights of U.S. Consuls to issue U.S. identification documents. Before unilaterally denying the rights of foreign Consuls to issue foreign documents to their nationals in the U.S., the U.S. government should at the very least engage in negotiations for the reasonable reciprocal recognition of foreign IDs.

If the U.S. government fails to take these steps, U.S. citizens and businesses could be without legal protection and unable to function abroad. Furthermore, the U.S. could be open to an international lawsuit. By adopting the Optional Protocol to the Vienna Convention on Consular Relations Concerning the Compulsory Settlement of Disputes, the United States agreed that any disputes about the interpretation or application of the provisions of the same Vienna Convention "shall lie within the compulsory jurisdiction of the International Court of Justice."

7. Eight hundred police departments, various local governments and at least 80 banks have accepted the matricula, because it increases public safety, national security and our economic competitiveness by enabling the reliable identification of millions of Mexicans living and working in the U.S.

When deciding upon the legality of accepting foreign IDs, we must ensure that whatever measures we take in the name of national security are actually effective. Common sense also dictates that we should not enact measures that will be detrimental to public safety and national security. Many jurisdictions are accepting the matricula because it very clearly increases public safety.

The Inter-Agency Commission must take into account that perfectly legal Mexican immigrants and tourists may use the Mexican consular ID, because it is safer and easier to carry than a passport. Banks may also prefer the matricula, because its security features are in full compliance with the Patriot Act and it is a much more reliable form of identification than a Mexican passport.

The matricula has a number of extremely sophisticated security features, including a digitized photo, in-person consular interviews and review of supporting documentation, and standards for supporting documentation that are more demanding than those used for U.S.-government issued IDs. Furthermore, the matricula decreases robberies of Mexican nationals and increases public safety. Eight hundred local police departments accept the matricula because it is extremely helpful to be able to accurately identify people.

Many Mexicans arrived here without a passport, and in any case, the Mexican passport is not nearly as fraud-proof as a matricula. Without the Mexican consular ID, many migrants would be without any reliable identification, either because they do not have access to U.S. documentation or because their application for immigration status is still pending. It is much better for police to be able to identify people, including suspects, witnesses, and people who come forward to report crimes and suspicious activities, than to be unable to accurately identify people and locate them in the future. As Chief Moose of Montgomery County, Maryland explained to D.C.-area residents during the sniper crisis, we all need for immigrants to be able to report information without fear of immigration consequences.

Acceptance of the Mexican consular ID has a proven track record of increasing public safety. On the other hand, it is not at all clear how failure to recognize the matricula and the inability to identify millions of Mexicans living and working here in the U.S. would actually assist in the primary mission of the Department of Homeland Security, e.g., "to prevent terrorist acts within the United States." Furthermore, part of the official "primary mission" of the new Department of Homeland Security is to "ensure that the overall economic security of the United States is not diminished by efforts, activities, and programs aimed at securing the homeland."

8. The only viable alternative to acceptance of the matricula is to legalize the millions of Mexicans who are performing vital work and sustaining the U.S. economy.

While Representative Tancredo and the anti-immigration groups seem to be worried about securing our borders by making it impossible to recognize foreign IDs, it is obvious that their real concern is illegal immigration. The reality is that there are 8-9 million undocumented immigrants living and working here in the U.S., and about half of them are Mexican. This is in large part because undocumented workers are an essential part of the U.S. economy. A recent study by Northeastern University found that more than half of new workers in the 1990s were undocumented immigrants. They are doing work that U.S. citizens and residents do not want. In January, Alan Greenspan acknowledged that, due to the aging of the native U.S. workforce, a surge in immigration is our only hope for undoing massive fiscal deficits and moving towards economic recovery.

It is not a good idea to leave millions of people without any means to legally identify themselves. As President Bush has said, undocumented Mexicans come here because they are willing workers going to willing employers. Instead of pushing good people who are undocumented immigrants even further into the shadows, the administration should re-open the legalization negotiations that were underway on September 3, 2001. Recent statements by Secretary of State Colin Powell and National Security Advisor Condoleezza Rice, along with recent statements by President Bush himself, confirm that legalization is entirely logical if not essential in the context of the need to protect our collective national security.

Conclusion:

For all these reasons, the Inter-Agency Commission studying the validity of consular IDs should confirm that recognition of the Mexican consular ID and similar consular IDs is legal. The Administration should also realize that the *matricula* is only a stop-gap measure, and look into alternatives for providing U.S. legal identity and documentation to the millions of Mexicans and other foreign nationals who are working as the backbone of the U.S. economy.

MALDEF STATEMENT SUBMITTED BY REP. STEVE KING AS REBUTTAL TO STATEMENT SUBMITTED BY REP. JACKSON LEE

Despite FILE's "Legal Objections" to Acceptance by U.S. Institutions of the *Matricula Consular* and Other Foreign-Issued Consular ID Cards, Acceptance of the Mexican Consular ID is Safe and Legal

The Mexican American Legal Defense and Educational Fund ("MALDEF") is a national, nonpartisan, nonprofit Latino civil rights group defending the civil rights of Latinos for 34 years. MALDEF would like to clarify several points of law for the House Judiciary Committee ("Committee") and its Immigration, Border and Claims Subcommittee ('Immigration Subcommittee" or "Subcommittee"), as the Committee has decided to review the legality of accepting consular identification documents ("IDs"). MALDEF has previously submitted a brief into the record by the Ranking Member on June 19, 2003. MALDEF has taken an interest in this issue because it affects Latino immigrants, many who are stunned to see that the safe and fraud-proof documents issued by their countries of origin being denigrated. Latino immigrants, like most other community members of this country, care deeply about personal safety and national security. They are simply trying to find a way to identify themselves to conduct their everyday lives, professing a right to an identity that most of us accept as fundamental.

Rather than review arguments and information previously provided, we limit this submission to address the "Legal Objections to Acceptance by U.S. Institutions of the *Matricula Consular* and Other Foreign-Issued Consular Identification Cards" submitted to the Subcommittee by "Friends of Immigration Law Enforcement" ("FILE")("FILE's Objections"). FILE's objections, cast as legal arguments, are largely exaggerated, unfounded and without merit. In addition, because the issue of the consular document is already under study by the Inter-Agency Task Force of the Federal Government, we respectfully request the Subcommittee to defer to the Task Force and its security experts regarding the legality of accepting consular IDs. Absent deferral, this Subcommittee should consider a fair and impartial review of the law and the facts before taking any action.

1. Final Treasury Regulations Provide For More Than Sufficient Security Protections

On June 8th, the Department of Treasury issued Final Regulations pursuant to the Patriot Act that would permit financial institutions to accept foreign consular IDs. Under the very strict provision of the Final Regulations, financial institutions can only accept foreign IDs if they are convinced that such IDs are safe and fraud-proof. Under the Patriot Act and its purpose to ensure national security, the rules and procedures "must enable the bank to form a reasonable belief that it knows the true identity of the customer." Financial institutions must have their own Customer Identification Program ("CIP") to review the security of each foreign ID, according to high standards of due diligence. Furthermore, the Final Regulations also recognize that there are millions of non-citizens who may need to present non-US identification documents. The bottom line is that the Final Regulations require that whatever identity documents a bank accepts, such documents should enable the bank to accurately identify its holder.

2. The New Safe ID Act Disproves FILE's Allegation that Mexican Consular IDs are Supported by Insecure "Breeder Documents"

FILE and others allege, without substantiation, that the documents underlying the matricula are not secure. Yet, the Mexican Government has explained to the U.S. Government how it authenticates the underlying documents required to receive a *matrícula*. Mexico created a modern, fraud-proof form of ID through a national voter ID. In cases where the Mexican national voter ID is not available, the Mexican consulates require applicants to tender a passport, military registration card, U.S. alien registration card and/or Mexican social security card in order to receive a *matrícula*. In each and every case, an applicant needs a birth certificate demonstrating Mexican nationality, plus two of the above-mentioned identification documents. These documents are verified through the consular review process. Furthermore, if the underlying documents cannot be authenticated, a Mexican consular ID will not be issued. According to the Mexican government, a significant portion of applications for *matrículas* are indeed rejected on those grounds. Many other anti-ID-fraud measures have been put into place to ensure the safety of the Mexican consular ID. That is why the Mexican consular ID is accepted by over 800 U.S. police departments.

If accepted, FILE's position also implicates basic international relations. The U.S. "generally adheres to the Vienna Convention on Consular Relations because it terms are consistent with international customary law." (Customary international law is international common law, e.g. it is enforceable whether or not a country signed a treaty agreeing to it.). If the U.S. does not accept the safest and most fraud-proof form of Mexican ID, under the Vienna Convention on Consular Relations, there is no reason that the Mexican government would have any obligation to accept U.S. passports, much less the U.S. drivers' licenses and other alternative forms of ID it routinely accepts from the millions of U.S. tourists, business travelers, and residents in Mexico.

Moreover, the Vienna Convention already provides the legal means for the authentication and certification of international legal documents, to which the rules of parity and reciprocity apply. Those who do international business are already familiar with these rules. If the U.S. does not respect the Vienna Convention, U.S. documents might not be accepted overseas, or certified by foreign consulates as required to make foreign investments, and the United States would not be able to verify the authenticity of the foreign documents needed for any international venture made here. Since globalization, rules for the authentication of foreign documents are indeed one of the most common modern applications of this line of international legal conventions. The U.S. could not function in the global economy if we did not have the protections of the Vienna Convention, which would be put in jeopardy by failing to accept Mexican consular IDs.

Finally, the new Safe ID Act just passed by this Congress and signed into law by President Bush on April 30, 2003, should assuage any concerns about the authenticity of underlying documentation used to procure a foreign ID. The Safe ID Act, found in Section 607 of the PROTECT Act, permits the U.S. to prosecute any form of document fraud, including for foreign documents.

3. Consular IDs Do Not Provide Immigration Benefits and Therefore Are Not Subject to the Exclusive, Plenary Power of the Federal Government to Regulate Immigration

Contrary to allegations made by anti-immigrant witnesses at the last Subcommittee hearing, it is very clear that Mexican consular IDs do not provide any immigration benefits whatsoever.

The ability to prove one's identity is not an immigration benefit. Under the U.S. Constitution, every person is entitled to due process of law. Without the ability to identify one's self, a person cannot report crimes, and if they are accused of any crimes, they can hardly realize constitutional due process rights. Whether or not a consular ID helps immigrants' fundamental due process rights, every human being has the right to identify his or herself.

For many years now, immigrants and foreign entities doing business in America have been able to open U.S. bank accounts. It is also convenient that U.S. citizens abroad can conduct financial transactions through foreign banks and foreign branches of U.S. banks. The ability to open a bank account does not confer any immigration benefits. In fact, it confers substantial benefits to the U.S. economy, benefiting citizens and immigrants alike.

Many public safety and national security benefits are realized by everyone in the United States through the acceptance of Mexican consular IDs. Acceptance of consular IDs could either be a federal or a state issue. While foreign policy and national security issues are the responsibility of the federal government, it is the state that is primarily responsible for public safety, under the police power. Accepting Mexican consular IDs thus is either a federal national security matter, or a state public safety matter.

However, because consular IDs do not confer immigration benefits, it is not up to the branches of the federal government charged with immigration matters to regulate consular IDs. This is because U.S. law differentiates between regulating immigrants, which is a state matter, and regulating immigration, which is uniquely a federal matter. How immigrants identify themselves clearly falls into the category of regulating immigrants, which is a matter for the states, absent national security concerns.

4. FILE Cannot Show that Accepting the Matricula Violates Criminal Laws

FILE has repeatedly posited, with no support, that acceptance of Mexican consular IDs could run afoul of the criminal provisions of the INA. Absent any showing of intent, their position has no merit. Federal courts have uniformly held that intent in the form of knowledge or reckless disregard must be shown for a criminal violation to be proven under the INA. If this were not the case, anyone, for example, who unwittingly hired independent contractors to do renovations in their home, or ate produce picked by undocumented labor, would violate the criminal laws.

Moreover, the sole case cited by FILE to attempt to prove its theory is completely inapplicable to the issue of Mexican consular IDs. In the Oloyede case, the defendant was convicted of "aiding and abetting illegal immigration" because he knowingly sold fraudulent U.S. documents to persons he knew were illegal immigrants. The defendant, an immigration lawyer himself, procured and sold fraudulent documents. The Fourth Circuit Court of Appeals found that:

> "The evidence at trial showed a distinct pattern of appellants luring well-educated, employed aliens to Cooper's office by offering to sell them a legal status they could not otherwise obtain."

Therefore, the element of encouraging illegal immigration was based upon a finding of actively and knowingly producing fraudulent documents, which in turn knowingly encouraged illegal immigration. In contrast, Mexican consular IDs are not fraudulent documents. And unlike the false immigration papers procured by this unethical attorney, Mexican consular IDs do not provide or purport to provide any immigration benefits. Therefore, they do not "encourage illegal immigration," because they do make immigrants feel they have the right to work legally in the U.S., that they are not subject to deportation, and that they can travel back and forth freely to their homeland. None of these "benefits of citizenship" are realized through a consular ID.

In Oloyede, the Fourth Circuit Court also found that, under the statutory language of INA, a second element of proof of intent is required. Defendants must have not only knowingly encouraged illegal immigration, but they must have acted "knowing that [the immigrants'] residence is or will be in violation of law." By accepting a Mexican consular ID, a bank or a police department has no reason to know that the person is not in legal status. It is not within the jurisdiction of banks or anyone except the federal government (and its legal delegates, with appropriate constitutional protections) to be verifying immigration status. Indeed, research released by the Congressional Research Service demonstrates that entire categories of people with legal immigration rights would not have US-issued immigration documents. These individuals would be obvious beneficiaries of the consular ID.

FILE's RICO argument is similarly infirm. Absent an underlying crime, there can be no liability under a Racketeering Influenced and Corrupt Organizations ("RICO") Act. Because acceptance of Mexican consular IDs is not a criminal violation of the INA, there can be no RICO violation.

5. Even FILE Concedes That It Probably Could Not Prevail on Its Admittedly Stretched Theory of Negligence

FILE's Objections show the inherent weakness of their claims that those who accept Mexican consular IDs could be held negligent. FILE cannot cite to a single case supporting this attenuated theory of causation. FILE alleges that:

> "While it is unclear what findings a jury will make in these cases, many jurors will likely be sympathetic to a U.S. citizen who is killed or injured by an illegal alien, especially when that illegal alien is present in the country due to the illegal policies of a bank, a state, or a municipality."

These circumstances are entirely too remote to credibly prove causation. First, as the Treasury Department has just confirmed, it is not illegal for a bank to accept Mexican consular IDs. Second, regardless of whatever sympathies our conjured jury may feel, there is a serious question whether a case such as this hypothetical one would even go before to a jury since a court would first have to conclude that a plaintiff had proven a *prima facie* case-that is to say-that defendants' negligence was the cause of the events that produced the injury. Thus, a court would have to first find that the bank's acceptance of a consular ID caused the citizen's injury by the bearer of the ID. Even before the days of tort reform, such causation would be too remote for a bank to be held liable under a negligence theory.

Conclusion:

After carefully scrutinizing the law, this committee should conclude that none of the arguments FILE has raised in its Legal Objections are meritorious. FILE neither showed that acceptance of Mexican consular IDs and similar consular IDs would be unconstitutional, failed to prove any violations of federal law, and did not prove that acceptance of Mexican consular IDs would be negligent. MALDEF also urges this Congress to carefully evaluate the public safety, national security and economic benefits that acceptance of Mexican consular IDs provides. Please feel free to contact us with any questions, or requests for further information about the security and legality of Mexican consular IDs.

PREPARED STATEMENT OF THE HONORABLE SHEILA JACKSON LEE, A REPRESENTATIVE IN CONGRESS FROM THE STATE OF TEXAS

The subject of this hearing is the federal government's response to the issuance and acceptance of the consular identification cards issued by foreign governments. We all know, however, that only one consular identification card is of concern at this hearing. That card is the Matricula Consular that the Government of Mexico has been issuing at consulates around the world for more than 130 years.

The Mexican consulates issue these cards to create an official record of its citizens in other countries. The Matricula is legal proof of such registration. This registration facilitates access to protection and consular services because the certificate is evidence of Mexican nationality. It does not provide immigrant status of any kind, and it cannot be used for travel, employment, or driving in the United States or in Mexico. The Matricula only attests that a Mexican consulate has verified the individual's identity.

I am only aware of one federal agency that has taken a position on consular identification cards in its regulations, the Department of Treasury. In regulations promulgated pursuant to the USA PATRIOT Act, the Treasury Department set forth minimum standards for financial institutions that relate to the identification and verification of any person who applies to open an account.

These regulations specifically address the use of government-issued documents as evidence of nationality or residence. The regulations permit the acceptance of government-issued documents evidencing nationality or residence and bearing a photograph or similar safeguard. 68 Federal Register § 103.121(b)(2)(iii)(4).

In view of the fact that the Matricula is an acceptable identity document under Treasury Department regulations promulgated pursuant to the USA PATRIOT Act, it is not apparent why the card should be rejected by any other government agency.

Opponents of the Matricula will argue that the document is not secure. I disagree. I am confident that the Matricula is a secure form of identification. The person requesting a Matricula must produce an original birth certificate and an official Mexican identification card such as a passport or a federal electoral card, and his photograph will be taken by the consulate office, on the consulate premises.

In addition, the Matricula has been modernized with the use of new technologies to improve its security features. The Mexican government uses security standards in making the Matricula that are similar to the ones used by the United States Government in its own official documents.

It has visible security features such as green security paper with the official Mexican seal printed in a special security pattern, and a colored hologram with a seal that appears over the holder's photograph and changes color from green to brown.

It also has security features that are visible only under fluorescent light. The fluorescent light reveals the letters "SRE" across the front of the card. An infra red band appears on the upper back of the card.

In case this is not enough, there are security marks visible only with the use of a special decoder. The decoder reveals the word "Mexico" printed on the left side of the card, next to the holder's photograph. "Matricular Consular ID Card" is printed at the bottom. And, "SRE" is printed three times on the right side.

In addition to hearing about the federal government's response to the Matricula, we need to learn how local governments are responding to it, which is why I invited a representative from the Government of Montgomery County, Maryland, to speak at this hearing.

Montgomery County Maryland has many Hispanic residents. County Executive, Douglas Duncan, recently announced that Montgomery County would accept the Matricula Consular as identification for all County services. I am anxious to hear about why Montgomery County adopted this policy. More Mexican nationals will be affected by the practices of state and local government than by the practices of our federal government.

Thank you.

RESPONSE TO POST-HEARING QUESTIONS SUBMITTED BY REP. HOSTETTLER TO ROBERTA S. JACOBSON, ACTING DEPUTY ASSISTANT SECRETARY OF STATE FOR THE BUREAU OF WESTERN HEMISPHERE AFFAIRS

United States Department of State

Washington, D.C. 20520

RECEIVED
JUL 2 5 2003
Immigration and Claims

July 17, 2003

Dear Mr. Chairman:

Following the June 26, 2003 hearing at which Deputy Assistant Secretary Roberta S. Jacobson testified, additional questions were submitted for the record. Please find enclosed the responses to those questions.

If we can be of further assistance to you, please do not hesitate to contact us.

Sincerely,

Paul V. Kelly

Paul V. Kelly
Assistant Secretary
Legislative Affairs

Enclosure:
As stated.

The Honorable
John N. Hostettler, Chairman,
Subcommittee on Immigration, Border Security, and Claims,
Committee on the Judiciary,
House of Representatives.

Questions for the Record Submitted to
Deputy Assistant Secretary Roberta S. Jacobson
Chairman John N. Hostettler (#1)
Sc. on Immigration, Border Security, and Claims
Committee on the Judiciary
June 26, 2003

Question:

In the debate concerning the Matricula Consular, some of its proponents have cited and implied responsibilities under the Vienna Convention on Consular Relations, raising issues about international reciprocity. In this regard, please tell the Committee whether or not the following statements are correct:

A. The United States has no responsibility under the Vienna Convention to recognize the Matricula Consular because the United States does not require Mexico to recognize a U.S.-issued consular card.

B. While the Vienna Convention allows governments to issue passports and other forms of identification, the Convention in no way requires any government to officially recognize such documents.

Answer:

A. The Vienna Convention on Consular Relations does not specifically refer to the issuance or the recognition of consular identification cards. The Vienna Convention provides broad authority for states to carry out consular functions to help, assist, and protect their nationals. The exercise of these authorities by consular officers of a sending state is not dependent on the reciprocal exercise of the same authorities by consular officers of the host state in the sending State. (In other words, Mexico is entitled to provide protection to Mexicans in the United States even if the United States decided not to provide protection to Americans in Mexico.) The United States has been aggressive in asserting its rights to help, assist and protect Americans under this Convention.

B. The VCCR lists among consular functions the ability to issue "passports and travel documents to nationals of the sending State". (Article 5(d)). It does not specifically address whether receiving States must officially recognize identification documents issued by a sending State. Generally the question is not "recognition" of a passport or travel document, but rather acceptance of the document for a particular purpose. For example, for visa issuance purposes, a passport must comply with the passport definition in the Immigration and Nationality Act, and in the future, for purposes of participation in the visa waiver program, a person may be required to have a machine readable passport that meets internationally adopted standards.

Questions for the Record Submitted to
Deputy Assistant Secretary Roberta S. Jacobson
Chairman John N. Hostettler (#2)
Sc. on Immigration, Border Security, and Claims
Committee on the Judiciary
June 26, 2003

Question:

Ms. Jacobson stated that the Administration has convened an inter-agency working group to evaluate the use of consular ID cards and to make recommendations.

A. We have been informed that until recently, the State Department headed up this group. Is that correct?

B. Which agencies are involved in this working group?

C. How long has the working group been considering these issues?

D. What were the findings and recommendations of the agencies involved in this working group?

Answer:

A. It is correct that the Department of State headed up the Interagency Working Group (IWG) formed to evaluate the use of consular ID cards and to make recommendations. The period of Department of State leadership of the IWG was from January until late April 2003, when the Homeland Security Council assumed the leadership role on this issue.

B. Agencies which have been involved in the working group include the Departments of State, Homeland Security, Treasury,

Justice, Transportation, Education, Health and Human Services, Labor as well as HSC, NSC and DPC.

C. The IWG has been considering these issues since it formed in January 2003.

D. The Administration, under the guidance of the Homeland Security Council, is currently working with a sense of urgency in developing policy on the acceptance of consular identification cards as a valid form of identification in the United States. The development of this policy is taking some time because the issue is complex and will have far-reaching ramifications. One policy determination has already been made. Foreign consular ID cards do not establish or indicate lawful U.S. immigration status and should not be viewed as valid for that purpose, nor do they establish a foreign national's right to be or remain in the United States. Work on additional policy is ongoing and additional results should be available shortly.

**Questions for the Record Submitted to
Deputy Assistant Secretary Roberta S. Jacobson
Chairman John N. Hostettler (#3)
Sc. on Immigration, Border Security, and Claims
Committee on the Judiciary
June 26, 2003**

Question:

Ms. Jacobson noted that any policy on consular identification cards must address questions of security, reciprocity, and protection for Americans abroad.

A. What are the State Department's specific concerns in this regard?

B. What documents, other than passports, does the United States issue to its citizens abroad annually? Please state how many of these documents the United States issued last year. Please also describe the general circumstances under which the recipients of the documents received them, and state whether those individuals are eligible to receive passports.

C. How many consular identification cards did the Government of Mexico issue in the United States last year?

D. Who accepts U.S.-issued consular cards?

E. Does the State Department lobby localities in any other countries to accept U.S. consular identification cards for domestic identification purposes? Please describe.

Answer:

A. The standard document used by U.S. citizens living or traveling outside the United States is the U.S. passport. However, especially in contiguous countries like Mexico, Canada and Caribbean nations, American citizens often travel with other, less secure documents. For example, American citizens may enter many of these countries with only a birth certificate as evidence of citizenship. The United States also issues a limited number of consular cards of identity to U.S. citizens, and a larger number of transportation letters, which are used in lieu of passport for direct return to the United States, generally in emergency circumstances. The Department of State would not wish to have other countries refuse to accept the identification documents borne by U.S. citizens. In emergency situations, it is vital that the United States government can move quickly to protect the lives and interests of U.S. citizens who may be in danger.

B. The Department issues only a small number of consular cards of identity. U.S. Cards of Identity are generally issued to U.S. citizens who are being returned to the United States under escort by U.S. law enforcement under Extradition or Prisoner Transfer treaties. Many of these cards are issued in Mexico to U.S. citizen prisoners who are being returned to the United States under the U.S.- Mexico prisoner transfer treaty. The most common identification document issued to U.S. citizens abroad is the passport, but we also issue transportation letters to facilitate rapid return of a citizen to the United States in critical situations when it is not feasible to issue a U.S. passport.

C. The Embassy of Mexico informed us that approximately 1,200,000 cards were issued in calendar year 2002.

D. Other governments, including the Government of Mexico, accept the U.S. consular card of identity. Inspectors of the Department of Homeland Security also accept these cards to allow the U.S. citizen bearer to enter the United States.

E. We have not needed to lobby other countries to accept our consular cards of identity. However, we regularly engage with host country officials around the world on a wide variety of issues related to the protection of U.S. citizens.

Questions for the Record Submitted to
Deputy Assistant Secretary Roberta S. Jacobson
Chairman John N. Hostettler (#4)
Sc. on Immigration, Border Security, and Claims
Committee on the Judiciary
June 26, 2003

Question:

Ms. Jacobson noted in her testimony that Mexico has issued consular cards to its citizens in the United States for over 100 years, but only recently has begun "vigorous efforts to secure acceptance of the card by local governments and financial institutions at a time of heightened security concerns."

A. What have those efforts consisted of?

B. Given the fact that, post-September 11, we do have heightened security concerns, why has the Mexican government decided now to seek acceptance of these cards?

Answer:

A. It is our understanding that Mexico's efforts to gain acceptance of the redesigned consular identification cards consist of providing written, verbal, or electronic information about the card while simultaneously or soon after requesting that the card be accepted as valid identification. The Government of Mexico has provided this information to a host of organizations including: state governments, local governments, private corporations, and law enforcement offices.

B. Since taking office in December 2000, the Fox Administration has made a concerted effort to engage the Mexican population living abroad. It is believed that seeking acceptance of the Mexican consular identification card is an example of their efforts - a method to assist Mexicans living in the United States.

Questions for the Record Submitted to
Deputy Assistant Secretary Roberta S. Jacobson
Chairman John N. Hostettler (#5)
Sc. on Immigration, Border Security, and Claims
Committee on the Judiciary
June 26, 2003

Question:

It would appear that, of the State Department components, the Office of Foreign Missions would have more authority to regulate consular issuance of identification cards, and consular lobbying efforts on behalf of those cards. Is there any reason that the State Department did not send a representative from OFM, instead of Ms. Jacobson, to testify at this hearing?

Answer:

The Department decided to send Ms. Jacobson to testify on the issue of consular identification cards, as we understood that the Mexican case was of primary interest to the Subcommittee. In an effort to be responsive to the Subcommittee's concerns, we selected Ms. Jacobson, who was Acting Deputy Assistant Secretary for Mexico and Canada in the absence of her supervisor and who, as the Director of the Office of Mexican Affairs, has had close involvement in the issue.

Questions for the Record Submitted to
Deputy Assistant Secretary Roberta S. Jacobson
Chairman John N. Hostettler (#6)
Sc. on Immigration, Border Security, and Claims
Committee on the Judiciary
June 26, 2003

Question:

As reported in the media, some critics of the domestic acceptance of consular ID cards by U.S. states and localities contend that foreign governments' promotion of the use of these cards by illegal aliens has, as one of its motives, the desire to create a de-facto immigration amnesty program. Is there any evidence of that motive?

Answer:

We understand that registration of citizens and protection of their welfare is a strong motive for the issuance of consular identification cards.

Questions for the Record Submitted to
Deputy Assistant Secretary Roberta S. Jacobson
Chairman John N. Hostettler (#7)
Sc. on Immigration, Border Security, and Claims
Committee on the Judiciary
June 26, 2003

Question:

Questions have been raised about acceptance of Mexican-issued Matriculas Consular in Mexico.

A. Ms. Jacobson stated in her testimony that it was her belief that "an increasing number of Mexican banks in the northern part of the country . . . accept the Matricula." Please provide the Subcommittee with a list of those banks.

B. Is it true that only a handful of Mexico's states accept the Matricula Consular as a form of ID? If so, what is the reason that so few Mexican states accept the cards?

C. Please provide a list of the Mexican states that accept the Matricula Consular for identification purposes.

Answer:

A. While the Mexican consular identification card is designed to be used by Mexicans outside of Mexico, we have been informed that Serfin, Bancomer, Banamex, and Scotia/Inverlat have offices accepting the Mexican consular identification card in Northern Mexico. Banks in central and southern Mexico have not embraced the card as they receive few requests to honor them.

B. The Department is unaware of the acceptance level of the Mexican consular identification card within Mexico.

C. The Department does not have such a list, but is requesting this information from the Embassy of Mexico.

Questions for the Record Submitted to
Deputy Assistant Secretary Roberta S. Jacobson
Chairman John N. Hostettler (#8)
Sc. on Immigration, Border Security, and Claims
Committee on the Judiciary
June 26, 2003

Question:

Aside from the Vienna Convention, does the State Department have any other ability to regulate the activities of consular officers in the United States? Please describe the authorities that the State Department has to regulate the activities of foreign consular officers in the United States.

Answer:

See answer to question 10(C).

Questions for the Record Submitted to
Deputy Assistant Secretary Roberta S. Jacobson
Chairman John N. Hostettler (#9)
Sc. on Immigration, Border Security, and Claims
Committee on the Judiciary
June 26, 2003

Question:

We have been told that one of the main problems with the Mexican consular card, the Matricula Consular, is that Mexico has no centralized databases to verify true identities of applicants, or to cross-check who has applied for or received the ID cards.

Various media reports have indicated that the Government of Mexico intends to correct that problem sometime in the future. Some reports have speculated that it would be a matter of months; others have talked about years; and still others have speculated that Mexico may never complete such a task. In this context, please respond to the following questions:

A. What do we actually know about the efficacy, the scope, the completeness, and the accuracy of whatever database Mexico may have for its birth certificates?

B. Would Mexico allow U.S. law enforcement access to such information for purposes of verification or investigation of crimes or terrorism?

Answer:

A. The Mexican Civil Registrar system does have computerized records; however, the electronic records are not centralized either physically or through a common database.

B. While we have not engaged the Mexicans specifically on this issue, Mexico has demonstrated itself as a partner in the war on terrorism. Mexico has also expressed a willingness to improve the security of the card. In addition, there is anecdotal evidence that local U.S. law enforcement agencies have requested and received assistance from Mexican consular officials in verifying the veracity of Mexican consular identification cards. Finally, the Mutual Legal Assistance Treaty (MLAT) facilitates investigations that require either evidence or assistance from Mexican authorities; the validation of documents, such as the Mexican consular identification card, to assist in criminal investigations would fall into this category.

Questions for the Record Submitted to
Deputy Assistant Secretary Roberta S. Jacobson
Chairman John N. Hostettler (#10)
Sc. on Immigration, Border Security, and Claims
Committee on the Judiciary
June 26, 2003

Question:

The Foreign Missions Act gives the Secretary of State broad authority over foreign missions in the United States. The Senate Report on that act states that the Office of Foreign Missions has responsibility for assuring that the national security interests of the United States are taken into consideration when foreign governments seek to operate missions in the United States.

A. In light of the fact that the 19 September 11 hijackers were aliens in the United States, does the State Department believe that controlling immigration is a national security interest of our country?

B. Does the State Department believe that the United States has the ability, under the Foreign Missions Act, to regulate or limit efforts by foreign government officials to lobby state and local officials to accept consular identification cards?

C. If the United States does not have the ability to regulate or limit efforts by foreign government officials to lobby state and local officials under the Foreign Missions Act, does the U.S. government have any authority to regulate or limit those efforts? If so, what authority does the U.S. government have?

Answer:

A. Yes.

B. Much of the work of U.S. Embassy and Consulate officers in other countries could be described as lobbying foreign officials: "federal", state or local, in order to advance the national interests of the United States. The Department therefore would not wish to take actions to curtail the activities of foreign diplomats in the U.S. if such actions would lead to a curtailment of our vital diplomatic and consular work in the other country. It is particularly important not to constrain the ability of a consular officer to assist U.S. citizens in foreign countries and very often this requires communicating with state and local authorities. In this regard, Article 38 of the Vienna Convention on Consular Relations provides that in the exercise of their consular functions, consular officers may address the competent local authorities of their consular district.

The Foreign Missions Act (FMA) provides authority to regulate certain activities which the Secretary determines are "benefits" to foreign missions. However, it also provides that "nothing in this chapter shall be construed to limit the authority of the United States to carry out its international obligations...." (22 USC 4310) Thus, the Congress has recognized that while the authorities provided to the Secretary under the FMA are extremely broad, these authorities will be exercised consistent with the United States' obligations under the VCCR or other international obligations.

C. We are not aware of any problems in this area. All members of consular missions are required under the VCCR to respect local law. If foreign consular officers or employees are engaged in improper activity, there are a range of weapons in our arsenal on which we may rely. For example, we could actively engage the foreign government in a range of diplomatic efforts, including protests, or we could declare the individual persona non grata. If the consular officer or employee has engaged in criminal activity, he is subject to prosecution, or immediate expulsion.

Questions for the Record Submitted to
Deputy Assistant Secretary Roberta S. Jacobson
Chairman John N. Hostettler (#11)
Sc. on Immigration, Border Security, and Claims
Committee on the Judiciary
June 26, 2003

Question:

We have been told that the State Department has been approached by countries that are planning to issue consular identification cards for domestic acceptance in the United States. Members of Congress have already made public a copy of a cable from the U.S. Embassy in Nicaragua, discussing Nicaragua's plan to issue consular cards in the U.S. for domestic acceptance.

We have been told that the following countries are issuing, or are planning to issue consular cards for domestic acceptance in the United States. Please state whether the State Department has exchanged cables, had meetings, or received diplomatic notes from these countries announcing their intention to do this:

a. Haiti

b. Ecuador

c. Nicaragua

d. Honduras

e. El Salvador

f. Guatemala

g. Mexico

h. Argentina

i. Brazil

j. Chile

k. Uruguay

l. Paraguay

m. Barbados

n. Panama

o. Costa Rica

Answer:

We have had communication on this issue with Mexico and Nicaragua. Several Central American countries have told us informally in recent months that they examining the feasibility of matricula consular issuance. We would be happy to provide you with a status report on their deliberations in the near future.

Questions for the Record Submitted to
Deputy Assistant Secretary Roberta S. Jacobson
Chairman John N. Hostettler (#12)
Sc. on Immigration, Border Security, and Claims
Committee on the Judiciary
June 26, 2003

Question:

Does the State Department have any plan to take action in the event that the Iranian, Syrian, North Korean, Libyan, or Sudanese government announces that it will be issuing consular cards in the United States.

Answer:

The Department, in coordination with other agencies, would address these issues as appropriate depending on the specific situation.

Questions for the Record Submitted to
Deputy Assistant Secretary Roberta S. Jacobson
Chairman John N. Hostettler (#13)
Sc. on Immigration, Border Security, and Claims
Committee on the Judiciary
June 26, 2003

Question:

Recently staff learned that China may be issuing consular identification cards to their nationals unlawfully present in certain European countries. Does the State Department have information in that regard?

Answer:

The State Department has no information on the issuance of consular identification cards by China in countries other than the United States.

Questions for the Record Submitted to
Deputy Assistant Secretary Roberta S. Jacobson
Chairman John N. Hostettler (#14)
Sc. on Immigration, Border Security, and Claims
Committee on the Judiciary
June 26, 2003

Question:

This Subcommittee has been told that passports that have been issued by foreign nations are more secure and reliable than those nations "consular identification cards," because passports are governed by and issued in accordance with international standards.

A. Please state whether passports are generally issued in accordance with international standards. If passports are issued in accordance with international standards, please identify the body that sets those standards, and identify the treaties and/or international agreements under which that body operates. Please also identify the nations that issue passports in accordance with those standards.

B. Please state whether that regulating body or any other organization regulates the issuance of "consular identification cards," such as the Mexican government's Matricula Consular. If so, please identify the regulating body for those documents, and the treaties and/or international agreements under which that body operates. Please also provide a copy of the international standards "consular identification cards" are issued.

C. Please provide a list of the nations that currently issue passports that do not contain photographs of the bearer.

D. Please provide a list, by class and/or nationality, of all aliens in the United States who are unable to obtain passports from their country of nationality or citizenship. In submitting that list, please provide a brief description of the reasons that each class or nationality of aliens is unable to obtain a passport.

Answer:

A. The International Civil Aviation Organization (ICAO) sets standards for passports under the authority of the 1944 Chicago Convention held under the aegis of the emerging United Nations. It does not "regulate" the issuance of passports. No such international regulatory organization exists. While technically advisory in nature, the ICAO standards are adhered to by many, but not all, countries. We do not have a comprehensive list available of countries which issue passports in accordance with all or part of the ICAO standards.

B. We are not aware of any international regulatory or standard-setting organization for consular identification cards.

C. We are not aware of any countries that issue passports without photographs.

D The Department of State does not keep track of aliens once they are in the United States. That is a function of the Department of Homeland Security.

○